THE CAMBRIDGE COMPANION TO

AQUINAS

The Cambridge Companion to
AQUINAS

Edited by

Norman Kretzmann
Cornell University

and

Eleonore Stump
St. Louis University

CAMBRIDGE
UNIVERSITY PRESS

Published by the Press Syndicate of the University of Cambridge
The Pitt Building, Trumpington Street, Cambridge CB2 1RP
40 West 20th Street, New York, NY 10011-4211, USA
10 Stamford Road, Oakleigh, Victoria 3166, Australia

First published 1993

Printed in the United States of America

Library of Congress Cataloging-in-Publication Data
The Cambridge companion to Aquinas / edited by Norman Kretzmann
and Eleonore Stump
p.   cm.
Includes bibliographical references and index.
ISBN 0-521-43769-5. – ISBN 0-521-43195-6 (pbk.)
1. Thomas, Aquinas, Saint, 1225?–1274.   I. Kretzmann, Norman.
II. Stump, Eleonore, 1947–
B765.T54C29   1993
189'.4 – dc20   92-31977
                                                                         CIP

A catalog record for this book is available from the British Library

ISBN 0-521-43769-5 hardback
ISBN 0-521-43195-6 paperback

CONTENTS

v

vi   Contents

CONTRIBUTORS

JAN A. AERTSEN is Professor of Philosophy at the Vrije Universiteit in Amsterdam. He is the author of *Nature and Creature: Thomas Aquinas's Way of Thought* and of many articles on the medieval doctrine of the transcendentals.

DAVID B. BURRELL, C.S.C., holds a dual Professorship in theology and philosophy at the University of Notre Dame. He is the author of *Aquinas: God and Action; Knowing the Unknowable God: Ibn Sina, Maimonides, Aquinas,* and of many articles on medieval philosophy and theology.

MARK D. JORDAN is an Associate Professor in The Medieval Institute of the University of Notre Dame. His published studies of Aquinas include *Ordering Wisdom: The Hierarchy of Philosophical Discourses in Aquinas* and "The Alleged Aristotelianism of Thomas Aquinas."

NORMAN KRETZMANN is Susan Linn Sage Professor of Philosophy at Cornell University. He has written widely on medieval philosophy and philosophy of religion and was the principal editor of *The Cambridge History of Later Medieval Philosophy.*

SCOTT MACDONALD is Associate Professor of Philosophy at the University of Iowa and the editor of *Being and Goodness: The Concept of the Good in Metaphysics and Philosophical Theology.* His articles include "Ultimate Ends in Practical Reasoning: Aquinas's Aristotelian Moral Psychology and Anscombe's Fallacy."

RALPH MCINERNY is Michael P. Grace Professor of Philosophy and the Director of the Jacques Maritain Center at the University of

Notre Dame. Among his many books and articles on Aquinas are *Ethica Thomistica: The Moral Philosophy of Thomas Aquinas* and *Aquinas on Human Action.*

JOSEPH OWENS, C.Ss.R., an emeritus member of the Pontifical Institute of Mediaeval Studies at the University of Toronto, has contributed many books and articles to the study of Aquinas and of ancient and medieval philosophy, most notably *The Doctrine of Being in the Aristotelian Metaphysics* and *St. Thomas Aquinas on the Existence of God: Collected Papers.*

PAUL E. SIGMUND is Professor of Politics at Princeton University and the author of *Natural Law in Political Thought* and *St. Thomas Aquinas on Politics and Ethics.*

ELEONORE STUMP is the Robert J. Henle Professor of Philosophy at St. Louis University. She is the author of several books and articles in philosophy of religion and medieval philosophy, including *Dialectic and Its Place in the Development of Medieval Logic* and "Aquinas on the Foundations of Knowledge."

JOHN F. WIPPEL is Professor of Philosophy and Academic Vice-President of the Catholic University of America. His many articles and books on medieval philosophy include *Metaphysical Themes in Thomas Aquinas* and "Truth in Thomas Aquinas."

NORMAN KRETZMANN *and* ELEONORE STUMP

Introduction

I. AQUINAS'S REPUTATION

People familiar with Thomas Aquinas's work know that he ranks among the greatest philosophers, but the number of such people is still smaller than it should be. Anthony Kenny described and gave one reason for this state of affairs more than a decade ago, when it was even more deplorable than it is now:

Aquinas is little read nowadays by professional philosophers: he has received much less attention in philosophy departments, whether in the continental tradition or in the Anglo-American one, than lesser thinkers such as Berkeley or Hegel. He has, of course, been extensively studied in theological colleges and in the philosophy courses of ecclesiastical institutions; but ecclesiastical endorsement has itself damaged Aquinas's reputation with secular philosophers. . . . But since the Second Vatican Council [1962–65] Aquinas seems to have lost something of the pre-eminent favour he enjoyed in ecclesiastical circles. . . . This wind of ecclesiastical change may blow no harm to his reputation in secular circles. (Kenny 1980a, pp. 27–28)

The prognosis with which Kenny ends his diagnosis was being slowly borne out even before he published it. Philosophers, especially those in the Anglo-American tradition, have been bringing Aquinas into secular philosophical discussions. The philosophers of religion among them have, understandably, taken the lead in this process. It was natural that they began looking into Aquinas because of their special interest in his philosophical theology. But Aquinas's systematic approach to philosophical theology led him to include in it full treatments of virtually every area of philosophy, regarding which he always shows how in his view the existence and nature of God is related to the area's subject matter. Consequently, philoso-

I

phers of religion who first read Aquinas in connection with a narrow, twentieth-century conception of their specialization have been taking up appreciative investigations of other aspects of his thought, and they are gradually being joined by philosophers who have no professional interest in religion.

Since this book is intended to help speed the process of engaging philosophers as well as students in the study and appreciation of Aquinas's philosophy, it makes sense to begin by trying to dispel the familiar, apparent obstacles to a wider recognition of Aquinas's value as a philosopher.

II. THE STATE OF THE TEXTS

It seems safe to say that Aquinas is better known, at least by name, than any other medieval philosopher. From the viewpoint of contemporary philosophy, however, even the best-known medieval philosopher is likely to seem more remote philosophically than Plato and Aristotle. To some extent this odd situation testifies to the achievements of a group of outstanding philosophical scholars in the latter half of this century who have devoted themselves to the study and presentation of ancient philosophy in ways that have shown its relevance to contemporary philosophy. But their recent achievements were made possible by the fact that for a long time almost all the texts of ancient philosophy have been available in good printed editions and, to a very large extent, in English translations, often in several versions. On the other hand, all corresponding efforts on behalf of medieval philosophy are bound to be enormously hampered by the contrasting state of the relevant texts. The works of medieval philosophers are in many cases entirely unedited and unavailable in print, or at best – even in the case of Aquinas – incompletely edited. The editions that exist are often less good than they should be, and only a very small proportion of the edited texts have been translated into English or any other modern language.

The great disparity between the current state of the materials for the study and teaching of ancient philosophy, on the one hand, and of medieval philosophy, on the other, is entirely unwarranted. There are many more medieval than ancient philosophical works, and most of them have yet to be studied. Since a good proportion of those that have been studied exhibit intellectual scope and sophistication as impressive as any in the history of philosophy, the exploration of this medieval material, much of which is brand new to twentieth-century readers, is likely to be rewarding. And exploration is what it takes – pioneering exploration, with all the excitement and risk that accompany such enterprises. Before the texts of medieval philosophy can be studied and properly assessed, they have to be dug out of unreliable, unannotated printed versions four or five hundred years old or from the medieval manuscripts themselves (which are still numerous despite the devastation in Europe during and since the Middle Ages). Special training is required even for reading the old editions, which are typically printed in an abbreviated Latin; and the manuscripts, which are obviously much more important sources than the old, uncritical editions, can be deciphered only by people trained in Latin paleography. Making a critical edition based on more than one and sometimes many manuscripts demands further skills along with great care and patience. As matters stand, then, most texts of medieval philosophy are literally inaccessible except to highly specialized scholars, only a few of whom are likely to share the interests of contemporary philosophers and thus to invest the extra time and effort required to make this material fully available.

Nevertheless, a small but slowly growing number of philosophers have glimpsed some of the intriguing philosophical material to be found in medieval texts on even such unlikely topics as grammar and logic and have been equipping themselves to make some of it available to their colleagues and students. The editions, translations, and philosophical articles and books that have appeared during the past twenty-five years or so have begun to affect the perception of medieval philosophy by philosophers in general. A great deal remains to be done, and all of it involves hard work. But no other area of philosophical scholarship is so rich in unexplored material or so likely to repay the effort required to bring it to light in ways that will stimulate its philosophical assessment. As might be expected, much more scholarly attention has been given to Aquinas's philosophy than to that of any other medieval philosopher, but even his works – more extensive than those of Plato and Aristotle combined – need better editions and translations and further, deeper exploration.

III. MEDIEVAL PHILOSOPHY'S PLACE IN THE
HISTORY OF PHILOSOPHY

The works of the medievals in general would probably be more accessible now if their philosophical value had been recognized earlier, but in that respect, too, history has been unjust to medieval philosophy. The unwarranted disparity between medieval and ancient philosophy as regards not only their texts but also their apparent relevance to post-medieval philosophy has its historical roots in the achievements of the renaissance humanists. The intellectual gap between *ancient* and medieval philosophy seems to have been a natural consequence of the cataclysmic historical events associated with the barbarian invasions, the fall of Rome, and the rise of Christianity. But, more than a thousand years later, an even wider gap appeared between medieval and modern philosophy that can be attributed not to historical events on the grand scale but to the humanists' attitudes shaped by broad cultural considerations more than by specifically philosophical positions. The humanists extolled the ancients, naturally condemned the medieval scholastics against whom they were rebelling, and arrived on the European scene simultaneously with the development of printing, which gave their views an immediate and lasting influential advantage over those of their medieval predecessors. The humanists' views divided medieval from modern philosophy not only by rejecting scholasticism as literarily benighted and hence linguistically, educationally, and intellectually barbarous but also by portraying the philosophy of their own day as the first legitimate successor to the philosophy of antiquity, especially to that of Plato. Of course, many views promoted by the humanists have gone the way of their insistence that education consists almost entirely of the study of the Greek and Latin classics. The effect of their wholesale rejection of medieval philosophy on cultural grounds lasted longer partly because it was reinforced by the Protestant reformers' simultaneous and equally vehement rejection of medieval philosophy on the basis of its association with Catholicism, and partly because the rejection coincided with a growing disaffection toward traditional Christianity among many of the educated elite.

The success of the humanists' deliberate attempt to resume the development of philosophy as if the thousand years of medieval philosophy had never happened can be seen in early modern philosophy. With the exception of Leibniz, the best-known philosophers of the seventeenth and eighteenth centuries mention "the schoolmen" only to denigrate their thought. In fact, however, as historians of modern philosophy have shown, early modern philosophers sometimes owed a large, unacknowledged debt to scholasticism.

Medieval philosophy, then, is useful for understanding the thought of both the periods that surround it. The contribution medieval philosophers make to our understanding of ancient philosophy is perfectly explicit, since they make it in their many commentaries on Aristotle, of which Aquinas's are especially careful and insightful. And understanding the contribution medieval philosophy makes to modern philosophy, seeing the continuities as well as the rifts between the Middle Ages and the Enlightenment, will deepen our understanding of the work of the moderns.

IV. THE SCHOLASTIC METHOD IN MEDIEVAL PHILOSOPHY

Even if an open-minded, experienced reader of ancient, modern, and contemporary philosophy overcomes the traditional historical obstacles just discussed and looks into a good English translation of one of Aquinas's books, he or she is likely to be daunted by the unfamiliar, unusually formal organization of the discussion. Aquinas wrote *Summa contra gentiles*, the most obviously philosophical of his big theological works, in chapters grouped into four books; but even that sort of arrangement, common in later philosophical texts, is made unusual in Aquinas's version by the fact that many of his hundreds of chapters consist almost entirely of series of topically organized arguments, one after another.

The literary format that is characteristic of Aquinas's (and other scholastic philosophers') work, the "scholastic method," is a hallmark of medieval philosophy. Treatises written in this format are typically divided into "questions" or major topics (such as "Truth"), which are subdivided into "articles," which are detailed examinations of particular issues within the topic (such as "Is there truth in sense perception?"). The examination carried out in the article begins with an affirmative or negative thesis in answer to the article's yes/no question, and the thesis is then supported by a series of arguments. Since the thesis is typically opposed to the position the au-

thor will take, its supporting arguments are often called "objections." Immediately following the objections is the presentation of
at least one piece of evidence on the other side of the issue – the *sed
contra* ("But, on the other hand . . ."). The *sed contra* is sometimes
an argument or two, sometimes simply the citation of a relevant
authority – just enough to remind the reader that, despite all the
arguments supporting the thesis, there are grounds for taking the
other side seriously. The body of the article contains the author's
reasoned reply to the initial question, invariably argued for and often
introduced by pertinent explanations and distinctions. The article
then typically concludes with the author's rejoinders to all the objections (and sometimes to the *sed contra* as well), so that the form of
the article is that of an ideal philosophical debate.

The scholastic method, derived from the classroom disputations
that characterized much medieval university instruction (and made
it more interactive and risky than the sort we're used to), is the
methodological essence of scholastic philosophy and helps to explain its reputation for difficulty. But scholastic philosophy is hard
and dry for much the same reason as a beetle is hard and dry: its
skeleton is on the outside. Argument, the skeleton of all philosophy,
has been on the inside during most of philosophy's history: covered
by artful conversation in Plato, by masterful rhetoric in Augustine,
by deceptively plain speaking in the British empiricists. Once one
gets over the initial strangeness of scholastic philosophy's carefully
organized, abundant, direct presentation of its arguments, that characteristic will be appreciated as making scholastic philosophy more
accessible and less ambiguous than philosophy often is. And the
scholastic method – laying out the arguments plainly and developing the issues in such a way that both sides are attacked and
defended – provides an opportunity, unique among the types of philosophical literature, for understanding the nature of philosophical
reasoning and assessing its success or failure. Jan Aertsen (in Chapter 1) explains the origins of scholasticism's specific literary forms
and Aquinas's uses of them.

V. MEDIEVAL PHILOSOPHY AND THEOLOGY

The most formidable obstacle to contemporary philosophers granting medieval philosophy the attention it deserves is the still wide-

spread suspicion that it merely helps itself to carefully selected bits and pieces of philosophy in order to serve the purposes of theology, or that medieval philosophy simply *is* theology of a sort that might occasionally fool an unwary reader into thinking it is philosophy.

We can begin to dispel this misconception by observing that medieval philosophy's connection with theology is like philosophy's many connections with other disciplines in other periods, and that philosophy has been noticeably affected by one or another influence during most of its history. For instance, from the middle of the nineteenth century until the present, the dominant influences on philosophy seem to have included first biology and geology, then physics and mathematics, and now, perhaps, a combination of physics, neurophysiology, and computer science. Still, medieval philosophy, the longest of the traditionally recognized periods in the history of philosophy, is also the one most clearly marked by a single outside influence, and that influence is unquestionably theism of one sort or another – Christianity in most of western Europe, Judaism or Islam elsewhere. Until relatively recently, the influence of theism was considered to have permeated all of medieval philosophy. It did not; a great deal of medieval philosophy – logic, semantic theory, and parts of natural philosophy, for instance – could have been written by altogether irreligious people, and perhaps some of it was.

Theism's influence also used to be considered to have been unhealthy for medieval philosophy. It might have been so if the philosophy really had been confined to theological topics, but it wasn't; or if the medievals typically had developed, say, their theories of inference, of signification, or of acceleration with only religious purposes in view, or had applied religious criteria of some sort in assessing those theories; but they didn't. Of course, they did spend a lot of their time thinking carefully about religious and theological issues, somewhat as twentieth-century Anglo-American philosophers have done with linguistic issues, because they thought those issues were even more fundamental than (and hence explanatory of) many traditional philosophical issues. To that extent they might be fairly described as preoccupied with theism, but certainly not to the exclusion of other concerns or in such a way as to distort their philosophy into preaching or to obliterate the boundary between it and dogmatic theology.

As Anthony Kenny and Jan Pinborg have pointed out, during the Middle Ages

The most advanced scholarly research in philosophy . . . was made by students or teachers in the faculty of Theology (especially in the thirteenth and fourteenth centuries). . . . That is why so much of the study of medieval philosophy is concerned with theological texts. But this historical connection does not entail that philosophy and theology could not be studied separately, or that theological goals determined philosophy and made it unfree and unphilosophical. There are large sections of pure philosophy in theological texts, often to the extent that theological authorities thought it necessary to intercede and demand a stricter limitation to theological problems.

(Kenny, 1982, p. 15)

Philosophers have always been particularly, and legitimately, concerned with the influence of religion on philosophy, because of religion's reputation for anti-intellectualism and its tendency to try to settle disputes by simply citing doctrine. But the professional attitude of medieval philosopher–theologians toward religion was determinedly *anti*-anti-intellectual, and in their professional capacity they saw doctrine primarily as part of their subject matter to be analyzed and argued over, rather than as an argument-stopper. In particular, no open-minded philosophical reader can study even a few pages of Aquinas without recognizing a kindred spirit, even when Aquinas is working on an unmistakably theological topic such as creation, God's knowledge, or the Incarnation. Aquinas is at least as concerned as we are with making sense of obscure claims, exploring the implications and interrelations of theoretical propositions, and supporting them with valid arguments dependent on plausible premises. And he is no less concerned than any responsible philosopher has ever been with the truth, coherence, consistency, and justification of his beliefs, his religious beliefs no less than his philosophical ones.

Still, theology is not philosophy, and if any medieval philosopher's work seems correctly characterized as theology, Aquinas's does (as Mark Jordan explains in Chapter 9). His active academic career was as a member of the Faculty of Theology; his biggest, most characteristic works seem to be altogether theological in their motivation; and he was officially designated a Doctor of the Church. But the modern philosophical reader should understand that although Aquinas's motivation may be most readily described as theological, what he produces in acting on that motivation is thoroughly, interestingly philosophical. Some of the most fully developed and traditionally recognized components of Aquinas's philosophy are presented below in chapters by John Wippel, Norman Kretzmann, Scott Mac-Donald, Ralph McInerny, and Paul Sigmund, each of whom inevitably and quite naturally refers to connections between the particular philosophical subject matter and Aquinas's theological concerns.

A closer look at Aquinas's lifelong enterprise of philosophical theology will show that even its motivation can be construed as fundamentally philosophical. In Aquinas's Aristotelian view, all human beings by their very nature want to understand, and to understand a thing, event, or state of affairs is to know its causes; consequently, the natural human desire to understand will naturally, or at least ideally, spur the inquiring mind to seek knowledge of the first cause of all. Aquinas of course thinks that human beings have relatively easy access to particular knowledge of the absolutely first cause through divine revelation in Scripture. But he is convinced that a great deal of such knowledge can also be obtained through a standard sort of application of reason to evidence available to everyone without a revealed text. He is also convinced that even propositions conveyed initially by revelation and available only in that way – such as the doctrine of the Trinity – can be instructively clarified, explained, and confirmed by reasoning of a sort that differs from other philosophical reasoning only in its subject matter. Wippel's chapter (4) includes a discussion of the close connection between philosophy and theology in Aquinas's metaphysics, and Eleonore Stump's chapter (10) shows that even in Aquinas's commentaries on Scripture itself there is a good deal of philosophical material.

Of course, Aquinas is not simply a philosopher–theologian but the paradigmatic *Christian* philosopher–theologian. Nonetheless, he thought that Christians should be ready to dispute theological issues with non-Christians of all sorts. Since Jews accept the Old Testament and heretics the New, Christians can argue with them on the basis of commonly accepted authority; but because some non-Christians – "for instance, Mohammedans and pagans – do not agree with us about the authority of any Scripture on the basis of which they can be convinced . . . it is necessary to have recourse to natural reason, to which everyone is compelled to assent – although where theological issues are concerned it cannot do the whole job" (SCG I.2.11). It is even more surprising that Aquinas differed from most of his thirteenth-century academic Christian contemporaries in the breadth and depth of his respect for and sense of partnership with the Islamic and Jewish philosopher–theologians Avicenna and Maimonides. As David Burrell explains in Chapter 3, Aquinas saw them as valued co-workers in the vast project of clarifying and supporting revealed doctrine by philosophical analysis and argumentation, uncovering in the process the need to investigate all the traditionally recognized areas of philosophy in a newly discerned web of relationships among themselves and with theology.

VI. AQUINAS'S ARISTOTELIANISM

Some scholars impressed with Aquinas's achievements in general and sympathetic with his intellectual Christianity have insisted on viewing him as a theologian rather than a philosopher. They have taken a narrow view of philosophy, one that coincides better with Aquinas's thirteenth-century understanding of *philosophia* than with our use of "philosophy," and on that basis they have been willing to classify only Aquinas's commentaries on Aristotle as philosophical works. Certainly those commentaries are philosophical, as purely philosophical as the Aristotelian works they elucidate. But if they constituted all the philosophy Aquinas had produced, no one could reasonably rank him among the great philosophers. As Jordan says below, Aquinas wrote those commentaries to make sense of Aristotle's philosophy, not to set out a philosophy of his own. Our appreciation of his outstanding value as a philosopher depends on our seeing his ostensibly theological works as also fundamentally philosophical, in the way suggested above and developed differently by Aertsen and by Jordan (Chapters 1 and 9).

Aquinas's aim in those many works of his requires him to take up traditional philosophical issues often, especially in metaphysics (see Wippel's Chapter 4), philosophy of mind (Kretzmann's Chapter 5), epistemology (MacDonald's Chapter 6), ethics (McInerny's Chapter 7), and politics and law (Sigmund's Chapter 8). Even a casual reader of any of those detailed discussions will notice that Aquinas very often cites Aristotle as a source or in support of a thesis he is defending, and a reader who knows Aristotle well will recognize even more of Aquinas's philosophy as Aristotelian. In those circumstances it's only natural to wonder whether Aquinas isn't merely Aristotle's most talented and prominent follower. Again, even scholars entirely friendly to Aquinas and impressed with his achievements as a philosopher have sometimes presented him as simply the consummate Aristotelian, adopting the term "Aristotelian–Thomistic" as the best short characterization of Aquinas's philosophical positions. Joseph Owens in Chapter 2 provides a careful, thoroughly critical analysis of that still prevalent view, effectively dispelling the notion that Aquinas's philosophy is fundamentally an extrapolation of Aristotle's, adjusted here and there to suit Christian doctrine.

VII. CONCLUSION

Having explained and, we hope, removed the traditional obstacles to taking Aquinas's philosophy as seriously as that of any other philosopher of the first rank, we invite the reader to consider the contributors to this Companion as ten specialized guides to important components of Aquinas's thought and intellectual background. Besides discussing some of the salient features of his or her special topic, each contributor points out many more related, interesting issues that must be looked for in Aquinas's works themselves and elucidated in articles and books selected from a vast secondary literature. No book this size, no five-foot shelf of books this size, could be a fully satisfactory companion to all aspects of Aquinas's thought, but the ten contributors hope to have provided a Companion to Aquinas that will suffice to introduce him to new readers and to show them and others the way to a wider knowledge and a deeper appreciation of his philosophy.

1 Aquinas's philosophy in its historical setting

I. INTRODUCTION

Thomas Aquinas was born at the end of 1224 or the beginning of 1225 in Roccasecca, not far from Naples. He was the scion of a prominent noble family, the counts of Aquino. Aquinas received his earliest education at the Benedictine Abbey of Monte Cassino. In 1239 he went to the University of Naples to study the liberal arts.

In Naples Aquinas became acquainted with the relatively new Order of Friar Preachers, better known as the Dominicans. Like the Franciscans, whose order was founded during the same period, the Dominicans were mendicants, radicalizing the evangelical ideal of poverty. Unlike the Benedictines, the Dominicans did not tie themselves to one specific cloister. Their life was therefore marked by a high degree of mobility. The Dominicans were the first religious order to make devotion to study one of its main objectives; in keeping with this aim they established study houses in university cities throughout Europe. In 1244 Aquinas decided to join the new order, much against the will of his family, who apparently had other plans for him. He was detained for a year in the family castle of Roccasecca, but his family finally accepted Aquinas's decision.

For his study of theology, the superiors of the Dominican Order sent Aquinas to Paris, then the intellectual center of Christendom, and next to the *studium generale* of the Dominicans in Cologne. There he studied from 1248 to 1252 with Albert the Great, who was named *Doctor universalis* in the Middle Ages because of his wide-ranging scholarly interests. To complete his theological training Aquinas returned to the University of Paris (1252–1256). During these years the theological faculty there harbored an air of hostility toward the mendicants. Dominicans and Franciscans had obtained chairs in the faculty, and the secular masters feared that their guild would come to be dominated by members of these religious orders. They refused to admit Aquinas, as well as his Franciscan colleague Bonaventure, as a master. Only through papal intervention was their resistance brought to an end.

From 1256 to 1259 Aquinas was occupied as a master in theology at the University of Paris. He next taught for ten years in the Italian cities of Orvieto, Rome, and Viterbo. At the request of his order, Aquinas in 1269 became a professor in Paris for a second time. The growing doctrinal tensions between some masters in the Faculty of Arts and the theologians demanded his attention. With two publications, Aquinas took a stand in the discussions, as we shall see (sect. 4). In 1272 he was ordered to set up a school of theology in Naples. On March 7, 1274, Aquinas died, only forty-nine years old.[1]

From this summary of his career one point is clear: Aquinas, like many other great medieval thinkers, was a *theologian* by profession. He always saw himself as a master of the "sacred doctrine." This fact can embarrass the historian of medieval philosophy. A good illustration is the experience that Etienne Gilson, one of the most prominent figures in the study of medieval philosophy in our century, describes in his intellectual autobiography, *The Philosopher and Theology*. His doctoral dissertation of 1913 dealt with Descartes. Through his inquiry into the French philosopher's sources he had come to the conclusion, contrary to the generally accepted prejudice, that there was a truly original philosophy in the Middle Ages. He elaborated this insight in his studies of Thomism and the philosophy of Bonaventure. Gilson's newly acquired certainty of the existence of a "medieval philosophy" was, however, shaken by critics. They objected that neither in Aquinas nor in Bonaventure is there a distinctive philosophy. "There remained for me only theologies," Gilson writes.[2]

But, as this book itself will help to show, it is unthinkable that the historian of philosophy is left with little to say about Aquinas's work, which is more complex than the term "theology" suggests.[3] An indication of this complexity can be found in a document of his contemporaries. On May 2, 1274, the rector of the University of Paris and "all the masters teaching in the Faculty of Arts" sent a letter to the general chapter of the Dominicans meeting in Lyons. In that letter they expressed their grief at the death of Friar Thomas and made known their wish that his final resting place should be Paris, "the noblest of all university cities." Their letter had another purpose as well. The masters requested the Dominicans to send them "some writings of a philosophical nature, begun by [Thomas] at Paris, but left unfinished at his departure." In addition, they requested the sending of translations that "he himself promised would be sent to us," namely, Latin versions of the commentary of Simplicius on Aristotle's *De caelo* and of Proclus's exposition of Plato's *Timaeus*.[4]

This document is remarkable for more than one reason. Masters in the Faculty of Arts (not Theology) were showing their interest in Aquinas's writings "of a philosophical nature." (It has been suggested that the masters were referring here to his Commentary on Aristotle's *Metaphysics*.)[5] Moreover, Aquinas apparently possessed commentaries on philosophical texts to which the masters of arts did not have access. The picture that emerges from this letter is that Aquinas engaged in a thorough study of the philosophical tradition, both of Aristotelianism and of Platonism. What is especially intriguing from our view of the academic disciplines is that a professional theologian took the trouble to write a commentary on unquestionably philosophical works by Aristotle – not only on the *Metaphysics* but on several others as well.[6]

In this chapter Aquinas's attitude towards philosophy, his leading sources, and the aims of his philosophical interest are clarified in two complementary ways. First, his writings, which are very voluminous in spite of his relatively early death, will be placed within the historical context of the thirteenth century. An overview of his work and its philosophical relevance will be provided in connection with the most important intellectual developments in this period – the rise of the university, the reception of Aristotle, and the conflict between the faculties (sections II–IV). Subsequently, Aquinas's view of philosophy and of its relationship to theology will be elaborated in a more systematic way (sections V–X).

II. UNIVERSITIES AND "SCHOLASTIC" THEOLOGY

The first development that shaped thirteenth-century thought was the rise of universities. The life and work of Aquinas were marked by this new institution, which was perhaps the most important contribution of the Middle Ages to western culture. Certainly it is impossible to imagine intellectual life in our own day without the university.[7]

The rise of universities in the thirteenth century was part of a more general social development. Originally, the university was nothing other than a special case of the corporations and guilds, which in this period arose in cities everywhere in western Europe. Just as those who were active in the same craft or trade united to form a guild to protect and further their interests, so masters and students joined together to form a *universitas*. As a result, higher education was institutionalized for the first time and thus became tied to fixed rules and forms. In the statutes of the university even the curriculum was set, as were the tasks of the master and the requirements a student had to satisfy to attain first the degree of *baccalaureus* and later that of *magister*, the degree that carried with it "the right to teach" (*licentia docendi*).

The basis of education in the medieval university was the *lectio*, the reading and exposition of a text. An essential difference from the present-day system of education is that the text was not chosen by the master himself; instead, an "authoritative" text was prescribed in the statutes. This form of education led to the development of a sophisticated hermeneutics. To understand the authoritative author's intention, much attention was devoted to items such as the multiple senses of words and "the properties of terms" – the effect of a word's syntactic context on its semantic function. The established format of the university *lectio* also accounts for the fact that the genre of the commentary was so frequently used during this period. But the term "commentary" is to be taken in a broad sense here, for medieval commentators dealt with the content of a basic text in many different ways, ranging from line-by-line explications to increasingly original essays, sometimes dependent only thematically on the original.

The second task of the master was to hold disputations "a number of times" throughout the academic year. The *disputatio* about a question set by the master was a regular part of university training. Almost always the form of the question demanded an affirmative or a negative reply, thus presenting an issue with two sides. One of the bachelors (counterparts of today's graduate students, broadly speaking) was required to respond to the arguments advanced on both sides. On the day following the dispute, the master met his students for the *determinatio* or resolution, carefully weighing the arguments pro and con and formulating a systematic answer to the disputed question. The written version of a series of these questions, arguments, and resolutions forms the genre of the *quaestiones disputatae*. This pattern of education naturally led to the development of a system of refined techniques of argumentation.

The *lectio* and the *disputatio* provided students with logical-semantic training that clearly left its mark on the philosophical and theological treatises of the thirteenth century. "Scholasticism," a term often used as a synonym for medieval thought, gives expression to this close connection between the way of thinking and the methods used in the "schools." Both the form and content of Aquinas's writings must be understood in their scholastic context.[8]

In the theological faculty, where Aquinas carried out his academic duties, the course of study lasted eight years, following the six years required to obtain the degree of bachelor of arts. During the final years of a bachelor's study of theology, he was required to lecture on the *Sentences*, a collection of doctrinally central, often difficult texts from Scripture and the Church Fathers, compiled by Peter Lombard (d. 1160). A Commentary on the *Sentences* was the formal requirement for the degree of master of theology; it can be compared with the modern Ph.D. thesis. Aquinas lectured as *sententiarius* at Paris from 1252 through 1256. Aquinas's Commentary, his first great systematic work, displays original features. He does not follow the scheme Peter Lombard had used to arrange the texts that make up the *Sentences*. Lombard had structured his work on the basis of a statement made by Augustine in *De doctrina christiana* (I, c. 2), according to which "all teaching (*doctrina*) is either about things or about signs." On Aquinas's scheme, things are to be considered according to the pattern of their proceeding from God as their source (Trinity, creation, the nature of creatures) and insofar as they return to him as their end (salvation and atonement).[9] This scheme of *exitus* and *reditus* is derived from Neoplatonism and plays a fundamental role in Aquinas's thought. The origin and end of things are one and the same. The dynamics of reality is a circular motion (*circulatio*).

The authoritative text that formed the basis of the *lectio* in the theology faculty was the Bible. The master in theology was thought of as primarily a "Master in the sacred Page." Aquinas's lecturing on the Bible resulted in several scriptural commentaries, to which relatively little attention has as yet been devoted.[10] His most important commentaries are those on Job, the Psalms, Matthew, John, and the letters of Paul.

Scholastic Bible commentaries are of a different character than their modern counterparts. An example can clarify this. Modern commentaries explain the opening passage of the Gospel of John ("In the beginning was the Word") by pointing to the historical background of the terms "beginning" and "Word" (*Logos*). Aquinas begins his commentary by asking what a beginning is and what a word is. His explanation of "word" starts from Aristotle's well-known statement (*De interpretatione* 1, 16a4) that words are signs of the "passions" or "conceptions" of the soul. But then Aquinas introduces an idea that is not found in Aristotle in this form, namely, that the immediate significates of spoken words are themselves also called "words." This observation leads to an extensive reflection on this "inner" word, the formation of which he describes as the terminus of the intellective operation.[11] The conception of the inner word is the essential completion of knowledge and is therefore found in every nature that has the ability to know. Aquinas's next step is to explain the differences between the human word and the divine word, and to use all these observations to explain the nature and activity of the Word that was in the beginning. As this example shows, Aquinas does not hesitate to base the exposition of a biblical text on philosophical reflections.[12]

Aquinas also held disputations, usually once every two weeks. His *quaestiones disputatae* include *De veritate* (On Truth), *De potentia* (On the Power of God in the creation and conservation of things), *De malo* (On Evil), *De spiritualibus creaturis* (On Spiritual Creatures) and *De anima* (On the Soul). These titles reveal the broad range of Aquinas's interests – theological in their motivation but often philosophical in content. In addition to the regular disputations, disputations of a somewhat different character were held twice a year at the University of Paris during the penitential seasons of Advent and Lent. The subjects on these occasions were determined not by the master but by his audience. Thus such a disputation could be about any theme (*de quolibet*). We also have a collection of Aquinas's *quaestiones quodlibetales*, which often afford a good impression of the live issues of the day.

In addition to these various sorts of works that resulted directly from Aquinas's duties as a theology professor, there are writings that were not the product of his university teaching. Among these, his two great theological syntheses deserve special attention.[13] For Dominican missionaries in the Moslem world he wrote the *Summa contra gentiles* (SCG). His intention in this work is to make "the truth of the Catholic faith" manifest even to those who hold beliefs opposed to it. Aquinas observes (SCG I.3) that there is "a twofold mode of truth" in what Christians profess about God. Some truths about God, for example, that God is triune, surpass the ability of human reason to prove. But other truths can be reached by natural reason, for instance, that God exists, that there is one God. Such truths have been proved demonstratively by the philosophers, he maintains. On the basis of this distinction Aquinas unfolds the structure of his *Summa* (I.9). He will proceed in the first three books "by the way of reason," by bringing forward both necessary ("demonstrative") and probable arguments, dealing with God in himself, with creation, and with the ordering of creatures to God as their end. In the fourth book he will use reason in another way, clarifying truths that surpass reason and are known only by revelation. Particularly in its first three books, SCG is an important source for Aquinas's philosophical views.

During his Italian period (1259–1269), Aquinas began a second synthesis, the *Summa theologiae* (ST). This work, Aquinas's main achievement, is structured according to the scholastic method of the disputation: it is constructed entirely of *quaestiones*, which are again divided into subquestions, *articuli*. Every "article" follows a fixed pattern. A yes/no question is raised, giving rise to an examination of two contradictory possibilities, such as "Does God exist?" (ST Prima pars, question 2, article 3 [Ia.2.3]). The development of the article's question consists of four parts that begin with fixed formulas:

1. "It seems that it is not so" (*Videtur quod non*), the introduction to arguments supporting the negative reply (the "objections"). In ST Ia.2.3 Aquinas puts forward the well-known argument from evil.

2. "On the contrary" (*Sed contra*), the introduction to arguments or authoritative pronouncements, supporting the opposite reply. Here Aquinas cites an authoritative text, Exodus 3:14, where God says of himself, "I am who am." Since this

part of the development almost always prefigures Aquinas's reasoned reply, it is often meagre in itself, simply reminding the reader that there are good reasons for taking the other side seriously.

3. "I reply that it must be said that . . ." (*Respondeo dicendum quod . . .*), the beginning of the master's own doctrinal explanation, supporting the reply he favors. Here Aquinas presents five proofs for the existence of God, the so-called "five ways."

4. Finally, Aquinas offers rejoinders to the objections that were raised at the beginning. In the construction of an article, two characteristic elements of the scholastic method work together: authority and argument. The first two parts often rely heavily on authority, the third and fourth are based almost entirely on rational argumentation.

This construction is instructive in another respect as well. In the first question of ST Ia Aquinas argues that theological science proceeds from the articles of faith, which are revealed to human beings in the Bible. For a believer who subscribes to the articles of faith, the existence of God is not in question. Yet Aquinas presents proofs for it in ST Ia.2. In one of his quodlibetal questions he gives a motive for this procedure. A master who resolves a theological question exclusively on the basis of an authority and not on grounds of rational argumentation (*ratio*) makes no contribution to knowledge (*scientia*) and sends his audience away empty.[14] If theology aspires to be a systematic theoretical inquiry, it must make room for philosophical reasoning.

From this overview of Aquinas's theological works – his commentary on the *Sentences*, biblical commentaries, disputed questions, and *Summae* – it is obvious that his conception of theology is broader than what is usually understood as "theology" today. It is a "scholastic" theology because of its distinctive use of philosophy.[15] Aquinas himself acknowledges that theologians diverge because of their different philosophical positions. Augustine and the majority of the saints followed Plato's views in philosophical matters that do not touch faith, but others followed Aristotle.[16] It is therefore important to find out what philosophy Aquinas followed. Other writings of his provide the answer.

III. PHILOSOPHY AND THE ARTS FACULTY OF THE MEDIEVAL UNIVERSITY

The second development that shaped thirteenth-century western European thought was the reception of the complete works of Aristotle in Latin translations. The early Middle Ages had known only his logical works, but from the middle of the twelfth century his other writings also became available in translation. The acquisition of this new philosophical literature had far-reaching consequences for intellectual life. The English historian David Knowles has justifiedly spoken of it as the "Philosophical Revolution" of the thirteenth century.[17] Until that time medieval thought had been oriented mainly toward Augustine, Boethius, and Pseudo-Dionysius the Areopagite, who were all strongly influenced by Platonism. In Aristotelianism it was now furnished with a comprehensive, often technical philosophy, in which human beings and other things in the physical world were understood not in terms of their participation in ideal Forms but on the basis of their own inner principles or natures.

The study of Aristotelian philosophy acquired a place of its own in the medieval university. In the arts faculty, which provided the course of studies that prepared the student for the other faculties, the works of Aristotle became the basic texts for the *lectio*. This change in the curriculum did not go unchallenged. The resistance was strongest from the ecclesiastics, whose suspicion of the "naturalistic" thought of Aristotle was wide and deep. In 1210 a provincial synod prohibited the University of Paris from "reading" Aristotle's works on natural philosophy "on pain of excommunication." But this prohibition, which was renewed more than once during the decades that followed, was not a universal one. The natural philosophy of Aristotle was studied at the University of Naples while Aquinas was a student there. (Naples was part of the kingdom of Sicily, one of the centers where the works of Aristotle were translated from Arabic into Latin.)

The study of Aristotle spread rapidly through the universities. It was officially approved at the University of Paris on March 19, 1255. At that time the Faculty of Arts stated officially that the lecture program must include all the works of Aristotle: his logical writings, of course, but also those about natural philosophy, metaphysics and ethics.[18] This decree can be viewed as the final seal on the fact that the once primarily preparatory arts faculty had developed in the thirteenth century into a philosophy faculty. There the student was trained for six years in the thought of Aristotle, who had become known to all as "the Philosopher." Scholastic theoretical discussion of all sorts would henceforth be based on the Aristotelian conceptual framework.

One of the most striking aspects of Aquinas's work is that a considerable part of his writings consists of commentaries on "the Philosopher." This is the more remarkable because such work did not belong to his proper academic duty: he was never a master in the arts faculty. Yet he apparently recognized in the reception of Aristotle a tremendous challenge to Christian thought and therefore considered it worth the effort to analyze Aristotelian philosophy thoroughly. That his commentaries were highly regarded may be seen from the letter the masters of the arts faculty wrote shortly after his death.[19]

Aquinas took pains to secure reliable translations of Aristotle and his Greek commentators. In this respect he received assistance from another friar, the Flemish Dominican William of Moerbeke, who revised older translations and made new translations directly from the Greek. Aquinas wrote no fewer than twelve commentaries, a number of which remained uncompleted at his early death in 1274. He commented on *De interpretatione*, the *Posterior Analytics*, the *Physics*, *De caelo*, *De generatione et corruptione*, *Meteora*, *De anima*, *De sensu et sensato*, *De memoria et reminiscentia*, the *Metaphysics*, the *Nicomachean Ethics*, and the *Politics*. His commentaries are not those of a historian but of a philosopher, and his intention is always to seek the truth of what the Philosopher has thought. In one of his commentaries (In DC I.22) he says expressly that "the inquiry of philosophy has as its purpose to know not what men have thought but what the truth is about reality."

Aquinas's intense engagement with Aristotle's thought profoundly influenced his own. He adopts essential insights from Aristotle, as is especially evident in his theory of knowledge.[20] He rejects the view that a human being has innate ideas. The basis of human knowledge is sense experience. "It is natural to a human being to attain to what is intelligible through objects of sense, because our knowledge originates from sense" (ST Ia.1.9). Aquinas also rejects Augustine's idea that we need divine illumination to attain certain knowledge. The human intellect has a "natural light" that is itself sufficient for the knowledge of truths.[21] The way to intellective cognition passes from sensory cognition through abstraction: the intellect abstracts the intelligible content from sense images. Aquinas's frequent reproach to the Platonists is that they project our necessarily abstract mode of knowing onto the mode of being of things, which leads them to hold incorrectly that what is abstracted in the intellect is also "separate," abstracted from physical things, in reality.[22]

Yet it would be decidedly incorrect to consider Aquinas's thought to be simply a continuation of Aristotelianism, as many older discussions suggest by such terms as "Aristotelian–Thomist philosophy." His thought contains essentially Platonic elements. As we have seen, even at the beginning of his career in his Commentary on the Sentences, Aquinas used the neoplatonic scheme of the *exitus* and *reditus* of all things as a fundamental principle of organization. Recent studies have shown that the notion of "participation" plays a central role in Aquinas's metaphysics.[23] He thinks of the relation between created being and God in terms of participation, a concept Plato had introduced to express the relation between visible things and the Forms, and a concept Aristotle had sharply criticized.

Aquinas deals extensively with "the views of the Platonists" in his Commentary on the *Liber De causis* ("The Book on Causes"), a work by an anonymous Muslim author. This treatise was also part of the arts curriculum at Paris, because it was thought to be a work of "the Philosopher." To Aquinas goes the credit for having been the first in the Middle Ages to have recognized its true *auctoritas*. In his commentary he points out that this work is an excerpt from the *Elementatio theologica* of Proclus.[24] Aquinas was able to arrive at this insight because he was the first to have a copy of the Latin translation of the *Elementatio*, completed in 1268 by William of Moerbeke. Aquinas must have made a careful study of Proclus's work, for in his commentary he refers again and again to the original propositions from the *Elementatio* on which the author of *De causis* was drawing. Thus Aquinas's commentary on *De causis* can likewise be considered a commentary on the neoplatonic philosopher Proclus.

Most unusual in the thirteenth century was Aquinas's writing of commentaries on two works by Boethius, *De trinitate* and *De hebdomadibus*.[25] The complete title of the latter work is "How can substances be good in virtue of the fact that they have being when they are not substantial goods?" Boethius reduces this to the question whether beings are good by their own substance or by participation in something else. Boethius's text was the starting point of Aquinas's reflection on the notion of participation. His commentary on *De hebdomadibus* is therefore essential for our understanding of his interpretation of the doctrine.

In the Prologue to his commentary on the *De divinis nominibus* ("On the divine names") of Pseudo-Dionysius, Aquinas provides an evaluation of Platonism. He wants to justify Dionysius's Platonic way of speaking of God as "the Good itself" and "the *per se* Good." He describes the Platonists as wanting to reduce every composite thing to simple, abstract principles. That is why they posit the existence of separate, ideal Forms of things. They apply this approach not only to the species of natural things but also to that which is most common, namely, good, one, and being. They hold that there is a first principle, which is the essence of goodness, of unity, and of being – a principle, Aquinas says, that we call God. Other things are called good, one, or being because of their derivation from the first principle. In the continuation of the Prologue, Aquinas rejects the first application of the Platonic method, subscribing to Aristotle's criticism that the Platonists project our abstract mode of knowing onto the mode of being of things. But with regard to the first principle itself, he recognizes the legitimacy of the Platonic approach.[26] The reduction to abstract principles is justified only at the level of that which is most common, being, one, and good. These general properties are called "transcendentals" in medieval philosophy, because they transcend the Aristotelian categories. The first "separate" principle is Being itself; other things participate in being.

Aquinas's conceptions, like those of any other thinker, cannot simply be reduced to his leading sources. His originality appears clearly in the philosophical treatise *De ente et essentia* ("On Being and Essence"). It is one of his earliest works, written even before he became a master in theology, but in it one already finds essential features of his metaphysics. In chapter 4 he discusses the essence of the "separated substances," or spiritual creatures, such as angels. (This issue engaged Aquinas a great deal – he even devoted a particular treatise to it, *De substantiis separatis* – and it provides a context in which the deepest intentions of his metaphysics can be recovered.) At stake is the ontological structure of finite substances. This structure cannot consist in the (Aristotelian) composition of form and matter, for *separated* substances, although substances, are separated from matter. Yet although such substances are pure forms, they do not have complete simplicity. They have their being (*esse*) not of themselves, but from something else. Aquinas's thesis, which remains distinctive for his ontology, is that all creatures are marked by the non-identity of their essence and their *esse*.[27]

IV. "THE CONFLICT OF THE FACULTIES"

The constellation of the medieval university bore within it the seeds of conflict. The Faculty of Arts had in fact developed into a philosophy faculty where Aristotle's rational account of the world was taught. In the course of the thirteenth century, the writings and Aristotle commentaries of the two great Islamic philosophers Avicenna and Averroes also became available for this program. But the study of the arts was still preparatory for the theology faculty, in which the doctrine of the Christian faith was explained and systematized. Greek and Arabic philosophy on the one hand and Christian theology on the other make divergent statements about human beings and the world, and both sides claim truth. The truth claims of philosophy and theology were the cause of what one might name (following Kant) "the conflict of the faculties."

The Faculty of Arts of the University of Paris, called by Albert the Great "the city of philosophers," after 1260 tended to make the study of philosophy independent of theology. A group of young masters, led by Siger of Brabant, defended the autonomy of philosophy and of natural reason. In their analysis of Aristotle they arrived at conclusions that were in conflict with Christian doctrine. Thus Siger of Brabant taught "the eternity of the world" (that is, that the universe has always existed) and "the unicity of intellect" (that there is only one intellect for all mankind). This development in the Faculty of Arts increasingly disturbed the theologians. Bonaventure was one of the first to warn against "the untrue conceptions of the members of the arts faculty."[28] In 1270 the bishop of Paris condemned thirteen theses that were taught by masters in the arts. In this intellectual crisis Aquinas also took a stand. During his second professorship in Paris he published treatises on the two principal controversies.[29]

The controversy over the unicity of intellect stemmed from an obscure passage in Aristotle's *De anima*. In the third book he investigates intellect, "that with which the soul knows and thinks." He describes it as "separate"; only the intellect is "immortal and eternal" (430a17–23). The Arabic philosopher Averroes, so highly regarded as an interpreter of Aristotle in the thirteenth century that he was called "the Commentator," had read this passage as claiming that the intellect is one and the same for all human beings. For if intellect is "separate," it is not pluralized over individuals. This view struck the theologians as particularly shocking, because it was incompatible with the Christian doctrine of individual immortality and personal moral responsibility.

Aquinas reacted with his treatise *De unitate intellectus* (certain manuscripts add to this title "*contra Averroistas*"). Although Siger of Brabant is not named, this work is directed primarily against him. The Averroist view of the unicity of intellect implies that the rational soul is not the substantial form of the human body. But this position is untenable for Aquinas, for two reasons. First, it is contrary to Aristotle's own conception. Aquinas makes this clear through an extensive exegesis of *De anima* and an investigation of the Greek commentators. His conclusion (ch. 2) is that Averroes "was not so much a Peripatetic as a corrupter of Peripatetic philosophy" (*philosophiae peripateticae depravator*). This conclusion, which preserves the compatibility of Aristotelianism with Christianity, must have strengthened Aquinas in his conviction that it was worthwhile for a theologian to write commentaries on the works of Aristotle. Second, the Averroist position is not only exegetically but also philosophically untenable. Aquinas's basic argument rests on the evident fact "that this individual human being understands" – a fact that remains inexplicable if the substantial form of a human being does not include intellect, the principle of this activity.

The most striking aspect of *De unitate intellectus* is that the argumentation is purely philosophical. In the Prologue Aquinas says that it is not his intention to show that the Averroist position is incorrect because it contradicts the truth of the Christian faith – that is evident to everyone, he observes. His intention is to show that this position contradicts "the principles of philosophy." He wants to challenge Siger of Brabant on his own terrain, not through "documents of faith," but on strictly rational grounds.

The second issue regarding which the Christian tradition was opposed to Greek philosophy was the thesis of "the eternity of the world."[30] Aristotle, in the *Physics*, had concluded that the world was beginningless because of the impossibility of explaining an absolute beginning of motion. Masters in the Faculty of Arts adopted this conclusion as philosophers. But Christian doctrine holds that the world did begin to exist: "In the beginning God created the heavens and the earth."

Aquinas also devoted a separate treatise to this controversy, his *De aeternitate mundi*. After having expressed the doctrine "that the world's duration had a beginning," he immediately raises the problem "whether the world could have always existed." He argues that the whole problem comes down to the question of whether the concepts *created by God* and *eternal (beginningless)* are contradictory. At this point it becomes clear against whom this treatise is really directed. Aquinas is opposing not the masters in the Faculty of Arts, but fellow theologians. Bonaventure had argued that the idea of "an eternal created world" contains an inner contradiction. Creation *ex nihilo* necessarily implies a temporal beginning.[31] According to Aquinas, on the other hand, creation "from nothing" means that things are caused by God in their complete being, but this ontological dependence does not necessarily imply a temporal beginning. A cause does not necessarily precede its effect in duration, but can be simultaneous with the effect. An eternal creation is *possible*, philosophically speaking. No compelling arguments can be adduced for the "novelty" of the world. Neither, for that matter, can the opinion of the philosophers, that the world is necessarily eternal, be proved. Aristotle's arguments for the eternalist position are not demonstrative and conclusive, but only probable. That the world had a beginning we know only on the basis of divine revelation.[32]

The fact that in *De aeternitae mundi* Aquinas defends the possibility of an eternal creation against theologians is worth noting. He intends to provide a metaphysical deepening of the concept of creation by pointing out that it is not the concept of *beginning* but that of *original dependence of being* that necessarily belongs to its essence.[33] Aquinas's view provoked fierce reactions from theologians. A few years after his death the Franciscan William de la Mare put together the *Correctorium Fratris Thomae*, which contained 118 points of criticism. One of the views most objectionable to William was

Brother Thomas's rejection of the demonstrability of the world's temporal beginning.[34]

V. "ALL HUMAN BEINGS BY NATURE DESIRE TO KNOW": THE LEGITIMACY OF PHILOSOPHY

The preceding sections have explained the role of philosophy in Aquinas's thought by placing his works in the "scholastic" context of the thirteenth century. But this picture should be complemented by a more direct consideration of Aquinas's own relationship to philosophy.

An appropriate point of departure is a text from the "Philosopher" – the renowned opening statement of Aristotle's *Metaphysics* (980a21): "All human beings by nature desire to know." This authoritative text must have struck a special chord in the university milieu. Aquinas refers to it in various contexts and also in his theological works. Aristotle's statement puts into words something that Aquinas regards as essential for human beings. The desire to know is "natural," a desire rooted in human nature. Human beings, precisely because they are human, aim at knowledge as their end. Hence Aristotle can even say that *all* human beings desire to know. This is not an empirical observation, but a pronouncement about the essence of humanity.

This ontological aspect is elaborated by Aquinas in his Commentary on the *Metaphysics* (1.1–4). Unlike Aristotle, who merely makes the pronouncement, Aquinas advances three arguments for the desire to know. The first is based on the thesis that each thing naturally desires its perfection. Something is perfect insofar as it is fully actualized, not insofar as it is in a state of potentiality. The desire of a thing for perfection is the desire for the actualization of its naturally essential potentialities. What does this mean for human beings? That by which a human being is human is intellect. Now, through his cognitive powers a person has access to all things, but only potentially. Human beings possess no innate knowledge of reality. Knowledge is the actualization of the natural human potentialities, the perfection of the human being. That is why human beings naturally desire to know. On the basis of this argument Aquinas draws the conclusion that all scientific, systematic knowledge (*omnis scientia*) is good, since knowledge is the perfection of the human being as such, the fulfillment of its natural desire.[35]

With this conclusion Aquinas opposes another tradition in the Middle Ages that was especially powerful in the monastic world. This tradition discerns and deplores human "curiosity", an unvirtuous desire to know in human beings. Bernard of Clairvaux (1090–1153), one of the leading figures in twelfth-century intellectual life, writes: "There are people who want to know solely for the sake of knowing, and that is scandalous curiosity."[36] The authority behind this tradition is Augustine.

In Book X, 35 of the Confessions, Augustine deals at length with the vice of curiosity. He calls it "a vain desire cloaked in the name of knowledge." Curiosity is the temptation to seek knowledge for its own sake. For Augustine, "knowledge" has an instrumental meaning. It must be subservient to human salvation and oriented to faith. God and the human soul are the only things worthy of being known. From this perspective Augustine criticizes the inquiry of philosophers into the nature of things: "Because of this morbid curiosity . . . men proceed to search out the secrets of nature, things outside ourselves, to know which profits us nothing, and of which men desire nothing but to know them."

For Aquinas, however, the human desire to know is not a vain curiosity. Following Aristotle, he sees the desire to know as natural. It arises from human nature and is directed to human perfection. The Augustinian tradition of condemning the vice of curiosity accordingly plays no role in Aquinas's work, stamped by the new world of the university. In the part of ST that deals with the theme of curiosity, he claims that "the study of philosophy is legitimate and praiseworthy (licitum et laudabile) in itself."[37] Human beings marvel at things and desire to know the causes of what they see.

VI. THE PROGRESS OF PHILOSOPHY

Individually and as a species, we make only gradual progress in the knowledge of the causes. What was dealt with imperfectly by the first philosophers is brought nearer to completion by their successors.[38]

Aquinas sketches this historical progression in ST Ia.44.2. He raises the question "Is prime matter created by God?" In discussing this question he brings together notions from two different traditions. "Prime matter" is a basic concept in Aristotle, the philosophical expression of a common supposition of Greek thought, namely, "nothing comes from nothing" (ex nihilo nihil fit). Every instance of becoming requires a substratum, and prime matter is the ultimate substratum. "Creation," however, is a fundamental notion in Christian doctrine. As the first objection in this article suggests, it seems to be difficult to connect the two notions because prime matter itself cannot come to be, since it is the substratum of every becoming. If prime matter were to come to be, it would already have to be before its coming to be. "Therefore, prime matter cannot have been made." Greek philosophy and Christian doctrine seem irreconcilable. In his reply Aquinas explains the history of philosophical reflection about the origin of being. "The ancient philosophers gradually, step by step as it were, advanced in the knowledge of the truth." Three main phases can be distinguished in the progression of philosophy as he sees it.[39]

The first step was taken by the pre-Socratics. They were still so tied to sense-objects that they believed only material things exist. They held that matter is the "substance" of things and that all forms are accidents. They posited one or more substrata (water, fire, etc.), which they regarded as the ungenerated and indestructible principles of all things. To the extent to which they acknowledged change in the substratum, it consisted only in "alteration," a change of its accidental forms.

The second stage in the progress of philosophy was reached when philosophers understood that there is a distinction between "matter" and "substantial form." While for the pre-Socratics the substratum was "actual" and "becoming" only an "alteration," later philosophers posited a prime matter that is purely potential and is brought into actuality through a form. Aquinas regards it as one of Aristotle's great merits that with his doctrine of the potentiality of matter he made it possible to acknowledge a *substantial* change, or "generation."[40]

Aquinas emphasizes, however, that the final step had not yet been taken, for generation, too, presupposes something. The philosophers of the first and second phases considered the origin of being under some particular aspect, namely, either as *this* being or as *such* being. As a result, the causes to which they attributed the becoming of things were particular. Their causality is restricted to one or another category of being: accident (as in the first phase) or substance (as in the second). Even the Aristotelian doctrine of matter and form is inadequate to account for the radical origin of things.

The third phase in the progression began when some thinkers (*aliqui*) raised themselves to the consideration of being as *being*.[41] In this metaphysical analysis they assigned a cause to things not only insofar as they are *such* (by accidental forms) and *these* (by substantial forms), but also considered according to all that belongs to their *being*. This procession of all being from the universal cause is not a change or a becoming, because it no longer presupposes anything in that which is caused. It is creation, *ex nihilo*.

Aquinas's view of the progress of philosophy has two striking features. The first is that philosophical reflection proceeds from a particular to a more universal consideration of being. Aristotle's thesis that prime matter is ungenerated concerns the particular mode of becoming in nature – the sort analyzed in the Aristotelian categories. At this level it holds that "Nothing comes from nothing." But for Aquinas this is not ultimate. "We are speaking of things in connection with their coming forth from the universal principle of being. From this coming forth, not even matter itself is excluded" (ST Ia.44.2, ad 1). The origin considered by the metaphysician is transcendental: it concerns being as such, not merely being as analyzed into natural categories. In this context Aquinas elaborates his thesis that all created things are marked by the composition of essence and *esse* (which he had already developed in *De ente et essentia*, and his doctrine of participation). Things have received their *esse* from that which is Being itself, and their relation to this creating cause is the relation of participation in being.

A second striking feature of Aquinas's view is that the idea of creation appears as the result of the *internal* development of thought, independent of the external aid of revelation. That the world is created is not only a datum of faith but also a philosophical insight. Aquinas defended this philosophical notion of creation, the production of being absolutely, against theologians in his treatise *De aeternitate mundi*. Reason can prove that the world's being had an origin, but not that the world had a temporal beginning.

VII. THE NATURAL DESIRE TO KNOW GOD

In his Commentary on the *Metaphysics* (1.4), Aquinas advances yet another argument for the thesis that "all human beings by nature desire to know." This third argument is of special interest because it connects Aristotle's pronouncement with a neoplatonic idea. Aquinas argues that it is desirable for each thing to be united to its principle or source, since it is in this union that the perfection of each thing consists. For this reason circular motion is the most perfect motion, because its terminus is united to its beginning. Only by means of intellect is a human being united to its principle. Consequently the ultimate end for human beings consists in this union. "Therefore, a human being naturally desires to know."

In this argument Aquinas introduces the neoplatonic doctrine of the circular motion of reality, known to him from Proclus and Pseudo-Dionysius.[42] The perfection of an effect consists in the return to its principle. That from which things come forth turns out to be their end: source and goal, beginning and end, are identical.

As we can see in Aquinas's Commentary on the *Sentences*, he adopts the neoplatonic conception of the emergence and the return of things, although with certain modifications. Things come to existence not in a step-by-step procession from the first principle, but because they are all created by God. The "authority" of the *Liber de causis* is, Aquinas observes, not to be followed in its idea that lower creatures are created by means of higher substances.[43] His remark illustrates the critical way in which the scholastics deal with an authoritative text. God, as Creator, is the immediate origin of all things. Because he is the most perfect being, every creature naturally turns back to its principle. The end corresponds with the beginning. Therefore the final end of things is not any created substance, but God alone.

In the process of the return of creatures to God, the human creature occupies a special position. Only the rational nature has the capacity to turn to its origin "expressly."[44] Human beings alone are able to attain God through their activity. This return is enacted in the natural human desire to know.

Aquinas elaborates this idea in SCG III.25. By nature there is in all human beings the desire to know the causes of whatever they see. The search does not cease until it comes to the first cause, for "we consider ourselves to know perfectly when we know the *first* cause." Here Aquinas cites Aristotle's definition of "to know" (*Posterior Analytics* I 2, 71b10) but with an addition: perfect knowledge is knowledge of the *first* cause. Now the first cause of all things is God. Therefore, for us the ultimate end is to know God. The ultimate end of human beings and of every intellectual substance is called happiness, or beatitude. "Hence the happiness of any intellectual substance is to know God." Our desire to know is finally, in Aquinas's interpretation, the natural desire for knowledge of God. "First philosophy [that is, metaphysics] is entirely directed to the knowledge of God as its final end" (SCG III.25).

VIII. THE LIMITS OF PHILOSOPHY

Can philosophy actually attain this end? Aquinas's answer to this crucial question is negative, based on the special nature of the human intellect: it is the form of the body. For our intellective cognition we are dependent upon sense experience. "It is natural to human beings to attain to the intelligible through sensible things." Systematic knowledge extends only as far as sensory cognition. Of course, the senses are not the total cause of all our knowledge, but they do provide the indispensable material from which the intellect abstracts the intelligible content. From this it follows that human beings cannot know the essence of a substance that is not perceptible by the senses.

The only knowledge of God that philosophers can attain is a knowledge based on God's effects in our world. They can prove, as Aquinas does in his "five ways," *that* there is a universal cause, God; they can give an answer to the question whether He exists. But they cannot give anything like a full account of *what* God is; knowledge of the divine essence remains hidden to human beings. In this restricted philosophical knowledge, however, our desire to know is not satisfied, for we retain by nature the desire to know the essence of God.[45]

Aquinas argues that our perfect happiness, the fulfillment of our natural desire, can consist only in the contemplation of God's essence, in the vision of God (*visio Dei*), in which we see the answer to the question *what* he is. From this he draws the conclusion (ST IaIIae.3.6) that "our complete happiness cannot consist in theoretical knowledge," that is, in philosophy, broadly conceived. The vision of God surpasses our natural powers and capacities. This end of ours is literally supernatural.

With this conclusion, philosophy is caught in crisis. The final end for human beings seems unattainable by them. Aquinas discusses at length the solutions of Aristotle, the Greek commentators, and Islamic philosophers (SCG III.41–48), but he concludes that their solution are not acceptable. Philosophy offers no prospect of a fulfillment of human life. "Distress" (*angustia*) is the pregnant word Aquinas uses to characterize the situation (SCG III.48).

IX. THE NECESSITY OF THEOLOGY

In his Commentary on Matthew 5:8 ("Blessed are the pure in heart: for they shall see God"), Aquinas remarks that some hold that God will never be seen in his essence. But this view, he argues, is contrary to Scripture and reason. First, the possibility of the vision of God is promised in Scripture, the foundation of the Christian faith. Through God's revelation the Christian is freed from philosophy's distress. He knows of a future fulfillment of human life, for in I John 3:2 he reads: "We shall see Him as He is," and in I Corinthians 13:12: "For now we see through a glass, darkly; but then face to face."

The impossibility of the vision of God is also contrary to reason, because human happiness is that in which human desire comes to rest. Now it is our natural desire, when we see an effect, to inquire into its cause. This desire will not come to rest until we reach the first cause, namely the divine essence itself. "Therefore God will be seen in his essence." Aquinas thus argues from the very phenomenon of the desire to know to its fulfillment. Implicit in this argument is the idea that the desire to know, because it is a natural desire, cannot be in vain; for the operation of nature is directed to its end by the Author of nature.[46] On the basis of this consideration Aquinas states repeatedly (for example, SCG III.51) that it must be *possible* for human beings to see God's essence.

In Aquinas's argumentation in this biblical commentary, the teaching of the Christian *faith* concerning the vision of God goes together with the finality of the *natural* desire to *know*. This synthesis is an indication that faith must not by any means be conceived of as an elimination of our intellectual nature, but rather as its perfection. The vision of God surpasses our natural powers. If we are to attain this supernatural end, our intellective power must be fortified. The "beatific vision" becomes a connatural end for human beings, if by God's grace some gifts are added to human nature. One of these gifts is the "light of faith," whereby the human intellect is illuminated concerning what surpasses the natural light of reason.[47]

This perspective shapes the opening of Aquinas's *Summa theologiae*. In ST Ia.1.1 he investigates the necessity of theology. Is theology not "superfluous" (obj. 1), considering the fact that the philosophical disciplines deal with everything that is, even God himself? Aquinas's reply stresses the necessity for human salvation of a knowledge based on divine revelation, in addition to the philosophical sciences based on human reason. First, "Human beings are directed to God as an end that surpasses the grasp of their reason." Hence certain truths must be made known to us by revelation if we are to direct our thought and actions to the supernatural end. And even concerning those truths about God which human reason is able to attain, divine revelation is not superfluous, for those truths are known only to a few people, and mingled with a great deal of error. For these reasons theology, a rational inquiry based on revelation, is necessary.

X. THE RELATIONSHIP BETWEEN PHILOSOPHY AND THEOLOGY

The circular motion of emergence and return is closed in the vision of God. This end cannot be attained by philosophy. A different sort of teaching and learning is necessary to show the supernatural completion of the human desire to know. Aquinas's view of the relationship between philosophy and theology can be summarized in three principles. These principles correspond roughly to the three groups of his works discussed in sections II–IV above, namely (a) his theological writings, (b) his philosophical writings, and (c) his treatises related to the controversies between the theology and the arts faculties.

The first principle is that there is *harmony* between philosophy, guided by the light of natural reason, and theology, guided by the light of faith. It is impossible that a theological truth contradict a philosophical truth. If that were the case, Aquinas argues, then necessarily one of them would be false. Consequently, since both the light of reason and the light of faith are from God, God would be the author of error. But to think of God as a deceiver is absurd. "If, however, in the writings of the philosophers one finds anything contrary to faith, it is not philosophy, but rather an abuse of philosophy stemming from a defect of reason."⁴⁸ A good example of this claim is Aquinas's reaction to the doctrine of the unicity of the intellect. His intention in *De unitate intellectus* is to show that this doctrine contradicts the principles of philosophy. In his view, a genuine "conflict of the faculties" is in principle impossible because a "double truth" is impossible.

The second principle is that "faith *presupposes* natural knowledge, as grace presupposes nature" (ST, Ia.2.2, ad 1). Natural knowledge is first and fundamental, because the gifts of grace are added to nature. Philosophy is not to be reduced to theology; it has its own work to do. Driven by the natural desire to know, it seeks the causes of what is seen and critically discusses the achievements of earlier thinkers. It is in this spirit that Aquinas writes *De ente et essentia* and comments on Aristotle.

The third principle is that "grace does not destroy nature, but *perfects* it" (ST Ia.1.8, ad 2). Faith is the perfection of natural knowledge. Aquinas advances this principle in order to explain why theology, the science that is based on the articles of faith, makes use of "human reason and the authority of philosophers." In his theological works he assigns philosophy an important place in the rational account of the truth of the faith. Aquinas is a theologian by profession. It is, however, not the professional philosophers of the thirteenth century, but the theologian Thomas Aquinas who belongs among the outstanding figures in the history of philosophy.

NOTES

Shortened references refer to the works found in the bibliography at the end of this volume.

1 The best study of Aquinas's life and work is Weisheipl 1983.
2 Gilson 1960, p. 106; English transl. in Gilson 1962.
3 See Jordan's Chapter 9, herein.
4 Denifle and Chatelain 1889, vol. I, n. 447. English transl. in Foster 1959, pp. 153–55.
5 See Weisheipl 1983, p. 316; also see Jordan's Chapter 9, herein.
6 See section III of this chapter and Owens's Chapter 2, herein.
7 On the university, see Cobban 1975; Kenny 1982, pp. 9–42.
8 For an excellent introduction to the intellectual background of Aquinas's works, see Chenu 1964.
9 In Sent I.2, division of the text.

10 See Stump's Chapter 10, herein.

11 See Kretzmann's Chapter 5.

12 This reflection has drawn the attention of the German philosopher H.-G. Gadamer, whose thesis is that language acquired special importance in medieval thought because of its theological interest in the Word. See Gadamer 1979, pp. 378–87.

13 His shorter, later *Compendium theologiae* often provides good summaries of positions he argues more fully in the two *Summae.*

14 QQ IV.9.3.

15 See Gilson 1960, p. 109. See also Jordan's Chapter 9.

16 In Sent II.14.1.2: "Expositors of Holy Scripture differed from one another because they were followers of various philosophers who had instructed them in philosophical matters."

17 Knowles 1962, pp. 221–34.

18 Denifle and Chatelain 1889, vol. I, n. 246.

19 Ibid., n. 447.

20 See MacDonald's Chapter 6, herein.

21 Cf. ST Ia.79.4; IaIIae.109.1.

22 See Henle, 1956, pp. 323–50. Also see Aquinas's critical comparison of Platonism and Aristotelianism in QDSC 3.

23 Geiger 1953; Fabro 1961; Kremer 1971; and Wippel 1987, 117–58. See also Wippel's Chapter 4 below.

24 Thomas Aquinas 1954, 3: "And so [this book] was apparently excerpted by one of the Arabian philosophers from that book of Proclus's."

25 See McInerny 1990.

26 In DDN, prol.: "But as regards what they had to say about the first principle of things, their view is perfectly true and in full agreement with the Christian faith."

27 See Wippel's Chapter 4.

28 Bonaventure, *Collationes in Hexaemeron* I, 9 (*Opera Omnia* V, 330).

29 See Van Steenberghen, 1980b.

30 See Dales 1990.

31 Bonaventure, *In Sent.* II, d. 1, p. 1, a. 1, q. 2 (*Opera Omnia* II, 22).

32 See Owens's Chapter 2.

33 See QDP 3.14, ad 8 (in contr.): "It belongs to the notion of creation to have a principle of origin (*principium originis*), but not of duration, unless creation is understood as the Faith understands it." See also Wippel's Chapter 4.

34 See Aertsen 1990 and Hoenen 1990.

35 In DA I.1.3: "It is clear that all scientific, systematic knowledge is good. But a thing's good is that in accordance with which the thing has its being completed or perfected, since that is what each thing seeks and

desires. Therefore, since scientific, systematic knowledge is the completion or perfection of a human being considered as such, it is its good."

36 Bernard of Clairvaux 1958, Sermo 36.

37 ST IIaIIae.167.1, ad 3.

38 See ibid. 97.1: "It seems natural to human reason to move to completion gradually from an incomplete state. In the theoretical sciences, for example, we see that those who first philosophized passed on incomplete results that were subsequently passed on by their successors in a more complete state."

39 For a more extensive analysis of this text, see Aertsen 1988, pp. 196–201.

40 QDSC 3: "Aristotle solves their difficulty by asserting that matter exists only in potentiality."

41 Who are these *aliqui*? A. C. Pegis (1946, p. 162, n. 9) suggested that Aquinas "has in mind those Christian thinkers who listened more to Genesis than to Platonism or to Aristotelianism." Yet there is at least one text in which Aquinas says that *quidam philosophi*, such as Avicenna, have recognized on the basis of demonstration that God is the Creator of things. See In Sent III.25.1.2, obj. 2.

42 See In DDN 1.3.94: "We must consider, further, that every effect is returned to the cause from which it proceeds, as the Platonists maintain."

43 QDP 3.4, ad 10: "This mistake – that lower creatures were created by God through the medium of higher beings – is found explicitly in the *Liber de causis*; and so its authority is not to be accepted on this point."

44 QDV 22.2.

45 See Wippel's Chapter 4.

46 See SCG III.156: "In connection with the works of God there is nothing in vain, just as in connection with works of nature; for it is from God that nature has this trait."

47 QDVC 10.

48 In BDT 2.3.

2 Aristotle and Aquinas

I. SIMILARITIES AND DIFFERENCES BETWEEN ARISTOTLE AND AQUINAS

Today a somewhat prevalent impression links Aristotle and Aquinas as though they both represented the same general type of philosophical thinking. *Prima facie* indications, it is true, may seem to point in the direction of a unitary trend in their basic philosophical procedures. Aquinas uses Aristotle's formal logic. Both of them reason in terms of actuality and potentiality; of material, formal, efficient, and final causes; and of the division of scientific thought into the theoretical and the practical and productive. Both regard intellectual contemplation as the supreme goal of human striving. Both look upon free choice as the origin of moral action. Both clearly distinguish the material from the immaterial, sensation from intellection, the temporal from the eternal, the body from the soul. Both ground all naturally attainable human knowledge on external sensible things, instead of on sensations, ideas, or language. Both look upon cognition as a way of being in which percipient and thing perceived, knower and thing known, are one and the same in the actuality of the cognition.

All these tenets are sharply outlined in both Aristotle and Aquinas. Closer similarity between two great thinkers, it might seem, would be hard to find. This may easily give occasion for a claim that, from a strictly philosophical viewpoint, Aquinas's thought coincides with Aristotle's despite differences of historical epoch and of cultural and religious background. In fact, these *prima facie* indications of basic coincidence were impressive enough to occasion a widespread acceptance of the label "Aristotelico–Thomistic" for the type of philoso-

38

phy promoted by Pope Leo XIII's 1879 encyclical *Aeterni Patris*,[1] the document that gave ecclesiastical backing to modern Thomism. There were, of course, other types of Neoscholastic thinking, chiefly Scotist and Suarezian, that looked to Aristotle for guidance while bypassing or opposing Aquinas. Outright identification of Aristotelian philosophy with Thomism was not at all unanimous in neoscholastic circles. A Neoscholastic could be strongly Aristotelian without being Thomistic.

Moreover, there are serious difficulties in finding one-to-one correspondence between important philosophical doctrines in Aquinas and their counterparts in Aristotle. For Aristotle, being and essence are identical in each particular instance. At most there could be a conceptual distinction between them, although it was more advantageous for practical purposes to regard them as identical.[2] Both were known through the same intellectual activity.[3] In Aquinas, on the other hand, there is an explicit claim that in all creatures there is a real distinction between a thing and its being. Being and essence, or quiddity, were known by radically different intellectual acts.[4] In fact, the real distinction between essence and existence could be regarded in neothomistic circles as the fundamental truth of Christian philosophy,[5] which pervaded the whole of Thomistic metaphysics. It was the nerve of the distinction between God and creatures. It was the basis for the demonstration of a real distinction between nature and faculties in creatures. It was essential for the proof of the indestructibility of the human soul, in contrast to the perishable character of the soul in other animals and in plants. It was everywhere crucial for Thomism. Yet it was very unAristotelian.

Likewise the "five ways" for demonstrating God's existence were regarded in Neoscholasticism as vital for Thomistic philosophical thought. Yet even the basic framework for these arguments is lacking in Aristotle, despite superficial structural resemblances. Aristotelian metaphysics reasons from the eternity of the cosmic processes and animated heavens to separate and immobile substance as final cause. Whether that separate substance was unique or a plurality seemed a matter of indifference to Aristotle, who left the question to the astronomers to answer, on the basis of the number of original movements they observed in the heavens. Heavenly bodies, endowed with souls, were required in order that each might love, desire, and strive after the perfection of the separate substances, each as best it could in its own distinctive way. Aquinas himself alerted his readers to Aristotle's firm belief in the sempiternity of cosmic motion and of time, since the reasoning supporting that belief was based upon those tenets.[6] In Aristotle there is no mention of efficient causality on the part of the separate substances. Each was aware of itself only, and unable to produce any actuality outside itself through efficient causality of its own.

This situation points to a radical difference between the philosophical thinking of Aquinas and that of Aristotle, despite Aquinas's use of the Aristotelian vocabulary. The philosophical phrasing employed by the two thinkers may to a large extent be the same, but the meanings attached to the same expressions can be very different for each of them. This gives rise to the general question of how philosophers can use the same terms yet understand them in radically different ways. In our own day that phenomenon can be readily explained in virtue of the different historical and linguistic circumstances in which various philosophers were brought up. Each thinks in the grooves in which he or she has been placed by these circumstances, and his or her way of thinking is to be probed and interpreted in the light of those circumstances. Especially in the context of these familiar considerations, one may ask how Aristotle and Aquinas could possibly have had the same basic way of thinking on the philosophical level when their cultural circumstances were so different. How could a thirteenth-century Christian theologian at the University of Paris philosophize in the same way as a Greek thinker in the pagan culture of fourth-century B.C. Athens?

II. HISTORICAL AND CULTURAL CIRCUMSTANCES OF ARISTOTLE'S THOUGHT

Aristotle lived in a civilization that had already experienced the triumph of pagan art in poetry, music, sculpture, painting, and architecture, and in the theater and in athletics, as well as in philosophy. He was the son of a medical practitioner, at home in the courts of Philip and Alexander and in Hermias's court at Atarneus and Assos. He was a student of Plato's and a participant in the activities of the Platonic Academy. Accordingly, he lived in firsthand contact with the best of Greek culture, in its multiple ramifications in medical and scientific research, political life, and intellectual activities. He had an exceptionally broad acquaintance with the civilization of his day. Through breathing this intense cultural atmosphere from his earliest years, Aristotle was amply conditioned to live out its fullness in his own personal thought. In his ethical works he insists repeatedly on the fundamental importance of this cultural habituation for shaping one's practical philosophy. Through this habituation, in fact, one originally acquires the starting points or first principles of moral philosophy. The rest of one's moral thinking proceeds from those culturally instilled first principles.

That conception of practical philosophy is explicit in the Aristotelian text. Can the same notion be extended to theoretical philosophy? Aristotle is not as explicit here. But in the *Metaphysics* (II 1, 993b14) he does say that the general habit of philosophical thinking has been handed down by one's predecessors who had exercised it in earlier times, as though it depended upon the training given by them. Likewise, in the same book (II 3, 994b32–995a3) he insists that we absorb instruction in accord with the habits we have acquired. So even outside the realm of practical philosophy, Aristotle seems to recognize clearly the need for correct upbringing from one's earliest years. The formative influence of one's cultural surroundings appears to exercise a determination over the direction that one's speculative thinking takes. The emotional overtones of gratitude toward one's predecessors indicate, in this context, deeply rooted tendencies of love for and devotion to the type of thought they have handed down. In any case, the dependence of one's philosophical thinking upon an ethos that has been transmitted allows at least the flexibility implied in the term "ethos," together with its firmness and its efficacy of habitual determination in one direction rather than another. It seems to extend to purely speculative philosophy the dependence upon cultural circumstances, at least to a certain degree, paralleling what Aristotle had insisted upon so strongly in the practical realm. The notion of a philosophy's essential dependence upon historical circumstances appears to be just as Aristotelian as it is postmodern, and any comparison of the thought of Aristotle with that of Aquinas should take that dependence into full account.

What relevant cultural circumstances and outlook need to be kept in mind when comparing Aristotelian thought with that of Aquinas? Greek culture was polytheistic, its mythologies entertaining a plurality of gods. It exhibits little, if any, yearning for a loving celestial father who exercises devoted and tender providence over every detail, even the smallest, of human life. True, St. Paul appealed to some of its poets, who asserted that we also are his offspring, but the close family feeling based on the Christian conception of grace was lacking. Human activity as a whole was directed toward this-worldly goals rather than to a life with a heavenly father after bodily death. Greek thought could indeed rise to admirable heights of beauty, and of esteem for goodness, in its poetry, art, drama, and philosophy. But focus on happiness in the present earthly life was dominant. This focus was far above the crassly material; nevertheless, its main thrust centered upon what could be obtained and enjoyed in one's lifetime on earth.

Corresponding to these cultural factors, Aristotle's philosophical thought followed a notion of finite form that had been cultivated with admirable success through Greek art and intellectual contemplation. The world was there before his eyes. Its existence posed no problem. The reasoning of Parmenides that nothing could come from nothing was accepted wholeheartedly. The cosmic processes were accordingly without temporal beginning and would never come to an end. The perpetually repeated rise and fall of civilizations assured the continuation of the moral training that was required for practical reasoning, and no divine revelation in this regard was looked for. Human happiness was attained in a complete lifetime on earth through intellectual contemplation of the mind's highest objects, or in a secondary fashion by exercising the practical virtues that make this contemplation possible. Concern for individuals physically, mentally, or economically incapable of this happiness is noticeably absent.

III. HISTORICAL AND CULTURAL CIRCUMSTANCES OF AQUINAS'S THOUGHT

A considerably different kind of philosophy is to be expected in a thinker whose habituation from earliest years was deeply Christian. Thomas Aquinas lived in the thirteenth century at a time when feudal civilization had already reached its peak and was showing signs of deterioration. The Aquinas family, members of the lower nobility, played its part in the feudal quarrels of the time and experienced the discouragements and reverses of changing political circumstances. Revolts intended for the better seemed invariably to make things worse. In one of his works Aquinas writes: "Indeed, if there be not an excess of tyranny it is more expedient to tolerate the milder tyranny for a while, than, by acting against the tyrant, to become involved in many perils more grievous than the tyranny itself. . . . This is wont to happen in tyranny, namely that the second [tyrant] becomes more grievous than the preceding, inasmuch as, without abandoning the previous oppressions, he himself thinks up fresh ones from the malice of his heart."[7] This pessimistic attitude toward efforts at political change stands in contrast to the buoyant élan of fourth-century B.C. Athens in regard to political life. But it bears witness to an attitude of relying on spiritual rather than temporal forces in working out one's happiness, an attitude that is perfectly logical when one's happiness on earth is placed in striving toward an eternal happiness to be attained after bodily death.

When Thomas was five years old, he was sent to the Benedictine monastery at Monte Cassino to begin his education in the arts. From that early age he saw the Christian monastic life firsthand and absorbed its spiritual atmosphere. While still in his early manhood he was caught up in the full flow of the intellectual enthusiasm that was sweeping through the universities of the day. He had become a Dominican friar, and he lived the Dominican religious life while completing his formal education at the order's *studia* in Paris and Cologne. At this time he launched wholeheartedly into the problems and controversies of the age, with an admiration for Aristotle that increased with the years. In the last decade of his life he was occupied predominantly with commentaries on the Aristotelian texts.[8]

It is not difficult to see the similarities and, at the same time, the profound differences in the respective intellectual formation and philosophical habituation of Aristotle and Aquinas. Like Aristotle, Aquinas had firsthand contact with the political struggles and turmoil of his century. Like Aristotle, he enjoyed the best educational opportunities of his time for philosophy. As his teacher Aquinas had Albert the Great at Cologne or Paris, just as Aristotle had had Plato and the Academy at Athens. But Aristotle, despite personal troubles occasioned by his Macedonian connection and his alien status at Athens, could still look forward to the triumph of pure philosophy in individual minds and in recurrent cyclic civilizations.

Aquinas, on the other hand, from his Christian home and family life and early acquaintance with monasticism, became habituated at an early age to regarding human happiness as above all earthly vicissitudes. From this viewpoint, success or failure in everyday life had only secondary importance. The one goal that really mattered was working toward an eternal happiness after death, in accord with the teachings of Christian faith. The supernatural and other-worldly destiny, it is true, consisted, as with Aristotle, in intellectual contemplation. But for Christian belief this intellectual contemplation was achieved through divine grace, not through unaided human effort. This meant that in the broadest outlook, the most important aim was to promote the teaching and work of the Church. The result was that Aquinas did all his writing as a theologian, not as a philosopher. Nevertheless, his Aristotelian formation permeates this theological work. To use his own metaphor, the water of philosophy was absorbed into the wine of theology.[9] Yet, it remained philosophy. And, to use the same figure of speech, philosophy was essential to his theological thinking as water is to wine, even though the water might be separated merely by distillation.

This Christian habituation and attitude inevitably make a profound difference in one's philosophical thinking. It has prompted the query "How could a Christian philosophize as though he or she had never heard of Christianity?"[10] The probative force of any philosophical reasoning has to be based solely on grounds naturally accessible to the human mind. No divinely revealed premises can be used for purposes of demonstration in philosophy. But what has been revealed is good, true, existent, and characterized by numerous other naturally knowable features. It can be an object of study under these naturally knowable aspects. To this extent the divinely revealed truths become an object of philosophical study. They remain as objects and do not become means of demonstration. But the Christian habituation toward them influences the selection of topics and the thrusts of interest, and in full accord with postmodern hermeneutic norms has to be taken into account in interpreting their philosophical meaning. The influence is reciprocal, insofar as the cultural interest concentrates attention upon a meaning the philosophical term can have, and that meaning, which otherwise might escape attention, enriches the notion in its use throughout purely philosophical areas.

IV. THE CONCEPT OF BEING IN ARISTOTLE'S AND AQUINAS'S THOUGHT

Any of a number of naturally attainable notions may serve as apt illustrations for the way philosophical thought bears upon supernaturally revealed objects, and how in turn the habituation toward those objects profoundly influences Aquinas's philosophy about them. The most outstanding is the notion of being, the object that specifies metaphysical inquiry. It is a notion taken from sensible things in both Aristotle and Aquinas.

Everything encountered in our perception is known as a being. If it happens to be a metal, a plant, an animal, or a human person, it is a substance. If it is a color, a size, or a relation, it is an accident and requires a substance in which it inheres. If it is right there before our eyes, it is actual. If it is to come into being in the future, it is still something potential and requires efficient causality to make it actual. If it undergoes change, it is temporal and is composed of matter that changes from one form to another. When we reason to things that have no matter and therefore no potentiality for change, we consider objects that are merely being, in contrast to becoming and perishing. They are the primary instances of being. All other things are beings through focal reference to them.

That is Aristotle's explanation of being. All beings exist in one way or another, either in reality or in thought. But Aristotle shows no special concern with existence as a philosophical notion. There is no real distinction between thing and being, they are known by the same mental activity, and it is easier in his metaphysics if no conceptual distinction is brought forward between the two.[11] A thing's being and what it is coincide. The problem of the world's needing a creator to make it exist does not arise, and an efficient cause is explained in terms of originating motion rather than of bestowing existence. Because it is utterly unchangeable, separate form has in itself and through itself the nature of being. All other things depend upon it through final causality for their permanence and in consequence for their being. In this way separate form is the primary instance of being, and everything else has being through focal reference to it.

Consider how this conception of being took on a drastically new significance when it was approached by Thomas Aquinas. He was conditioned by the reading of the sacred Scriptures, whose opening words declare that in the beginning God created heaven and earth. In philosophical language this meant that God was the first efficient cause of all other things. In this way, God was the primary instance of being. His was the nature to which all other beings had focal reference as beings. Further on, in Exodus (3:14) God reveals his own name in terms of being. "*Ego sum qui sum*" (I am who am) was the way the text read in the Vulgate translation. That was for Aquinas the "sublime truth" that the Christian knew about being.[12] It was the very name and nature of God. In Aristotelian language this meant that the primary instance of being was God, the God who was now revealed as a fond and loving parent deeply interested in and concerned with the children he had begotten in his own image and likeness. His efficient causality extended to everything that took place, insofar as he concurred as primary cause in everything done by his creatures, and conserved them all in existence. The focal reference through efficient causality was thereby all-pervasive.

Although this viewpoint was not Aristotelian, the Aristotelian notions were flexible enough to carry the enriched content of revelation. Some modern interpreters, it is true, find the union of the two incomprehensible. They claim that they are unable to see how the Aristotelian separate substance as primary mover can coincide with the loving and provident God of the Scriptures. The remote detachment and aloofness of the Aristotelian prime mover remains irreconcilable with the Judeo-Christian God. But Aquinas experienced no difficulty whatever in this regard. He approached the problem from the standpoint of the notion of being that he had found in Exodus. God is by nature being. That is the name and nature proper to him. No one else can have that nature, for according to the Scriptures strange gods cannot be tolerated. God alone has being as his nature. Philosophically the unicity of subsistent existence was indicated.

From this viewpoint of basic nature, God, in Aquinas's view, continued to be thoroughly remote from other things. No creature could have being as its nature. Its being necessarily is other than its nature and requires bestowal by an efficient cause. Ultimately being is bestowed by God as the primary efficient cause, through creation, conservation, and concurrence in the activity of every creature. This bestowal of existence by God extends to the smallest detail. It extends accordingly to the causality by which God makes human beings in his own image and likeness. In this way he makes them in truth his own children through grace, with all the affection and tenderness, interest and concern that this relationship implies. There is neither coldness nor insensitivity in this relationship of the primary being to his creatures, despite the infinite abyss that separates the basic natures of creator and of creature. From the viewpoint of existence and activity the relationship is extremely close and intimate.

But if the application of Aristotelian philosophy to the sphere of the sacred did not affect the sublimity or change the nature of the divine object, can the same be said with regard to the influence exercised upon those philosophical notions through their contact with theology?[13] In the present instance, what happens to the notion of being when it is used by Aquinas to explain this higher object? Aquinas is doing his own thinking. He has read that the proper name of God is being, the name that distinguishes the nature of God from the natures of all other beings. Being cannot be the nature of nor belong to the nature of any other thing. In every case the creature's being will remain distinct from the creature's nature. Being cannot come from the creature's own nature, for without existence there would be no creature to produce it. It has to come from something else: from the primary efficient cause. In the creation proclaimed by Genesis, moreover, there was nothing antecedent to receive the existence. There was only the giving of being.

This is a radical development of the Aristotelian notion of efficient causality. It continues to recognize the Aristotelian form as cause of being, but only under the activity of an efficient cause.[14] It makes efficient causality antecedent to all finite form, so that finite form is brought into being by reason of the existential actuality it limits and specifies.[15] Efficient causality now bears upon the whole of the finite thing and extends to the production of both matter and form through a creative act – the bringing of something into existence rather than the initiating of motion. In Aristotle matter was related to form as potentiality to actuality, but now the whole finite thing is seen as itself a potentiality to its own existence.[16]

So conceived, this is very different from the notion of being that had been developed by Aristotle. Yet it is readily brought under the general Aristotelian concept of actuality, which was adaptable enough to undergo the further extension. But it thereby brought out a metaphysical starting point that was not available to the ancient Greek thinker. The new notion was that of an actuality different from anything in the natures of sensible things, an actuality that had not been isolated in Aristotelian philosophy. Aristotle did not focus upon the existence of things, as an actuality distinct from their nature. Existence was taken for granted as the being of the things and as identical with them in reality. If taken as distinguished conceptually *from* the things, it would play no role in his metaphysics.[17]

With Aquinas, on the contrary, the being of the thing becomes identified with the aspect that is expressed by the term "existence." It is an aspect that stands in sharp contrast with a finite thing's nature. Being is present as a nature only in God. Everything else has to receive it as an actuality that comes from outside, from an efficient cause. In that framework, Aquinas can follow the structure of the Aristotelian reasoning from sensible things in their mixture of actuality with potentiality to an actuality that has no potentiality whatever. But whereas for Aristotle the actuality reached was finite form, for Aquinas it was infinite existence. This radical difference arose from the way actuality in sensible things was conceived. For Aristotle the things were actual through their form. For Aquinas the composite of form and matter was made actual by existence. Existence was in this way the ultimate actuality of every finite thing, and always distinct from the thing's nature.

Conditioned by his belief in the scriptural assertion that the name and nature of God is being, Aquinas could hardly help but give closer consideration to the way the being of sensible things is known. Just as strongly as Aristotle, he located the origin of all naturally attained knowledge in sensible things. He saw that they exist, and he was aware of what they are, certainly to the extent seen in Aristotle. But in his interpretation of Aristotle he had had Islamic predecessors, also conditioned by their religious belief that the world had received its existence from God.[18] He knew that they had distinguished the mental activity by which a thing's nature is known from the activity by which its existence is grasped.[19] They named these two activities in different ways. He himself, against the background of an Aristotelian classification, called the first of these mental activities the apprehension of a simple quiddity. (Later this was labeled "simple apprehension.") The second activity of the intellect was complex in contrast. It consisted in forming a proposition in which a predicate or verbal notion was either joined to or separated from a subject. It too was an apprehension. But where the first mental activity was the apprehension of the thing's quiddity or nature, the second activity was the apprehension of its existence.[20] (Later it became regularly known as "judgment.")

This basic epistemology is clear-cut. It means that human knowledge of quiddity or nature and human knowledge of existence have two radically different origins. Contrary to Aristotle's tenet, *what a thing is* and *that it is* are not grasped by the same intellectual activity. The result is that knowing what a thing is will never give knowledge of its existence. That is why for Aquinas the definition of what God is cannot serve as the basis for reasoning to his existence in an ontological argument. For that Anselmian reasoning to be conclusive, one would have to presuppose in the definition itself that God did in fact exist.[21] In Aquinas's own procedure, the reception of existence by the things in the actual world is shown to proceed ultimately from existence that subsists. The subsisting existence is then shown to be the nature or quiddity of God.[22] Actually existing is in this way presupposed by and included in the notion of God as it is reached philosophically by Aquinas. But no amount of reasoning on the basis of what things are can lead to any conclusion regarding existence.

This consideration has far-reaching consequences for Aquinas's metaphysics. As developed by him it means that human knowledge of what a thing is comes about by a "non-precisive abstraction" of the thing's quiddity from the individuals in which it exists.[23] Even the terminology here marks a sharp difference from Aristotle. Aristotle uses the term "abstraction" regularly, but only for mathematical entities. By "abstraction" he means that the objects of mathematics are taken by the mind in separation from the sensible qualities in which they are embedded in real things. After abstraction, substances remain for consideration only insofar as they are extended or countable. Correspondingly, in the extension of the term "abstraction" by Aquinas, the sensible thing's substantial and accidental natures are considered in separation from the individuals in which they exist in the real world. The notion *human* is abstracted from the individual women and men; the notion *animal,* from humans and other sentient beings; the notion of *living,* from these along with plants; and the notion of *body,* from living and non-living perceptible things. These abstracted notions ground our universal knowledge of sensible things.

Thus far the views of Aquinas correspond to those of Aristotle, even though Aristotle does not use the term "abstraction" in this regard. When the range is extended to things beyond the sensible world, a slight difference may be noted. Aristotle regards the sensible and the supersensible as coming under the one notion of *being*, because of the focal reference that all have to separate substance, the primary instance of being. Aquinas, on the other hand, looks upon a thing as a being because of its having the actuality of existence.²⁴ As he sees it, then, the reference is to the existence that is originally known through judgment. In regard to the extension of the notion *being* to the supersensible, he speaks of it not as taking place through abstraction, but rather through "separation". It involves a separation of the notion of *form* from the notion of *informing matter*. That separation is not made by abstraction, which requires that the intellect have before its gaze instances of the relevant types, as it does in the case of humans and animals and living bodies. But the intellect does not have before its gaze instances of both corporeal and incorporeal things, and so it cannot just abstract from them a notion that is common to both the sensible and the supersensible. So: "Through the operation by which it compounds and divides, it distinguishes one thing from another by understanding that the one does not exist in the other."²⁵ It is a separation made by the activity of judgment, not by that of simple apprehension.

In Aquinas, non-precisive abstraction makes possible the full identity of subject and predicate, allowing one to say that Socrates is a man or that a horse is an animal. As "non-precisive" indicates, it does not cut off or exclude any of the other features; it merely does not take them into consideration. Precisive abstraction, on the other hand, does cut off or exclude or prescind from the features left out by the abstraction. The result of precisive abstraction is expressed in English by abstract nouns, for instance by "humanity" in contrast to "human being." One cannot say that Socrates is his humanity in the way one says that Socrates is a human being. Nor is humanity animality in the way a human being is an animal. Nothing goes against Aristotle in this development of the doctrine of predication, yet it is a notable advance in philosophical understanding. It indicates new and original thinking on the part of Aquinas, enabling him to make the metaphysically crucial assertion that a nature may abstract from all existence without prescinding from any of the ways in which it may exist.[26] It shows him why one can know what a phoenix or a mountain of gold is without thereby knowing anything about its existence. Even the existence of either object in one's own thought is known through a judgment, and not through any kind of reflexive conceptualization.

The lack of any existence whatever in the thing's nature likewise allows Aquinas to see that the existence it has must come from something else, and ultimately from existence that subsists. It also gives a convincing explanation of how the same thing can exist both in reality and in one's cognition, and thereby of how the thing existing outside cognition is the same thing that is known. Similarly it explains how the knower and the thing known can exist as identical in the actuality of cognition. These important epistemological consequences follow the understanding of essence or nature as something known through conceptualization, while existence is known through a different act, namely judgment. For Aristotle the two were grasped by the same intellectual activity. Although he explained the fact of cognition by the union of knower and thing known in the actuality of cognition, and regarded the subject as united with the predicate by the copula in a proposition, he did not have the notion that these unions were brought about by an actuality over and above the thing's nature and grasped only by the act of judgment. The new vocabulary in Aquinas points to a deeper penetration into the topics that Aristotle had treated, and to an original method of handling them.

For Aquinas, then, existence as grasped through judgment was an actuality that had escaped the notice of Aristotle. Yet as Aquinas saw it, it was the actuality of every actuality and the perfection of every perfection. Without it an object would be simply nothing. In this way it permeates the metaphysics of Aquinas through and through. It is the basis on which Aquinas can take Aristotelian concepts into his reasoning and draw such different conclusions from them. When Aquinas reasons to an actuality without any potentiality at all, in a way that is at first sight Aristotelian, the object reached is not a finite form as it was in Aristotle. It is infinite existence, incapable of being pluralized but able to create and to know and to provide for creatures. Aristotle's pure actuality was confined to itself, unable to know anything else or to have interest in anything outside itself. It could be only a final cause, and not an efficient cause, a radically different kind of being from the pure actuality inferred by Aquinas.

The vital difference between the reasoning in Aquinas and the reasoning in Aristotle lies in the type of actuality from which each starts. Both commence with the things of the sensible universe. But the actuality that Aristotle sees in them is finite form, the form that actuates their matter. From that type of actuality he reasons to pure forms that are finite. Aquinas, in contrast, starts from the existential actuality that sensible things receive from something else. It is the actuality grasped through judgment, and not through conceptualization of finite natures. The existence thereby grasped is in fact limited by the nature it actuates. But in its own notion it contains no limiting factor. When it is reached as pure actuality, it is infinite. No limiting feature is possible in it.[27] Infinite in every perfection, this pure actuality is a creator and knows down to the last detail everything that has been created, and exercises love and providence. Radical difference in the actuality from which it starts, then, is what makes the Thomistic demonstration so different from the Aristotelian in its results despite whatever structural similarity may be seen in its procedure.

These considerations should be sufficient to make clear both the ways in which the philosophical thought of Aquinas is dependent upon and indebted to the work of his great Greek predecessor, and the radical difference between the two types of metaphysics that are developed respectively in their writings. The difference in their conceptions of being is all-pervasive. Other metaphysical concepts, such as those of truth, goodness, and relation, could likewise be explored to assess the differences and the similarities in the two philosophical procedures. The result would be substantially the same. The conditioning of Aquinas through his thirteenth-century Christian upbringing will be seen to lead him to starting points that were missed by his fourth-century B.C. predecessor, with the result that a new and profoundly original philosophy emerges. His philosophical vocabulary remains to a large extent the vocabulary of Aristotle. Nevertheless, the originality in his thinking forces him into expressions that at times are considerably different from Aristotle's. But even where the wording remains exactly the same, one must be alert to the possibility of deep change in meaning. Where the wording is different, however, deep originality may be suspected, as in the case of non-precisively abstracted concepts.

V. METHODOLOGICAL ISSUES

Two objections may be raised against this way of assessing the differences between the philosophical thought of Aristotle and that of Aquinas. The first is that this assessment judges them on the basis of late twentieth-century philosophy, to which neither owes allegiance. The second objection is that religious belief intrinsically influences the character of Aquinas's thought on philosophical matters, which places the difference between Aquinas and Aristotle outside philosophy proper.

Although these two objections are different, they evoke the same answer. The philosophical thought of Aquinas, as should be evident from this chapter, proceeds strictly from the external sensible things that are known by everyone regardless of religious belief. It uses only naturally evident starting points or premises for its demonstrative procedures. The whole problem lies in how it can isolate these starting points in a way that was not available to Aristotle, and yet in a manner that leaves them grounded solidly in external reality and not in any linguistic or historical habituation.

Common to both Aristotle and Aquinas is the tenet that all naturally attainable knowledge originates in external sensible things. By their efficient causality transmitted through the appropriate media, the external things impress their forms upon the human cognitive faculties, and thereby make the percipient be the thing perceived in the actuality of the cognition. The awareness is directly of the thing itself, and only concomitantly and reflexively of the percipient and of the cognitive acts. The external things remain epistemologically prior. From this viewpoint both Aristotle and Aquinas remain radically distinct from modern philosophers, who from Descartes on base their philosophy upon ideas or sensations or vivid phenomena, instead of immediately on external things themselves. Likewise, both Aristotle and Aquinas remain just as distinct from postmodern thinkers who look for their starting points in linguistic and historical formation. The two philosophers not only respect the overriding awareness of ordinary people that what is immediately and directly known is the world outside one's mind, but they also give a profound epistemological explanation of what everybody recognizes as a fact. Since this is the case, why can't the difference between them be explained solely in terms of the external sensible things from which both commence their philosophical reasoning? Would this not be a common standard by which both can be assessed, without recourse to any linguistic considerations?

It is true that both Aristotle and Aquinas start from sensible things. To that extent they present a common ground upon which they may be judged. Through that ground their similarities may be explained. But in those external sensible things Aristotle sees finite form as the highest actuality. Aquinas, on the other hand, sees existence as the highest actuality. Existence of itself is not finite, since it is originally the object of a judgment and not of conceptualization. What is attained through conceptualization is, like the Aristotelian form, something finite. The notions *table* and *red* are both of finite objects in the judgment "The table is red." But can the same be said about what is known through the copula "is"? What is thereby grasped is of course not something infinite. It is something that just in itself escapes the characterizations of either "finite" or "infinite." Taken just in itself it is open to either, but it is finite when received into a limiting subject, as in sensible things, and infinite when subsisting as a nature.

In this perspective both Aquinas and Aristotle are basing their philosophical thinking on the same sensible things, and in consequence they offer a common ground upon which both may be assessed. But that one common ground allows the things in it to be understood in radically different ways. It is rich enough to give rise to a number of different philosophies, such as those of Avicenna, Giles of Rome, Duns Scotus, and Suarez. In Aquinas it gave rise to the metaphysical study of things from the viewpoint of their existential actuality as grasped through judgment. What has to be accounted for is why Aquinas came to approach sensible things from this existential viewpoint. What led him to view things philosophically as existent in the sense that their ultimate actuality was something grasped originally through judgment?

Precisely here lies the answer to the present question. Aquinas was led by religious belief to look upon *being* as the proper name and nature of a creative and provident God. It was in consequence a nature different in reality from the nature of anything else. Where it was given to other things through efficient causality, it had to remain really distinct from their natures. This approach to external sensible things prompted the philosophical search for the way in which these sensible things were known through human cognition. From the viewpoint of their natures, they were known through simple apprehension or conceptualization. From the viewpoint of their being they were grasped through judgment. Here one was in the strictly philosophical realm. This was not something that was divinely revealed, but something available to unaided human reason. But prior to Aquinas nobody had approached sensible things in just that way. Islamic thinkers, also prompted by their belief that the world had been created, had distinguished between things and the existence that had been received from a cause.[28] They had assigned the grasp of each to a different type of cognition. In all this they were developing new philosophical thought, and their achievements were drawn upon by Aquinas on the purely philosophical level. Aquinas carried the philosophical development still further with his insight into the way that nature and existence were related to each other in creatures. Existence was seen to be the actuality of essence, the actuality of all actualities and the perfection of all perfections.

This purely philosophical development of course did not look to any revealed source for its notions of essence and existence and their relations to each other. It looked only at sensible things. It saw that their natures were known and universalized through conceptualization, while their existence was grasped in each instance through judgment. From these aspects as known in sensible things it reasoned in its own distinctive way to the infinitely perfect being that was the cause of all other existence. The reasoning was based on nothing that was not seen in the sensible things themselves. In this respect religious belief's function was comparable to that assigned by Aristotle to the dialectic that led up to the first principles of philosophical reasoning.[29] It led one to see the principles, but did not enter into the demonstrative procedure itself. The starting points of the philosophical process are firmly located in the existent sensible things, each of which stands in its own right epistemologically. The character of the philosophy is thereby intrinsically determined through the new starting points to which the dialectic led. But each of the things involved is an existent in itself, without requiring something ulterior to guarantee its legitimacy as a starting point for reasoning.

In its dependence upon the historical antecedents and personal education of its originator, the philosophical thinking of Aquinas need not seem at all different from the way anyone else is influenced by those factors. The reason, as contemporary hermeneutics insists, is that each philosopher has learned through language and thinks according to the particular circumstances in which she or he has been brought up. But this is still a far cry from the tenet that each thinker must take her or his starting points from the tradition itself. In that case each would be dependent upon predecessors, with those predecessors in turn dependent upon the circumstances and linguistic conditions brought about by their own historical antecedents, and so on in infinite regress. The differences between the philosophy of Aristotle and that of Aquinas are not being assessed here by the norms of this linguistic interpretation. That would be a tribunal neither of them could accept. These differences are being judged on grounds that may be observed by all in external sensible things. That is the final court of appeal. There is no infinite regress. Aristotle saw finite form as the highest actuality in sensible things; Aquinas saw existence as that actuality. The difference in the starting points of the two ways of thinking is clear-cut and is based on external things.

In this regard, in fact, the postmodern approach is bound by its own historical antecedents in a way that stretches as far back as Descartes. It cannot take seriously the approach from things in themselves. It is incapable of understanding how things in themselves may be epistemologically prior to thoughts and words. Still conditioned by the Cartesian asceticism of turning one's back upon the immaturity of sense cognition and taking one's ideas as the starting points for philosophical thinking, it finds incomprehensible the stand that the thing signified can be epistemologically prior to the sign. It is but going a step further to claim that language in its turn precedes thought in the genesis of human cognition, since through language thought is handed down from generation to generation. Yet language does not necessarily change thought. Image and idea remain the same. The visible solar system stays the same, whether conceived as geocentric or heliocentric. The thing itself is not changed by our thought about it. Nor by changing our language do we change our ideas, any more than by changing our ideas we change things. Rather, as Aristotle noted, all persons can have the same mental images even though they use different speech-sounds to express them.[30] Language, in fact, is checked by thought for its correctness, and thought by things.

Once the Cartesian origin of philosophy in ideas has been put aside, it is not difficult to see how things can be epistemologically prior to both thought and language, with sensible things themselves as the ground on which the differences between the philosophy of Aristotle and the philosophy of Aquinas are to be judged. Neither of them will fit into the modern or the postmodern settings. Yet neither gives rise to any "backwards" tendency. Each stands on its own feet. Both are valid today for understanding our own contemporary world, as well as for understanding any other world or any other philosophy. From that viewpoint both are philosophies for today or for any other epoch. They are both surprisingly up-to-date.

Both these ways of thinking, moreover, are to be judged by their accordance with the really existent sensible world, the sole tribunal to which they pay homage as philosophies. Each is led to its starting points by the urgings of its cultural circumstances, but each finds those starting points in naturally knowable things and not in the cultural tradition. In that fact lies the answer to the claim that their philosophic worth is to be assessed on the strength of postmodern hermeneutical principles, and to the charge that the philosophic thinking of Aquinas is based upon religious beliefs.

Yet each of the two philosophies has to be kept carefully distinct from the other. Aristotle's philosophy is based upon sensible natures, that of Aquinas upon sensible existents. To lump them together is to confuse their distinctive procedures and to deprive each of its own characteristic life. We would be left with merely the dead Aristotelianism of the Middle Ages and the uninspiring Thomism of the Neoscholastic textbooks. The picture could be blandly described as "dredging up from the depths of history and resuscitating a defunct (Thomistic) Aristotelianism."[31] On the other hand, when each is understood in its own setting, both Aristotle and Aquinas can be very much alive today, and each can play an important and much-needed role in our thinking.

NOTES

1 Leo XIII 1879, pp. 97–115. The title of Joseph Gredt's widely used neoscholastic textbook was *Elementa Philosophiae aristotelico-thomisticae* (Gredt 1937).

2   "... seeing that *one man* and *being a man* and *a man* are the same. ...
    Moreover, the *substance* of each individual is ... essentially a be-
    ing ..." Aristotle, *Metaphysics*, IV 2, 1003b26–33; tr. Apostle. It "would
    be even more suitable" (ibid., b26) not to see any conceptual distinction
    between being and unity in the way they are "one nature" (a23). The
    same reasoning that follows in this passage would extend the preference
    for lack of a conceptual distinction to the case of a thing and its being.

3   "... it belongs to the same power of *thought* to make known both the
    whatness and the existence of a genus." Aristotle 1982, *Metaphysics* VI
    1, 1025a 17–18.

4   "In the thing there are both the quiddity of the thing and its being. So in
    the intellect there is a double activity corresponding to those two. One
    activity, which is called 'formation' by the philosophers, is that by which
    the intellect apprehends the quiddities of things, and which is also called
    by the Philosopher in *De anima* III 'the understanding of indivisibles.' But
    the other activity comprehends the thing's being, by compounding an
    affirmation." Aquinas, In Sent I.38.1.3; cf. I.19.5.1, ad 7.

5   See Prado 1911. A balanced discussion of this problem of "la vérité
    fondamentale" may be found in Gilson 1960a, pp. 97–128.

6   Aquinas, In M XII.5.2496.

7   Thomas Aquinas 1949, pp. 24–25.

8   See Aertsen's Chapter 1 above.

9   "So those who use the works of the philosophers in sacred doctrine, by
    bringing them into the service of faith, do not mix water with wine, but
    rather change water into wine" (In BDT 2.3, ad 5; Thomas Aquinas 1987,
    p. 50). With Bonaventure, it was a question of the wine of sacred Scrip-
    ture, accompanied by a concern about the proportions of the mixture:
    "Indeed, not so much of the water of philosophy should be mixed with
    the wine of Sacred Scripture that it turn from wine into water" (*Colla-
    tions on the Six Days*, in Bonaventure 1960–1970, V, 291). On this topic,
    see Quinn 1973, pp. 814–15.

10 "Once you are in possession of that revelation how can you possibly
    philosophize as though you had never heard of it?" (Gilson 1940, p. 5).

11 See nn. 2–3 above.

12 Aquinas, SCG I.22.

13 See Jordan's Chapter 9, herein.

14 Aquinas, ST Ia. 104.1, ad 1.

15 Aquinas, QDP 7.2, ad 9.

16 See Wippel's Chapter 4.

17 See n.2 above.

18 See Burrell's Chapter 3.

19 Aquinas, In Sent I.38.1.3 See Rahman 1958, pp. 2–4.

20 "But our intellect, which has the source of its cognition in things that have composite being, apprehends that being only by composition and division." In Sent I.38.3, ad 2. See also MacDonald's chapter 6, herein.

21 Aquinas, ST Ia.2.1, ad 2.

22 Aquinas, DEE 4.94–146.

23 See MacDonald's Chapter 6.

24 ". . . the term 'being' is taken from the exercise of being, and not from the thing to which the exercise of being belongs." QDV 1.1, ad 3

25 Aquinas, In BDT 5.3. Thomas Aquinas 1986, p. 37.

26 "It is evident, therefore, that in its absolute consideration the nature of a human person abstracts from every kind of being, but in such a way that no prescinding from any of those kinds takes place." ("Ergo patet quod natura hominis absolute considerata abstrahit a quolibet esse, ita tamen quod non fiat precisio alicuius eorum.") DEE 3.68–70.

27 Aquinas, ST Ia.7.1 Cf. SCG I. 43

28 See Burrell's Chapter 3, herein.

29 ". . . dialectic, being exploratory, is the path to the principles of every inquiry." Aristotle, *Topics*, I 2, 101b3–4; Aristotle 1982, p. 145.

30 *De interpretatione*, 1, 16a5–8.

31 Madison 1988, p. 166.

3 Aquinas and Islamic and Jewish thinkers

I. AQUINAS'S ATTITUDES TOWARD AVICENNA, MAIMONIDES, AND AVERROES

The work of Thomas Aquinas may be distinguished from that of many of his contemporaries by his attention to the writings of Moses Maimonides (1135–1204), a Jew, and Ibn Sina (Avicenna) (980–1037), a Muslim. His contemporaries, especially in Paris, were responsive to the work of another Muslim, Ibn Rushd (Averroes) (1126–1198), for his rendition of the philosophical achievements of Aristotle, but Aquinas's relation to Averroes and to those who took their lead from him was far more ambivalent. Aquinas respected Rabbi Moses and Avicenna as fellow travelers in an arduous intellectual attempt to reconcile the horizons of philosophers of ancient Greece, notably Aristotle, with those reflecting a revelation originating in ancient Israel, articulated initially in the divinely inspired writings of Moses. So while Aquinas would consult "the Commentator" (Averroes) on matters of interpretation of the texts of Aristotle, that very aphorism suggested the limits of his reliance on the philosophical writings of Averroes, the *qadi* from Cordova. With Maimonides and Avicenna his relationship was more akin to that among interlocutors, and especially so with Rabbi Moses, whose extended dialectical conversation with his student Joseph in his *Guide of the Perplexed* closely matched Aquinas's own project: that of using philosophical inquiry to articulate one's received faith, and in the process extending the horizons of that inquiry to include topics unsuspected by those lacking in divine revelation.

We may wonder at Aquinas's welcoming assistance from Jewish and Muslim quarters, especially when we reflect on the character of his times: the popular response to the call to arms of the crusades as well as a nearly universal impression on the part of Christians that the new convenant had effectively eclipsed the old. Aquinas may have shared these sentiments, for all we know, yet his overriding concern in reaching out to other thinkers was always to learn from them in his search for the truth of the matters at hand. In this respect, he epitomized the medieval respect for learning, with its conviction that "truth was where one found it." So he was more inclined to examine the arguments of thinkers than their faith, trusting in the image of the creator in us all to search out traces of the divine handiwork, a theological premise that will prove useful in guiding our explorations into Aquinas's reliance on Jewish and Christian thinkers, and better than attributing to him an ecumenical or interfaith perspective *avant la lettre*. Yet it would not be untoward for *us* to note how other thinkers attempting to employ the inherited philosophy to elaborate their faith-perspective were for that very reason helpful to Aquinas in his vocational task.

It is worth speculating whether the perspective of Aquinas and his contemporaries was not less Eurocentric than our own. What we call "the West" was indeed geopolitically surrounded by Islam, which sat astride the lucrative trade routes to "the East." Moreover, the cultural heritage embodied in notable achievements in medicine, mathematics, astronomy, as well as the logic, philosophical commentary, translation, and original work in metaphysics begun in tenth-century Baghdad, represented a legacy coveted by western medieval thinkers.[1] Marshall Hodgson has called the culture that informed this epoch and extended from India to Andalusia "the Islamicate," intending thereby to include within its scope Jewish thinkers like Maimonides who enjoyed the protected status of *dhimmi* and contributed to Muslim civilization.[2] Christians like John of Damascus enjoyed a similar status, reserved by Qur'anic authority for "people of the book," yet the divisions in Christendom saw to it that thinkers in Paris were better acquainted with Muslim and Jewish writers than with their co-religionists in Islamic regions.

Aquinas's own geographic and social origins could well have predisposed him to a closer relationship with thinkers representative of the Islamicate than his contemporaries could be presumed to have had, in Paris at least. For his provenance from Aquino in the region of Naples, itself part of the kingdom of Sicily, reflected a face of

Europe turned to the Islamicate, as evidenced in the first translations commissioned from Arabic: "Latin, Muslim, and Jewish culture mingled freely in Sicily in a unique way that was peculiarly
Sicilian."[3] Moreover, in his later years, when his Dominican province asked him to direct a theological *studium*, Aquinas expressly
chose Naples (over Rome or Orvieto) for its location, and that for
intellectual reasons: "there was a vitality about Naples that was
absent from Rome or any other city in the Roman Province."[4] So it
might be surmised that these dimensions of his own personal history led him to be more open to thinkers from the Islamicate than
his co-workers from Cologne or Paris might have been. In any case,
the number and centrality of his citations from Avicenna and from
Moses Maimonides leave no doubt as to their place in his intellectual development. By styling that place as one of "interlocutor" I
have tried to finesse the vague historical category of *influence* in
favor of one more familiar to philosophers and theologians of every
age, and especially of those consciously working in a tradition of
inquiry, who treasure what they learn as a result of contending with
their predecessors' arguments, even when their interlocutors lie beyond the reach of actual conversation.

II. AVICENNA: THE DISTINCTION OF EXISTING
FROM ESSENCE

In his early monograph *De ente et essentia*, composed near the age of
thirty when he became Master of Theology at Paris, Aquinas dis-
played a rare metaphysical acumen in preparing the way for using the
philosophy of Aristotle to elucidate a universe created by a sovereign
God.[5] Presenting a lexicon of key philosophical expressions – *ens* ("a
being"), *essence* taken in itself and in its relation to *genus, species,*
and *differentia,* as well as essence in separate substances and in
accidents – Aquinas takes the opportunity to introduce a new level of
"composition" in created things beyond that established by Aristotle
of *matter* and *form.* His guide here is Avicenna, whose notion of
"essence in itself" gave him the key premise in the argument to a new
level of composition: "every essence or quiddity can be understood
without knowing anything about its *existing (esse)*" (DEE 4.6). This
fact is utilized as a sign that "*existing* itself cannot be caused by the
form or quiddity of the thing" (4.7), which then "must be potential

with regard to the *existing* it receives from God, and this *existing* is received as an actuality" (4.8). As form is actualization with respect to matter for Aristotle, so *existing* will be with respect to essence for Aquinas. The import of this famous "distinction" in his overall project will not appear until his treatment of creation, where *existing* will be identified as "the proper effect of the first and most universal cause, which is God" (ST Ia.45.5), but its role in Aquinas's reception of Aristotelian metaphysics has been comprehensively canvassed by Edward Booth.⁶ To appreciate the part that Ibn Sina played in the unfolding of that drama, let us try to understand its terms and something of the cast of players confronting Aquinas in his task of adapting a classical ontology to articulate a freely created universe.

The persistent problem bequeathed to posterity from Aristotle's *Metaphysics* concerns the relationship of existing individuals to their "intelligible natures" (or *rationes,* as the medievals identified them). It is clear that Aristotle meant *substance* to be exemplified paradigmatically by existing individuals, yet equally clear that "what makes something to be what it is," its essence (or "secondary substance"), comprises what is knowable about it. Which of the two has ontological primacy, and why? It is fair to say that the *Metaphysics* left this as a radical problem (or *aporia*), as Booth's assemblage of commentators on that seminal text will testify. What focused an otherwise abstruse metaphysical issue, however, was the avowal of a created universe. In Charles Kahn's admirable summary:

> *existence* in the modern sense becomes a central concept in philosophy only in the period when Greek ontology is radically revised in the light of a metaphysics of creation. . . . As far as I can see, [the early Christian theologians] remained under the sway of classical ontology. The new metaphysics seems to have taken shape in Islamic philosophy, in the form of a *radical* distinction between necessary and contingent existence: between the existence of God, on the one hand, and that of the created world on the other.⁷

The "sway of classical ontology" was confirmed and stamped by three figures spanning the third to the fifth centuries: Plotinus (205–270), his pupil and publicist Porphyry (232–305), and Proclus (410–485). (What is more, two books attributed to Aristotle and vastly influential among Arab and western thinkers – *The Theology of Aristotle* and *Liber de causis* – were in fact editions of Plotinus and Proclus, respectively.) Their neoplatonic tendencies neatly reversed the primacy of "first/second substance" in Aristotle, as they yoked ontology to logic with the less general serving the more universal. The most inclusive category of all will then be being (eis to einai), itself an emanation (for Plotinus) from the One. Of immense fascination to religious minds, whether pagan, Jewish, or Christian (and later Muslim), this systemic explanation of all things by an emanation that turns the increasing generality of substantial predication into a causal efflux can hardly be said to reproduce Aristotle's focal concern for individuals. The publication of the "Theology" under his name can only have been an act of pious deference, whose effect was to create the hybrid that the Arabs later encountered as "philosophy."

The western witness to the ensuing attempt to contain Aristotle within a neoplatonic scheme of emanation, while deferring to his concern for individuals, was Boethius (c. 480–524). His logical works tend to reproduce the Porphyrian tree in a manner reminiscent of Proclus (Liber de causis), yet he also comments on Porphyry's hesitation regarding the status of universals by considering them to be abstracted from experience as a means of giving experience an intelligible form.[8] In general, however, it seems that Boethius avoided judging "between Plato's separate ideas and Aristotle's universals,"[9] utilizing the realist conception of universals prior to things (ante res) when needing to express their containing priority, and the conceptualist view of them as dependent on things (post res) when deferring to Aristotle's insistence. When he does bring them together, it is to assert that an individual subject can be taken at once particularly and universally, although the being (esse) is clearly that of the subject. Aquinas commented on two of Boethius's works that exhibit a greater affinity to pseudo-Dionysius's monotheistic correction of Plotinus and Proclus: De trinitate and De hebdomadibus. In the latter Boethius identifies God with ipsum esse, carefully distinguishing "between the esse which makes God ipsum esse, and the ipsum esse of things which flow from him."[10] It is a notion on which Aquinas capitalized, but only after clearly discriminating esse from essentia, as we have seen.

Aristotle's central aporia will not admit of resolution, then, and even returns to threaten the urge to reduce the tension between species and individual by subsuming both in a larger emanation scheme. One maneuver, however, had not yet been attempted: distinguishing what constitutes the individual, namely its existing, from what makes it to be the kind of thing it is. As Kahn suggests, this move does not emerge until the Islamic philosophers, arguably first with al-Farabi (?870–?950), and clearly (though not yet coherently) with Ibn Sina. And the pressure to do so comes from the need to distinguish the "first being" (in al-Farabi) from all that is not first and derives from it. While not yet a coherent notion of creation, the concern to make a clear hiatus in the emanation scheme that he adopted made al-Farabi separate "a principle which has no essence as apart from *existing* (*huwiyya*) [from everything else that] must have [its *existing*] from something else" – namely the principle.[11] What will be required to keep the principle from being identified simply with the first in a logical scheme – in short, to secure a notion of creation – will be a way of clearly distinguishing *existing* from essence (*mahiyya*). So we are brought to Ibn Sina's wrestling with that task. Although it does not appear as clearly in him as it does later in Aquinas, that same distinction will allow one to overcome Aristotle's central *aporia*. Through a notion of creation, the difference of creator from creation will also mark what distinguishes the individual existent from its essential explanations. But that is to anticipate the story's final point.

Ibn Sina's discussions of *existing* (*mawjûd* or *anniyya*) as distinct from essence (*mahiyya*) are all in the context of distinguishing necessary being (*wajîb al-wujûd*) from possible being (*mumkin al-wujûd*).[12] And the consideration of universals-in-themselves, which might be said to prepare the way for the distinction, reminds us that "the providence of God accounts for something's being in so far as it is an animal."[13] Here he has in view the essence – the *haqîqa* – usually rendered by the specific term "man" or "animal." Ibn Sina, in short, is less preoccupied with Aristotle's quandary regarding the proper way to characterize existing individuals so as to secure their exemplary status, than he is concerned to find a way of characterizing essences so that their existence in things may properly be explained.

But that does not mean that such essences can exist apart; explicitly not, in fact (5.1, 204:14–17). As the essence of what may possibly exist, something other than itself must explain this animal's existing. For the essence as such is neither universal nor particular, one nor many; all it can explain is the thing's being an animal. (And, as we have seen, that is all that Aristotle seemed directly concerned to account for.) As for the individual animal's coming to be and passing away, as well as its continuing to exist as long as it does, it is this fact which, Ibn Sina insists, cannot be accounted for by the essence itself. Why not? Because all essences are essences of possible beings, and the "proper character [of such beings] is that they necessarily require some other thing to make them be actually (bil-fi'l mawjûdan)" (1.8, 47:10–11). There is only one whose existence is necessary, and that one, "the first, has no essence (mahiyya) except its existence (anniyya)" (8.4, 344:10). "Necessary being has no essence (mahiyya) except that it be necessary being, and this is its existence (anniyya)" (8.4, 346:11).

By insisting that the necessary being's essence (dhat) can be characterized only by its very existing (anniyya), Ibn Sina wants to avoid a misunderstanding that could jeopardize his entire enterprise: taking existence (wujûd) as a property contingently held by everything but the first being, who possesses it necessarily.[14] Such a reading would jeopardize his entire project, for it would make the distinction of necessary from possible being explicable by an independent understanding of modalities. (It would also require understanding wujûd as a property, a point that will emerge for comment.) Ibn Sina seeks rather for an independent way of characterizing "the first," which will then clarify his use of necessary/possible being. That is to present it as "sheer being, with the condition of negating anything understood as [adding] properties to it" (8.4, 347:10). The result is that such a one alone is utterly without potentiality, and "a unity, while everything else is a composite duality" (1.7, 47:18).

The statement just cited actually uses the ordinary Arabic word fard, or "individual," but it is better translated "unity" here since the entire chapter is concerned to show the radical unity attending necessary being. In the process of so distinguishing necessary from possible being, Ibn Sina succeeds in identifying a new mode of composition in everything that is not necessary. It is a "composite duality" – not that of matter and form, which he presumes throughout, but one of essence (mahiyya) and of some other factor that causes the individual thing to be. That factor is never identified as such, although it would be tempting to identify it as anniyya. The pair mahiyya/anniyya would then sound like essence/existence. Yet that factor is never isolated; anniyya expresses "the real existence of a particular individual" rather than identifying what it is that makes the individual exist.[15]

Moreover, the term that Ibn Sina consistently prefers, *mawjûd*, which is the participial form of *wujûd*, is probably best rendered "existing," as we do when we look for a participial form for "being" – once that term has been fixed as a noun! So we say that a being is an existing thing. Yet we have not thereby isolated a distinct factor, existence, which is why I have usually rendered *wujûd* as "being" rather than "existence" and *mawjûd* as "existing," saving "existence" (or "very existing") for *anniyya*.[16] Yet even here, following Frank, "existent" would render the usage more accurately. So once again, *existence* eludes us, yet we are on the track. It will continue to elude us in Ibn Sina, for he begins, as Anawati notes, "with essence in such a way as to arrive at the *existing* (*esse*) which affects it as though it were an accident."[17] It is in fact his treatment of the universal-in-itself that affords him the leverage to consider being (*wujûd*) as something that "comes to" the essence, while also guaranteeing that it *not* be considered as an accident properly so-called, that is, a property. His discussion (5.1) quickly leaves behind the general term "universal" (*kullî*) and concentrates on man or animal: "animal insofar as it is animal, and man insofar as it is man, that is in terms of their definition and meaning, without reference to other things accompanying them – nothing but man or animal" (5.1, 201:1–3). One cannot help but find this a congenial rendering of Aristotle's "secondary substance," or the formula. Universality, or predicability of many, belongs to the essence only upon further reflection regarding its role in discourse; hence it is an accompanying feature of "animal as animal."[18]

What Ibn Sina is reaching for is an essence prior to universality or particularity with no conditions, not even, he insists, one with the expressed condition *not* to attribute particularity or universality to it (5.1, 203:18). It is the essence taken by itself, without regard to existence, and hence short of the Platonic status of separateness. Such a one, he avers, can and indeed does "exist in reality," while the Platonic one – considered *as separate* – can exist only in the mind (5.1, 204:5–10). But how can we say it "exists in reality" if not separately? The Latin translation, which formed the basis for western interpretation of Avicenna, answers that unequivocally by translating "in reality (*fî'l-a'yân*) [as] *in sensibilibus* (in things which can be sensed)."[19] Such a rendering would leave no doubt as to Ibn Sina's Aristotelian commitments, and it is as plausible as any in rendering the Arabic expression *fi'l-a'yân*, which carries the original meaning of "upon observation." What is essential, after all, is that we arrest our consideration at the essence-itself – "animal insofar as animal" – which, if it were to exist, would exist in particulars. Yet the strategy of stopping short of that is to show that in itself no such essence can explain the presence of animals.

If we ask why it cannot do so, the question fairly answers itself. For the essence of all that is not necessary being is itself indifferent to existence or to non-existence; indeed, that is what it is to be possible being (1.6, 38:12–17). To have no cause is not to exist, and to exist such an essence "demands another thing which will make it be in actuality" (1.7, 47:12). There is no further question remaining beyond that implicitly put by Anawati: why select such a starting point? Nor can we expect Ibn Sina to answer that question; the best we can do is point to the neoplatonic manner of resolving Aristotle's quandary, and note the predilection of that tradition (and of much of philosophy) to focus on the formula itself.[20]

Standing in such a tradition, yet unwilling to give ontological primacy to what is more general, Ibn Sina sought a reason for giving primacy to existing individuals. Although the Aristotelian *aporia* did not structure his inquiry, it could not help but motivate it. Since that reason could not come from the formal side, it had to come from elsewhere. With matter a mere repository of possibility, it could come only from "the first" being whose very essence would be to exist. The image that comes to mind is of the Copernican system before Newton. As Bellarmine rightly saw, it remained a likely mathematical story without an account of the origin of movement.[21] The Plotinian emanation scheme remained a logico-aesthetic theory without an ontologico-kinetic source. Aristotle's prime mover accounted for the activity of the spheres governing generation and corruption; Ibn Sina's "first being" would account for the scheme's actually existing. No wonder Kahn insisted on the newness of this "notion of *radical* contingency, not simply the old Aristotelian idea that things might have been other than they in fact are . . . , but that the whole world of nature might not have been created at all: that it might not have *existed*."[22]

The prospect of a metaphysical rendition of that new situation must have directed Aquinas to Avicenna's "distinction" and led him to transform it the way he did. For Ibn Sina did not himself succeed in formulating a notion of creation corresponding to so radical a contingency, any more than he was able to identify *what* it was that united with essence to yield the composite dualities called *substances*.[23] Whatever it was, it had to "happen to" or "come to" essence or possible being (1.7, 47:12). And since the Arabic verb for "happen/come to," like the Latin *accidere*, in its noun form had translated Aristotle's "accident," Ibn Sina was said to have made of *existing* an accident. Kahn describes the new situation neatly: "for the contingent being of the created world (which was originally present only as a 'possibility' in the divine mind) the property of 'real existence' emerges as a new attribute or 'accident', a kind of added benefit bestowed by God upon possible being in the act of creation."[24]

It requires no exceptional philosophical acumen to show that *existing* cannot in any proper sense be an accident. For the grammar of that category – "what exists in another" – presupposes primary existents of which it can be an accident. If existing is taken to be that which enters into composition with essence to make a primary existent, then it could not itself be of such a sort as to presuppose itself. And if the contrast term for "existing" is not "substance" but "essence taken by itself," then Ibn Sina could well say that *existing* must *come to* such an item for it to exist as an individual, but would have no right to call what "came to" it an *accident* of it. Ibn Rushd (Averroes) belabored this point, intending it as a criticism of Ibn Sina; in our time Fazlur Rahman and Alexander Altmann have cleared the record.[25] Yet it took Aquinas's radically new metaphysical step in his early *De ente* (DEE) to fashion an adequate response by removing *existing* (*esse*) from the entire slate of Aristotelian categories, proposing that it be understood in terms of the master-analogy of actuality/potentiality. Its formal ontological status will have to await his treatment of creation, where he identifies the "*esse* received from God" (DEE 4.8) as "a relation to the creator as the origin of its existence" (ST Ia.45.3). *Relation-to-a-transcendent-agent* is the only possible way one can identify the *act* within each thing that is the expression of the activity whereby God "produces a thing without motion": creation. In one fell swoop, Aquinas has succeeded in restoring the primacy Aristotle intended for individual existing things, by linking them directly to their creator and by granting Avicenna's "distinction" an unequivocal ontological status. Yet as should be clear, this is more than a development of Avicenna; it is a fresh start requiring a conception of *existing* that could no longer be confused with an *accident*, and which has the capacity to link each creature to the gratuitous activity of a free creator. Only in such a way can the radical *newness* (*hudûth*) of the created universe find coherent expression, for the *existing* "received from God" will be the source of all perfections and need not presume anything at all – be it matter or "possibles."

III. MAIMONIDES: STRATEGIES OF CONCILIATION

If Avicenna gave the impetus to Aquinas's project of adapting the received philosophy of the Greeks to the larger project of elaborating a universe created and redeemed by the one God, it is fair to say that Moses Maimonides gave that project its critical shape. For the assistance that Aquinas most needed had to do with the respective criteria of reason and of revelation, and Maimonides's ongoing conversation with his student Joseph focused precisely on this point: the interaction of reason and of revelation in determining what one might responsibly hold.[26] In Aquinas's milieu, the translation of the *Guide of the Perplexed* must have been a boon, for the goal of his own project was questioned from two sides: the conservative Augustinians, who pretended to be invoking a pure tradition of faith against the "new learning," and the Latin Averroists, who were so enamored of Aristotle as to make of his teaching a virtual revelation for the philosophically minded.[27] Although Maimonides wrote his dialectical inquiry with Joseph in Judaeo-Arabic, it was translated into Hebrew in 1204, and thence into Latin by the 1220s. As Louis Gardet has shown, Aquinas gleaned all that he knew about the Muslim "theologians," the *mutakallimûn*, from the expositions available to him from the *Guide*.[28] But we are less concerned about information than strategy. Taking the central issue of creation as our focus, we will be able to see how Aquinas took his cue from Rabbi Moses precisely in the delicate domain of reconciling the deliverances of revelation with conclusions of reason. This will allow us to trace this tutelage in three critical areas: the "eternity" or temporal limitedness of the cosmos, the meaning-structure of divine names, and God's knowledge of singulars and the range of providence.

A beginningless world? Creation and "the distinction"

Since the free creation of the universe marked the divide separating medievals from the ancients, the task of reconciling biblical faith with Greek metaphysics found its natural focus there. The role of intermediaries is also crucial here, since the pagan thinker Plotinus provided the philosophers of a fledgling Islamic tradition with what looked like a promising pattern for articulating creation: the scheme of necessary emanation modeled on logical deduction. This allowed "al-Farabi and Avicenna [to] reconstruct the traditional notion of creation *ex nihilo* in terms of a Plotinian metaphysics that, given its compatibility with Aristotle's physics, they attribute or read into Aristotle's metaphysics. Thus for al-Farabi and Avicenna the eternal creation theory is *the* theory of Aristotle, although in its historical development Plotinus and Proclus are its real progenitors."[29] And the same can be said for Maimonides, who catalogues his "third theory," that of eternal emanation, as Aristotle's (2.13). This conflation is particularly significant, since it helps us to understand the appeal of the neoplatonic emanation scheme, when identified with Aristotle, to flesh out the lacuna in explanation which bedeviled his *Metaphysics*.[30] Moreover, linking this theory with Aristotle would pose a formidable obstacle to the program of Maimonides and Aquinas. Neither regarded the efforts of their companions in faith to prove the creation of the universe *de novo* to be very helpful. Quite the contrary, in fact, as both complain that the arguments adduced are of such poor quality that they could "furnish infidels with an occasion for scoffing, as they would think that we assent to truths of faith on such grounds" (ST Ia.46.2).

Maimonides is thinking of the *mutakallimûn*, the Muslim religious thinkers who "did not conform in their premises to the appearance of that which exists [as Aristotle had], but considered how being ought to be in order that it should furnish a proof for the correctness of a particular opinion" (1.71). For this purpose they elaborated an atomistic metaphysics running "counter to the nature of existence that is perceived so that they resort to the affirmation that nothing has a nature in any respect." Maimonides is referring specifically to the Ash'arite thesis that was intended to open the world of creatures to the direct action of God by withdrawing any intermediary structures like natures, whereas Aquinas focuses on their Christian counterparts, notably Bonaventure, who did not dally with an occasionalist thesis but nonetheless insisted that creation *ex nihilo* had also to be *de novo*.[31] That the arguments, good or bad, could be so easily shared testifies to the accuracy of Maimonides's contention that the "affirmation of the temporal creation of the world [is] common to all three of us, I mean the Jews, the Christians, and the Muslims" (1.71). So the divisions emerged within these communities rather than between them, and their origins were at once metaphysical and semantic: clarifying the precise import of the expressions used when the philosophical background favored certain understandings over others. Yet such confusions, as Wittgenstein has reminded us, can often illuminate the contours of the issues at stake. In this case, the terms "eternal," "*ex nihilo*," "*de novo*," and even "creation" itself are at issue.

Aquinas's monograph on this subject is entitled "On the Eternity of the World," yet he himself insists that "eternity, in the true and proper sense, belongs to God alone" (ST Ia.10.3). Like Maimonides, who does not hesitate to presume "the doctrine of the eternity of the world" in his demonstration of God's existence, *not* because he believes it but because he wishes "to establish . . . the existence of God . . . through a demonstrative method as to which there is no disagreement" (1.71), Aquinas will adopt the current parlance while explicitly noting, toward the end of the work, "that nothing can be co-eternal with God, because nothing can be immutable save God alone" (DAM 11, also 10). Yet the thrust of his argument is to show that there is no contradiction in asserting that "something has always existed, understanding that it was caused by God with regard to all the reality found in it" (DAM 1). So "eternal" in this discussion will mean "always existed," a predicate logically compatible with "the universe," even when we acknowledge its total derivation from God. The argument proceeds to clarify at each step the grammar of the other terms involved in explicating such a transcendent relation. *Ex nihilo* will then be parsed not according to its surface grammar, which would turn *nothing* into that *something* "out of which" the universe was made, but as a *façon de parler*: "the creature is made 'from nothing', that is, it is made 'after nothing', [where] the term 'after' unquestionably connotes order: . . . it is nothing before it is a being" (DAM 7, also 6). Similarly, *de novo* cannot mean "in time," as we often express this alternative – "that the world was created in time," but rather must intend "that its initial moment initiate time as well" (cf. ST Ia.46.1, ad 6).

Moreover, none of these grammatical clarifications could be attempted if *creating* were a process that takes time. Indeed, the claim that "creation cannot be called change except metaphorically, so far as a created thing is regarded as having existence after non-existence" (SCG II.37) formulates the nub of Aquinas's argument that one could *conceive of* the universe as always existing yet totally dependent upon its creator: if the activity of creating is inherently instantaneous, then there is no need that God temporally *precede* the universe to be its creator. So the press of controversy helps Aquinas to clarify a notion that had escaped al-Ghazali as well as Maimonides: that one could speak properly of a free creation without insisting that it had to be *de novo* (2.21).[32] Yet the prevailing philosophical climate, drawn so powerfully to the logical model of intellectual emanation as an elegant articulation of the origin of the universe, would have supported Maimonides's *prima facie* insistence that "in conceiving the world as *created*, we see it exhibiting purpose and design, expressing the will of a freely creating agent; [while] in understanding the world as *eternal*, we see it as displaying determinate and fixed laws that govern all natural phenomena, [so that] these two conceptual frameworks [would be] mutually exclusive models in terms of which nature is made intelligible to [us]."[33] So the notion of an "eternal creation" has the ring of an oxymoron, if "creation" contains the note of "free origination" – so powerful is the grip of the necessary emanation scheme.[34] Yet if Aquinas was able to escape that grip, it was no doubt due to the fact that Rabbi Moses had effectively prepared the way for negotiating the pitfalls in this debate, by mapping a way of distinguishing what is proper to the respective domains of demonstration (reason) and of revelation (faith).

Maimonides's strategy for dealing with this vexing question is disarmingly simple – one more testimony to his skill as a teacher and expositor. He introduces the extant views as three "opinions," thereby presaging the crucial step in his argument: none has the status of a philosophical demonstration. This ploy demands that he reduce the biblical view to "the *opinion* of all who believe in the Law of Moses, [namely] that the world as a whole . . . was brought into existence by God after having been purely and absolutely non-existent, and that God [who] had existed alone . . . through His will and His volition . . . brought into existence out of nothing all the beings as they are, time itself being one of the created things" (2.13). But such a dialectical move, like the presumption of the world's eternity in proving God's existence, in no way impugns his faith-commitment. The second opinion, said to be "the belief of Plato," has God creating from "a certain matter that is eternal as the deity is eternal," while the third, identified as "that of Aristotle," insists that the impassibility of deity entails that the universe "was not produced after having been in a state of nonexistence." He then focuses on Aristotle, "for it is his opinions that ought to be considered" (2.14), "to make it clear that Aristotle possesses no demonstration for the world being eternal, as he understands this" (2.15). What follows is a close reading of Aristotle to convince his "latter-day followers [who] believe that Aristotle has demonstrated the eternity of the world" that the master was quite aware of *not* having done so: that his form of argument corroborates his explicit statement: "that this doctrine was an opinion and that his proofs in favor of it were mere arguments [and] can Aristotle have been ignorant of the difference between mere [dialectical] arguments and demonstrations?" (2.15).

I have already suggested that such a picture of Aristotle, as espousing the eternal origination of the world, was really the work of al-Farabi and Avicenna, relying on Plotinus and Proclus. But never mind; that it was believed to be Aristotle's is part of what gave the scheme its authority. So all that Maimonides needed to do was to detach the scheme from that authority and so reduce it to one opinion among others. Then he could discuss the relative merits of the other two – those of Moses and Plato. It is only at this point that he has recourse to the *kalam* arguments of "purpose and particularization" (2.20): not, however, as demonstrations of anything, but solely as "arguments" in favor of the opinion of Moses that can better account for the fact that what we observe in the movement of the heavens does not follow the ideal requirements of Aristotle's scheme. Furthermore, since "the belief in eternity the way Aristotle sees it – that is, the belief according to which the world exists in virtue of necessity . . . destroys the Law in its principle, necessarily gives the lie to every miracle, and reduces to inanity all the hopes and threats that the law held out" (2.25), it would be absurd for believers to feel they had to espouse it short of its having been demonstrated. Had that been the case, Maimonides insists "we could interpret [the texts of the Torah] as figurative, as we have done when denying [God's] corporeality" (cf. 1.1–48), so "our shunning of the affirmation of the eternity of the world is not due to a text figuring in the Torah" (1.25), but to our freedom to affirm what we believe to be true in the absence of *proof* to the contrary. The dangler in his treatment is the "opinion of Plato, [which] would not destroy the foundations of the Law," and in accordance with which "it would also be possible to interpret figuratively the texts [of the Torah]." But given the fact that this too lacks demonstration, we are free to "take the texts according to their external sense and shall say: The Law has given us knowledge of a matter the grasp of which is not within our power, and the miracle [of the Torah itself] attests to the correctness of our claims" (2.25).[35]

That such matters are beyond our ken, since they have to do with the free activity of a divinity whose attributes we cannot know, is Maimonidean doctrine (1.51–60). What we can know are the results of divine action, revealed through nature as well as through the Torah. That these both reveal something of the divinity we know, however, requires "refuting the proofs of the philosophers bearing on the eternity of the world" (1.71), which would deliver to us a God who ruled by necessity; so Maimonides considers this to be the foremost task "of one who adheres to a Law." Aquinas certainly agreed, as his efforts testify, but he seemed in this matter more consistent than Rabbi Moses, for he eschewed employing any *kalam* arguments, leaving the matter solely to faith, and not wishing to reduce the affirmation of faith to an opinion among others, even for dialectical purposes. Yet his transformation of Avicenna's distinction of *existing* from *essence* allowed him a more positive characterization of this "matter the grasp of which is not in our power," as the "continual influx of *existing (esse)*" (ST Ia.104.3) on the part of an eternal God acting freely.

Naming God

It should be clear by now that both Maimonides and Aquinas were concerned primarily about a proper understanding of divinity, although the context was the way to characterize creation. And they each safeguarded God and the ways of God from the reductionist solvents of philosophy by recourse to a *via negativa*, yet always a disciplined one. Nowhere does this appear more clearly than in treating the "names of God," a topic on which Aquinas explicitly takes issue with Rabbi Moses, although, in practice, he espouses his critical concerns.[36] Their respective treatments presume the medieval parallelism between semantics and ontology: what may be said *of* God cannot be thought as a modification of the divine substance, which must be "One by virtue of a true Oneness" (1.50): "supremely one . . . because [it is] subsistent existence itself [and] altogether simple, not divided in any way" (ST Ia.11.4). Maimonides's prophetic insistence initiates his treatment of the multiple "names of God," while Aquinas's statement is the culmination of his metaphysical elaboration of the "formal features" attendant upon divine simpleness to show how our philosophical acumen must return us to a biblical faith.[37]

The context was set for Maimonides by the longstanding debate in the Islamicate on divine attributes, a discussion at once Qur'anic and philosophical in nature. It is customary for the Qur'an to punctuate its paranesis by recalling us to the feature of God apposite to the point being made – "He is the Wise, the Aware" (34:1), "the Merciful, the Forgiving" (34:2) – yet the overriding revelation respected the divine unity (*tawhîd*). So the earliest religious thinkers, the Mu'tazilites, exploited Greek philosophy to insist (according to Maimonides's summary) that "there is no oneness at all except in believing that there is one simple essence in which there is no complexity or multiplication of notions" (1.51). The later followers of al-Ash'ari objected to the results of this teaching, which in effect reduced the Qur'anic statements to metaphorical expressions. So they settled for acknowledging the reality of such attributes in one God, yet "without saying how (*bi-lâ kayf*)" that could be possible.[38] Maimonides mocks this intermediate position as inherently unstable: "some people engaged in speculation have ended by saying that His attributes . . . are neither His essence nor a thing external to His essence – these are things which are merely said" (1.51). So he will propose an entirely different approach to such expressions, familiar to him from the Psalms.

Since we can attribute nothing *to* a simple divinity, and since the prevailing context of God's Scriptures (as well as the Qur'an) speaks of God's deeds on behalf of the people, every such attributive statement is to be interpreted as expressing "an attribute of His action and not an attribute of His essence" (1.53), as "all His different acts [are] carried out by means of His essence and not . . . by means of a superadded notion" (1.52). Even the "attributes essential to" God, without apparent reference to divine activity on our behalf – "life, power, wisdom, and will" – "are not to be considered in reference to His essence, but in reference to the things that are created" (1.53). Indeed, what Moses himself was given to know (Exodus 34:6–7) "were simple pure attributes of action: *merciful and gracious, long-suffering*" (1.54). If this be all that God could communicate to Moses through a direct revelation, what more can we expect to glean of the divinity from the words of Scripture or the deliverances of reason? This does not keep us, of course, from regarding some of these expressions as "attributes indicative of a perfection likened to our perfections" (1.53), but we should realize that "the attributes ascribed to Him are attributes of His actions and that they do not mean that He possesses qualities" (1.54). What we can find significant in Maimonides's resolution of this question is the way he finesses the tangle of issues in the Islamic debate in favor of the spirit of the Hebrew scriptures' rendition of God.

Yet Aquinas finds Maimonides's stated position unstable and so takes him on directly, focusing on a corollary of his treatment: that all such terms, when applied to God, "are purely equivocal, so that their meaning when they are predicated of Him is in no way like their meaning in other applications" (1.56). Beyond that, since "there is no composition in [God], He cannot have an affirmative attribute in any respect" (1.58). The best we can do with such statements is to interpret "every attribute that we predicate of Him as an attribute of action, or, if the attribute is intended for the apprehension of His essence and not of His action, it signifies the negation of the privation of the attribute in question." Aquinas takes this to be "the view of Rabbi Moses: . . . that sentences like 'God is good', although they sound like affirmations are in fact used to deny something of God rather than to assert anything" (ST Ia.13.2). Aquinas does not object to the metaphysics implicit in Rabbi Moses' semantics, for he treats the practice of naming God immediately after securing the divine simplicity; he is rather concerned that "this is not what people want to say when they talk about God." The elaborate translation scheme that Maimonides proposes cuts against the grain of religious practice – presumably Jewish, Christian, and Muslim!

So Aquinas shifts the grounds of the discussion one step beyond those of his predecessor, employing some semantic tools unavailable to his interlocutors in the Islamicate, distinguishing between "the perfections themselves that are signified (*res significata*) – goodness, life, and the like – and the way in which they are signified (*modus significandi*)" (ST Ia.13.3). This distinction, gleaned from the twelfth-century explorations in the West of the various senses of Scripture, allowed him to insist that "so far as the perfections signified are concerned (*res significata*) the words are used literally (*proprie*) of God, and in fact more appropriately than they are used of creatures, for these perfections belong primarily to God and only secondarily to others. But so far as the way of signifying (*modus significandi*) these perfections is concerned the words are used inappropriately, for they have a way of signifying that is appropriate to creatures." The distinction regards the adaptations one must make in surface grammar to construct valid syllogistic arguments, but Aquinas had already put it to metaphysical use, reminding us that "in talking about simple things we have to use as models the composite things from which our knowledge derives. Thus when God is being referred to as a subsistent thing, we use concrete terms ['God is just'] (since the subsistent things with which we are familiar are composite); but to express God's simplicity we use abstract terms ['God is justice']" (ST Ia.3.3, ad 1).

This observation addresses one of Maimonides's recurrent concerns: that the very *form* of predication will mislead us into presuming that God "possesses qualities" (1.54). It also presupposes that in using the language appropriate to our condition we will be aware when the topic under discussion outstrips that language, and in what specific directions. Hence the focus on *perfections*, which Aquinas can suppose to represent traces of the creator, and whose semantic structure should reflect that fact. For not every term is susceptible of being distinguished in the way required: only those whose *meaning* can and must be said to outstrip their customary *use*, yet in a direction already intimated by that use.[39] This highly articulate grasp of analogous features of language differentiates Aquinas's treatment of "divine names" from that of Maimonides, who not only betrayed a rudimentary (and to Aquinas's mind, false) grasp of "terms used amphibolously" (1.56) but also emphasized the differences between scriptural and philosophical usage by the rabbinic adage: "the Torah speaks in the language of the sons of men" (1.53), that is, in ordinary parlance.[40] No doubt cutting the ties with our ordinary language reinforced his own convictions that the "names of God" that purport to signify essential attributes "are purely equivocal" (1.56). Yet Aquinas has shown how a speaker sensitive to distinctions already imbedded in our living language can use certain privileged terms of that language ("perfections") to point beyond our "manner of signifying" to "intend to signify" their source in God. So "the language of the sons of men" need not be misleading about the utter simplicity of the One, nor need one be a philosopher to use such terms correctly of God. For our native grasp of perfection terms demands that they outstrip their current descriptive sense if we are to use them properly – whenever we use them.

The upshot of this nearly direct exchange between the two is that Aquinas's resolution of the matter retains a generous dose of the "unknowing" that Maimonides sought to secure. Not, to be sure, in cutting all threads of meaning between, say, "knowledge" in our usage, and "knowledge" said of God as its object; yet neither does he demand that there be a shared "likeness in respect to some notion" (1.56). We may truly assert that God knows (res significata) without any sense of how it is that such is the case (modus significandi). Analogous usage for Aquinas is not to be explicated in terms of concepts but according to use, which could explain why many philosophers seem to have found the strategy elusive. In our reading of the two religious thinkers intent upon finding a way to speak of the utter oneness of God without distortion, however, it appears as though Aquinas's strategy responds to his predecessor's concerns without having to have recourse to the Rabbi's self-defeating insistence on "pure equivocity." For the grasp that we "composite beings" might be able to have of the "perfections signified" as they are in God's own self will ever be a tenuous one; indeed, it will comprise a via negativa every bit as taxing as that sketched by Maimonides in his culminating chapter on "divine names" (1.59).

God's knowledge of singulars and the range of providence

Maimonides's fourteenth-century commentator, Levi ben Gershon (Gersonides), located the decisive reason for his master's extreme agnosticism regarding divine attributes in the dilemma regarding God's foreknowledge and human freedom.[41] Maimonides insists that "it is in accordance with our Law that God's *knowledge* does not bring about the actualization of one of the two possibilities even though He knows perfectly how one of them will come about," and attributes all confusion on these matters to forgetting that "between our knowledge and His knowledge there is nothing in common" (3.20, emphasis added). So customary ways of generating the dilemma, "if God *knows that* something will take place, then it must occur," are rendered nugatory if the formula "knows that" does not function in connection with God the way the argument-form presumes it should. Insistent as he is about the matter, however, Maimonides does not leave it at that, but suggests a specific difference (inspired by Avicenna): "A great disparity subsists between the knowledge an artificer has of the thing he has made and the knowledge someone else has of the artifact in question" (3.21). In short, if we insist on comparing God's knowledge with ours, we ought to look not at our "knowings that" so much as the knowing that directs and issues in doing or making: "for in knowing the true reality of His own immutable essence, He also knows the totality of what necessarily derives from all His acts."[42] And while "it is impossible for us to know in any way this kind of apprehension, [it] is something extraordinary and a true opinion; . . . no mistake or distortion will be found in it."

So Maimonides accepts Ibn Sina's cue regarding the reversal of direction in knowing: from us who derive knowledge from existent things to the One whose knowing makes things exist. Yet the very necessity of Ibn Sina's scheme keeps that same One from knowing individuals "except in so far as they are universal" (8.6, 360:3). This will not suffice for a follower of the Torah, who must insist that "divine providence watches . . . over the individuals belonging to the human species" (3.17). Aquinas transforms the assertion into a theorem: "God's knowledge is the cause of things" (ST Ia.14.8) and "has the same extension as [God's] causality, [so] his knowledge must necessarily extend to individuals" (ST Ia.14.11). There is no hint of *how*, of course, for that regards the utterly basic relation of free creation; but we can know that whatever exists does so by participation in God's very existence, and only individuals exist. We are also freed from the specific bind from which Maimonides sought to escape, namely that God's knowing that something was to occur would determine its occurrence, since the practical knowing associated with the creator of things' very being is contemporaneous with the event itself and so must not be thought of as "foreknowledge."

At this point, Aquinas will take exception to a restriction that Rabbi Moses presents as "my own belief" – that for all species below the human, individuals are simply subject to chance: "I do not by any means believe that . . . this spider has devoured this fly because God has now decreed and willed something concerning individuals" (3.17) The argument here is with Ash'arite Islamic thinkers, whom he depicts as claiming that "every leaf falls through an ordinance and decree from God" (3.17). Aquinas does not have to deal with such a view, and so focuses on the immediate context of Maimonides's restriction: "intelligent creatures, because they have control over their own actions through free decision, come under providence in a special manner: blame or merit is imputed to them." But that is not to be taken "in the sense of Maimonides, who thought that God's providence has no concern for individual non-rational creatures" (ST Ia.22.2, ad 5). But in what sense does God have concern for them? In the measure that they fulfill their natures, which is (according to Aristotle) to contribute to the preservation of the species. So Aquinas's assertion seems to come to little more than Maimonides's denial, yet their statements differ according to the context of their concerns.

Where they differ considerably is in their respective characterizations of divine providence, which, for Maimonides, "is consequent upon the divine overflow" (3.17). That is, as he puts it in the concluding chapters of the Guide, "providence watches over everyone endowed with intellect proportionately to the measure of his intellect, [which allows such a one to attain] the perfection of the intelligibles that lead to passionate love of Him" (3.51). Yet while he seems to evoke the model of emanation to countenance a highly elitist providence, he will go on to note "that the end of the actions prescribed by the whole Law is to bring about the passion" (3.52) otherwise attained by "pure thought" (3.51). Where Rabbi Moses modifies an emanationist model to evoke something of divine grace, yet leaves the initiative with the individual (as he also does with prophecy [2.37]), Aquinas will carry the model of practical knowing to the level of God's interaction with individuals as well, in his elaboration of an elevation by God of each person to a new level of sharing in the divine life – a sharing communicated by the death and resurrection of Jesus. But that carries us into a new paradigm introduced by the Christian tradition's elaboration of the person of Jesus. It should suffice for us to have noted the considerable parallels between these exemplary Christian and Jewish thinkers; their differences are more readily apparent.

NOTES

1 Kraemer 1986, pp. 1–30.
2 Hodgson 1974, pp. 58–60.
3 Weisheipl 1983, p. 15.
4 Ibid., p. 296.
5 Thomas Aquinas 1983. For Maurer's rendering of *esse* as "being" (in this translation) I have substituted "existing." For an annotated edition of the original text, see Roland-Gosselin 1926.
6 Booth 1983. See also Burrell 1986a. In citations I have regularly altered his rendition of the Arabic *huwiyya* [lit., "thisness"] from "being" to "existing". See also Owens's Chapter 2.
7 Kahn 1982, p. 15. See Burrell 1986b, on which the following pages depend.
8 Booth 1983, p. 68.
9 Ibid., p. 66, n. 48.
10 Ibid., p. 74.
11 Ibid., p. 100.
12 For an account of the various terms the early Islamic philosophers adopted to translate key notions from Aristotle, see Shehadi 1982 *passim*.
13 References to Ibn Sina will be from Avicenna 1960a and Avicenna 1960b with citations by book and chapter, followed by page: lines. The French translation of Georges Anawati, Avicenna 1978 and Avicenna 1985, contains the Arabic pagination. The sections relevant to this inquiry are 1.6, 5.1, 8.4; the citation is from 5.1, 205:3.
14 The distinction between *mahiyya* and *dhat* is that between *quiddity* and *essence*, where *quiddity* answers the question "what [*quid, mâ*] is it?" (in proper terms: genus plus differentia), while *essence* will tolerate a less precise answer. So in answering "what is necessary being?" one will not be able to respond with a genus and a differentia, but can say something: it is *anniyya*. On this point (and several others) I have been assisted by Shehadi 1982, esp. p. 84.
15 On *anniyya*, see Frank 1956.
16 The abundance of terms can be confusing because the Islamic philosophers were refining them as they went along; al-Farabi's preferred

huwiyya (or "thisness") is gradually displaced by a set of terms that assume the more "abstract" cast of the original Greek. See Shehadi 1982, esp. p. 88.

17 Avicenna 1978, p. 78.

18 One is reminded here of Charles Sanders Peirce's preference for "general" rather than "universal," lest one pre-judge the issue by speaking of the "problem of universals." See Peirce 1960, 1.27, 1.422, 1.165, 5.429, 5.453, 5.503.

19 Avicenna 1980, pp. 236–37.

20 For a useful discussion of the background to Avicenna's notion, see Verbeke 1980, pp. 2*–19*.

21 Bellarmine's letter can be found in Drake 1957, pp. 162–64.

22 Kahn 1982, p. 8.

23 Verbeke 1980, pp. 30*–36*, 51*–68*.

24 Kahn 1982, p. 8.

25 For the objections of Ibn Rushd (Averroes), see Averroes 1954, I.236. See also Rahman 1958 and Altman 1969.

26 The *Dalâlat al-hâ'irîn*, or *Guide of the Perplexed*, is available as Maimonides 1956 and the more recent Maimonides 1963. I shall use Pines, amended as needed from Maimonides 1974.

27 For the Augustinians and their implicit philosophical commitments, see Gilson 1986; for the Latin Averroists, as well as later western and Islamic receptions, see Leaman 1988, "Averroism," pp. 163–78.

28 Gardet 1974.

29 See Seymour Feldman's clear summary of the positions in Feldman 1980, p. 293.

30 For an illuminating reading of Plotinus in this regard, see Gerson 1990, pp. 203–20; for a similar judgment on Aristotle, p. 140.

31 Aquinas's discussion of this matter has been collated in Vollert 1984. For the Ash'arite thesis, see Gimaret 1990.

32 Ghazali provides background for our discussion here, since it appears that Aquinas knew only his *Maqâsid al-falâsifâ*, intended to introduce the positions of the Islamic "philosophers" before refuting them in his *Tahâfût*; cf. Hanley 1982.

33 Feldman 1980, p. 294, whose expression "model" is utterly true to Maimonides's conception of our capacity to understand such matters.

34 For a study of confusions in Maimonidean scholarship on this matter, see Dunphy 1983.

35 Much has been made of Maimonides's maneuvers here and whether his stated preference for the "opinion" of Moses reflects his true position. For an assessment, see Dunphy 1989.

36 This is the consensus of recent writing: see Broadie 1987; Burrell

1986c, ch. 4: "Names of God: Attributes of Divine Nature"; and Miller 1977.

37 See my extended treatment of this issue in Burrell 1979, ch. 2: "The Unknown;" also Jordan 1983.

38 For a comprehensive treatment of this discussion, see Gimaret 1988; for an example of a classical commentary, see Burrell 1991.

39 On analogous terms, see Ross 1981, as well as Burrell 1973. For critiques of different accounts of analogy, see Sherry 1976a, Sherry 1976b, and Burrell 1985. See also Ashworth 1991.

40 For a review of the state of such semantics in the Islamicate, see Wolfson 1973.

41 Samuelson 1977, pp. 182–224.

42 This is Ibn Sina's contention: "it is not possible for the necessary existent to understand things from the things themselves . . . ; rather, because it is the principle of all existence, it understands from its own essence that of which it is the principle" (8.6, 358:13; 359:1).

4 Metaphysics

I. THE SUBJECT OF METAPHYSICS

For Aquinas metaphysics, first philosophy, and a philosophical science of the divine (*scientia divina*) are one and the same. Following Aristotle, he is convinced that there is a science that studies being as being. Like other theoretical sciences, metaphysics must have a given subject. According to Aquinas this subject is being in general (*ens commune*) or being as being.[1] Aquinas describes this science in that way in order to distinguish it from the less extended and more restricted subjects of the other theoretical sciences – natural philosophy (which studies being as subject to change and motion) and mathematics (which studies being as quantified).[2]

By emphasizing that the subject of metaphysics is being as being, Aquinas also establishes his position on an earlier controversy concerning the relationship between the science of being as being described by Aristotle in *Metaphysics* IV 1–2 and the "first philosophy" or "divine science" developed in *Metaphysics* VI 1. While the first approach emphasizes the nonparticularity of the subject matter of this science, the second seems rather to focus its study on one particular kind or range of being: separate and immaterial entity, or the divine. If Aristotle clearly attempted to identify these two as one and the same science at the end of *Metaphysics* VI 1, not all interpreters believe that he succeeded.[3]

Avicenna, for instance, had refused to identify the subject of metaphysics with God or the divine. Averroes, on the other hand, did precisely that. According to Aquinas, Avicenna, and Averroes, no science can demonstrate the existence of its own subject. Aquinas agrees with Avicenna that God's existence can be demonstrated in metaphysics, and not (merely) in physics, as Averroes held.[4] This forces Aquinas to eliminate God as the subject of metaphysics. At the same time, Aquinas holds that it belongs to one and the same science to study its subject and to pursue knowledge of the principles and causes of that subject. If being as being or being in general is the subject of this science, the metaphysician should reason from knowledge of this subject to knowledge of the cause or principle of all that falls under it, that is, under being as being. As Aquinas sees things, this principle is God. Hence he concludes not only that God is not the subject of metaphysics, but also that God is not included under its subject – being as being – as Avicenna seems to have held. Instead, God can be studied by the metaphysician only indirectly, as the cause or principle of what does fall under being as being. This approach enables Aquinas to defend the unity of metaphysics and the science of the divine in a way that appears to be unique among thirteenth-century thinkers.[5]

II. METAPHYSICS AND THEOLOGY

Aquinas distinguishes between the philosophical science ("metaphysics" or "first philosophy" or "divine science"), which studies God only indirectly as the cause of that which falls under its subject (being as being), and another kind of theology that has God as its subject and depends on belief in divine revelation for its principles.[6] Even so, Aquinas is convinced that there can be no real conflict between faith and reason or between faith and philosophy because, in his view, both derive from one and the same ultimate source: on the one hand, God viewed as the author of revelation; on the other hand, God viewed as the creative source of the human intellect and of the created universe, which it studies and from which it draws its principles. To admit that faith and reason could really be in contradiction with one another would be to acknowledge that in such a case one or the other was false. For Aquinas this would ultimately make God himself the author of falsity, which he rejects as impossible.[7]

The conviction that there must be harmony between faith and reason and between the theology based on revelation and the theology ("divine science") that is identical with metaphysics leads Aquinas to defend the theologian's right to use philosophical reasoning within theology. He singles out three different ways the theologian may employ philosophical thinking: (a) to demonstrate what Aquinas refers to as "preambles of faith," that is, truths about God that natural reason can prove, such as God's existence and unity, which, he states, faith presupposes; (b) to supply analogies that the theologian may use to clarify or illustrate mysteries of faith, such as Augustine's frequent use of philosophical analogies to illustrate the Trinity; and (c) to respond to attacks against religious belief by showing them to be false or at least not to have been demonstrated. Aquinas's identification of these three uses of philosophy by the theologian illustrates something of the confidence he had in employing philosophical reasoning in the development of his own theology.[8]

In SCG II.4 Aquinas distinguishes between the orders to be followed in philosophy, and in the teaching based on faith. In the case of philosophy one considers created reality in itself and moves from an examination of reality to a knowledge of God. One begins with one's discovery of being as being or being in general; in the course of one's effort to understand this, one should ultimately discover the principle or cause of that which falls under it, God. In the teaching based on faith, however, one first turns to a study of God and only thereafter examines created reality insofar as it in some way imitates or represents the divine reality. Since our interest here is in Aquinas's metaphysics, we shall follow the philosophical order in presenting his thought.[9]

III. DISCOVERY OF BEING AS BEING

If metaphysics has as its subject being as being, the very possibility of metaphysics presupposes that one can discover being as being. While Aquinas could have made this point more explicitly, there is good reason to think that he distinguishes two notions or concepts of being. The first, which we may describe as a primitive understanding of being, is open to every thinking human being and is implied in our more particular concepts and descriptions of reality. For instance, if we are considering a horse and identifying it as a sensitive-living-corporeal substance, we implicitly also acknowledge and recognize that it is a being. This is the kind of understanding of being that Aquinas seems to have in mind when he writes (citing Avicenna) that "being is that which the intellect first discovers as most known and into which it resolves all its other conceptions."[10]

Contemporary interpreters disagree over whether Aquinas thinks that this primitive understanding of being is reached by the intellect merely through its first operation (in which it recognizes what something is, without affirming or denying anything of it) or also requires its second operation – judgment (composition and division, in which the intellect affirms or denies). The better interpretation recalls that for Aquinas the notion of being ("that which is") is complex, including both quidditative and existential components – essence and existence. Hence both simple apprehension and some judgment of existence seem to be required for us to formulate this primitive notion of being.[11]

In any case, they are surely both required for the formulation of the notion of being that serves as the subject of metaphysics – the metaphysical notion of being. According to Aquinas, the things studied by natural philosophy depend on matter both to exist and to be understood. Hence we discover the subject of this science by an abstraction "of the whole," that is, abstracting something universal from the individuating conditions of matter.[12] The things studied by mathematics also depend on matter in order to exist, but they do not depend on sensible matter (matter as it is grasped by the external senses) in order to be defined. Hence its subject can be grasped by an abstraction "of the form," that is, by abstracting matter insofar as it is subject to the accidental form of quantity from the additional sensible qualities with which matter is always realized in fact.[13]

The things studied by metaphysics do not depend on matter in order to exist or to be understood. This may be so in the sense that they are never found in matter (God and separate entities) or in the sense that they are sometimes present in matter and sometimes not (substance, quality, being, potentiality, actuality, the one and the many, and so on). The subject of metaphysics – being as being – enjoys the last-mentioned kind of freedom from matter; it may or may not be found in matter and is therefore neutral in this respect. In addition to the positive judgment of existence required to formulate a primitive notion of being, discovery of being's freedom from matter in the sense just mentioned also requires a negative judgment on the part of the intellect. Through this second kind of judgment, which Aquinas calls "separation," one recognizes that being, in order to be realized as such, need not be material, changing, quantified, and so forth. By eliminating all such restrictions from one's understanding of being, one is justified in thinking of being as being. One has now formulated a metaphysical notion of being and is in position to set up a science that has as its subject being as being.[14]

Contemporary interpreters of Aquinas are divided over whether this discovery of being as being through separation requires prior knowledge that immaterial being in the stronger sense actually exists, that is, that God or other spiritual entities exist. In my opinion the better interpretation is that it does not require this, because Aquinas holds that it belongs to the metaphysician, as a goal or end of his science, to demonstrate that such reality does exist or, as he puts it, to reach knowledge of the principle or cause of the subject of metaphysics, God. Having said this, he could hardly presuppose prior knowledge that such an entity exists as a condition for one to discover metaphysics and to begin its work![15]

IV. ANALOGY OF BEING

Aquinas's views about the discovery of being as being lead to another closely related issue: What kind of unity must characterize the notion of being if it is to apply to each and every being and to the differences that obtain between beings? Aquinas's answer is framed in terms of his view that being is predicated analogically rather than purely univocally or purely equivocally. He criticizes Parmenides for having mistakenly thought that "being" or "that which is" is used in only one way. In fact, Aquinas counters, it is used in different ways. For instance, taken in one sense it means substance, and in another accident, with the latter sense allowing for different usages in accord with the various supreme genera or categories of accidents. Or again, being may be taken as applying both to substance and accident.[16]

The problem of analogy arises for Aquinas at two very different levels. On the one hand, it may be addressed at the level of beings insofar as they are discovered through sense experience and fall under being as being or being in general, the subject of metaphysics. It is at this horizontal level that we may ask how "being" can be meaningfully applied to substance and to the other categories. But this issue may also be addressed at what we may call the vertical level or, in Fabro's terminology, the transcendental level.[17] On this level one is concerned with explaining how "being" and like names may be meaningfully applied to different kinds of substance, including not only finite and created realities but even God himself. This section will concentrate on Aquinas's discussion of analogy at the horizontal or predicamental (categoreal) level. Analogy at the vertical or transcendental level will be considered after a discussion of Aquinas's argumentation for God's existence.[18]

In his very early treatise *De principiis naturae* Aquinas explains that something is predicated univocally when it remains the same in name and in intelligible content or definition. In this way the name "animal" is predicated of a human being and of a donkey. Something is predicated equivocally of different things when the name remains the same but its meaning differs in different applications. In this way the name "dog" may be said of a barking creature and of a heavenly body. Finally, something may be predicated analogically of different things that differ in definition but that are relevantly related to one and the same thing.[19] Aquinas illustrates this by using an example from Aristotle's *Metaphysics* IV 2. The name "health" is said of an animal's body, of urine, and of a medicinal potion, but not in the same way. It is said of urine insofar as it is a sign of health, of the potion as a cause of health, and of the living body as the subject in which health is present. And each of these usages is relevantly related to one and the same end – the animal's health.[20]

Guided by Averroes's Commentary on this same passage from Aristotle's *Metaphysics*, Aquinas distinguishes different causal orders that may ground analogical predication. Such predication may be based, first, on the fact that different secondary analogates are ordered to one and the same end, as in the example of health. Or, second, it may be based on the fact that the secondary analogates are ordered or related to one and the same agent (efficient cause). For instance, the term "medical" may be applied to a physician who possesses and works by means of the art of medicine, to another person who works without possessing this art but who has an aptitude for it, and finally, even to an instrument used in the practice of medicine, but in each case by reason of a relevant relationship to one agent, the art of medicine. Or, third, it may be that the analogical predication rests on the fact that different secondary analogates are ordered or related to one and the same subject. In this third way "being" is said of substance, quality, quantity, and other accidents.

The accidents are named by "being" because they are relevantly related to – that is, inherent in – a subject: substance.[21]

Aquinas thus agrees with Aristotle that "being" is said primarily of substance and of the other categories, and so on, because of their relationship to substance. Being, then, is not to be construed as a genus of which substance and the various accidents would be species. At the same time, we should not conclude from this that being is not realized in the secondary instances of being as well as in substance. According to Aquinas being is intrinsically present in accidents as well as in substance, but in a different way.[22]

As Aquinas sums this up in his Commentary on Aristotle's *Metaphysics*, weakest in their claim on being are those things that exist only in the order of thought: negations and privations. Somewhat stronger in their title to being are generation, corruption, and change or motion, because they are processes leading to substance or corruptions of substance. Higher in their claim upon being, but still with only a fragile degree of being since they exist only in something else, are quantity, qualities, and the properties of substance. Highest in its degree of being is substance, that which is most perfect because it enjoys being in itself.[23]

Frequently Aquinas makes the point that the intelligible content (*ratio*) corresponding to an analogical term is "partly the same and partly diverse" in its various analogical usages. He means that because each of the secondary things to which a term such as "being" is applied is differently related to the primary analogate (substance, in the case of being), the intelligible content of each of them will also differ. But because the various secondary analogates are relevantly related to some one thing (to substance, in the case of being), their intelligible contents are also partly the same.[24] In other words, Aquinas's theory of analogical predication is grounded on sameness and difference that obtain in reality.

Aquinas distinguishes between what may be called the analogy of "many to one" and the analogy of "one to another." In the first case analogous predication of a given name is justified by the fact that a number of different things are relevantly related to something prior to them. For instance, it is with reference to one and the same health that the name "healthy" may be predicated of an animal as its subject, of (the practice of) the art of medicine as its efficient cause, of food or medicine as that which preserves health, and of urine as its sign. But a term may also be predicated analogically of two things, not because of relationships both bear to some third thing, but simply because one is relevantly related to the other. For instance, in this same context Aquinas writes that "being" (ens) is predicated analogically of substance and of accident because of accident's relationship to substance, not because both are related to some third thing.²⁵ In QDP he also observes that "being" may be predicated analogically of quality and of quantity because of the relationship both bear to substance. This illustrates the analogy of "many to one." But "being" is said of substance and quantity because of quantity's relationship to substance (analogy of "one to another"). This suggests that the analogy of many to one ultimately rests on the analogy of one to another. As we shall see, when predicating names of God and created realities, Aquinas rejects the analogy of many to one and usually turns to the analogy of one to another. In QDV he rather surprisingly opts for an analogy of proportionality, but he returns to the analogy of one to another in subsequent discussions.²⁶

As we have seen, Aquinas denies that being is a genus. As he remarks in QDV 1.1, nothing can be added to being from without as if it were an extrinsic nature in the way a differentia is added to a genus or an accident to a subject. This follows from the fact that every nature is being essentially, that is, intrinsically. Therefore, something may be said to add to being only insofar as it expresses a mode not expressed by the name "being" itself. This in turn may happen in one of two ways. The mode expressed by "being" may be some more particularized mode of being, as with the accidents or categories. Or it may be a general mode that follows upon every being, as is true of what would later be known as the transcendental properties of being (especially *one, true, good*).²⁷

As for the categories, each of them is named as it is because it expresses a more particularized mode or way in which being is realized. For instance, the name "substance" signifies a special mode of being, being *per se*. The mode of being designated by each of the categories of accident differs from that of substance (and from the other accidents), but carries with it its relationship to substance.²⁸ And so in Aquinas's view the different modes or ways in which being is realized serve as the foundation for the different ways we understand and predicate being, that is, for analogical predication.²⁹

Aquinas accepts the reality of different levels of being and hence of different kinds of substances within the created universe – the hierarchy of being. It is fairly clear from his texts that "being" cannot be predicated of these different kinds univocally, but only analogically. Moreover, although this point is disputed by commentators, it seems that Aquinas must also defend analogical rather than univocal predication of "being" of different individual substances that fall within one and the same species.[30]

V. METAPHYSICS OF PARTICIPATION

Reference to Aquinas's theory of a hierarchy of being naturally leads to a consideration of his metaphysics of participation. His theories of analogy of being and participation in being are closely connected. The first addresses itself to the unity and the diversity involved in our understanding and predication of "being," and the second is concerned with the ontological situation that gives rise to such unity and diversity – that is, unity and diversity in reality. Aquinas's theory of participation of beings in being also lies at the heart of his answer to the problem of the One and the Many in the order of reality. Simply stated, how can there be many beings, each of which shares in being, and yet each of which is different from every other?[31]

In his Commentary on Boethius's *De hebdomadibus*, Aquinas quickly moves beyond the etymological explanation that to participate is "as it were, to take a part of something" and explains that "When something receives particularly that which belongs to another universally (or totally), the former is said to participate in the latter."[32] If a particular quality or characteristic is possessed by a given subject only partially rather than totally, the subject is said to participate in the quality or characteristic. Because other subjects may also share in that perfection, each is said to participate in it. No one of them is identical with it.[33]

Aquinas distinguishes a number of different ways in which participation may occur. (1) Human being is said to participate in animal because human being does not possess the total intelligible content of animal. In like fashion an individual (Socrates) is said to participate in human being. In these cases a less extended intelligible content is said to participate in a more extended intelligible content either as a species in a genus or as an individual in a species. Because intelligible contents (*rationes*) are at issue, this kind of participation may be described as "logical." (2) So too (2a) a subject participates in an accident and (2b) matter participates in form. Both may be described as instances of participation because the forms in question, whether accidental or substantial, while not restricted to any given subject when considered in themselves, are now limited to this or that particular subject. Since in both (2a) and (2b) distinct principles of being are involved, and since in each case a real composition results (whether of substance and accident or of matter and form), each may be described as a "real" or "ontological" participation. (3) Finally, an effect is said to participate in its cause, especially when it is not equal to the power of its cause. Under this third kind of real or ontological participation Aquinas seems to place participation of beings in existence (*esse*), the case of greatest interest here.[34]

Aquinas argues that existence (*esse*) cannot participate in anything else in the way a substance participates in an accident or matter in form. This is so because, although both a substantial subject and matter are signified concretely, existence is signified abstractly. Nor can existence participate in anything else in the way something less extended in intelligible content participates in something more extended, for there is nothing more general than existence in which it might participate. Therefore, he concludes that existence (*esse*) "is participated in by other things, but does not itself participate in anything else."[35] At the same time, he also comments that being (*ens*), even though it too is most universal, is expressed concretely. Therefore, a being can participate in existence (*esse*) in the way something taken concretely participates in something taken abstractly.[36]

At this point in Aquinas's text one would not be justified in thinking that either he or Boethius had concluded to any kind of real composition or diversity between a being, or concrete subject, and the existence (*esse*) in which it participates. But in the following context Aquinas notes that if something is to be the subject of an accident, it must participate in *esse* (or, as he had previously phrased it, in the act of being).[37] In other words, it must exist. And subsequently, in commenting on two other Boethian axioms, Aquinas concludes that just as existence (*esse*) and "that which is" differ intentionally (notionally) in the case of simple beings, they differ really in the case of composites. He concludes that there is only one

truly simple being and therefore only one being that does not participate in existence but is subsisting existence (*esse*). This is God.[38]

It should be emphasized that participation of a concrete being
(*ens*) in existence (*esse*) cannot be reduced to either Aquinas's first or
second general kind of participation mentioned above. It cannot be
reduced to the first type, since that involves a less general notion
participating in a more general notion and is, therefore, merely inten-
tional or logical; but participation of a being in existence (*esse*) is
real and leads to a real distinction between the participating subject
and that in which it participates. Nor can it be reduced to the second
type, because participation of a being in existence (*esse*) is more
fundamental than either the participation of matter in form or of a
subject in an accident. As Aquinas phrases it, if a subject is to exist,
it must first participate in existence (*esse*). So too, if a matter-form
composite is to exist, it must participate in *esse*. As suggested above,
it follows, therefore, that participation of beings in *esse* most naturally falls under Aquinas's third major type – that whereby an effect
participates in a cause.[39]

Two closely connected questions arise from this account of participation: (1) What does Aquinas understand by the existence (*esse*) in
which he claims existing entities participate? Does he mean by this
existence (act of being) viewed universally (*esse commune*)? Or does
he have in mind self-subsisting existence (*esse subsistens*), or God?
(2) Does he make his theory of real (extra-mental) composition of
essence and existence a necessary component of, or at least a necessary condition for, his metaphysics of participation?

As regards the first issue, Aquinas clearly refuses to identify *esse
commune* (existence in general) with self-subsisting existence.[40] He
also distinguishes existence in general from any abstract, universal
generic or specific concept. But by referring to existence as common
Aquinas does not mean that it exists as such apart from individual
existents, except conceptually, in the order of thought.[41] It is rather
the intrinsic principle present in, the act "common" to, every (substantial) entity that accounts for the fact that the entity actually
exists.[42]

At times Aquinas speaks of entities other than God as participating in existence in general (*esse commune*). For instance, in commenting on Boethius's *De hebdomadibus* he writes that there are
certain pure forms that do not exist in matter. Because each of them

determines (restricts) existence, no one of them is identical with it. Each of them "has" existence (esse). Suppose we admitted, with Plato, the existence of one subsisting immaterial form for human beings and another for horses. Such subsisting forms would not be identical with existence in general (esse commune) but would only participate in it. So too, if we grant the existence of immaterial forms (Aristotelian separate substances or Christian angels), each of these is a given specific form and each participates in existence (ipsum esse), that is, in esse commune.[43] Earlier in this same context he had noted that existence is most universal (communissimum). Therefore it is participated in by other things, but does not itself participate in anything else.[44] Or as he expresses this elsewhere, "Just as this human being participates in human nature, so does every created being participate, if I may so speak, in the nature of being; for God alone is his existence."[45] By participating in "the nature of being," Aquinas again appears to have in mind participating in esse commune.

In other texts Aquinas speaks of a caused or created being as participating in the divine existence (or in esse subsistens). Even though we have yet to consider Aquinas's argumentation for God's existence, we should bear in mind that in such texts he is taking this as granted either on the grounds of faith or as a result of philosophical demonstration.[46] For instance, in his Commentary on the Divine Names, Aquinas notes that the author (Pseudo-Dionysius) writes that all (other) things participate in God as their first exemplar cause,[47] and he identifies three differences in the way esse commune stands in relationship to God and to other existents: (1) While other existents depend on esse commune, God does not. Rather, esse commune itself depends on God. (2) While all other existents fall under esse commune, God does not; rather, esse commune falls under the power of God. Aquinas explains this by noting that God's power extends beyond (actually) created beings, presumably to all that could possibly be created. (3) All other existents participate in esse, but God does not. Rather, created esse is a certain participation in God and likeness of him. As Aquinas explains, by saying that esse commune "has" God Dionysius means that it participates in his likeness. And by denying that God "has" esse, he denies that God participates in it.[48] From this we may conclude that if esse commune participates in God and if other existents depend on esse (commune), they too participate in the divine *esse*. This squares with Aquinas's earlier remark that all (other) things participate in God as in the first exemplar cause.[49]

This final point is supported by the close connection Aquinas frequently draws between being by participation and being caused. For instance, in ST Ia.44.1 he writes that anything that exists in any way whatsoever is from God. If something is found in something else by participation, it must be caused in that thing by something to which it belongs essentially. After referring to his earlier discussions in ST of divine simplicity and divine unity, he recalls that he has there shown both that God is subsisting existence, and that subsisting existence can only be one. He concludes, therefore, that things other than God are not identical with their own existence, but only participate in existence. Hence things differing in the degree to which they participate in existence so as to exist more or less perfectly must all be caused by one first being that exists most perfectly.[50] Aquinas cites with approval Plato's view that before every many there must be a (higher) one (unity). He also finds support for this in Aristotle's statement in *Metaphysics* II to the effect that what is being and true to the maximum degree is the cause of all other being and truth.[51]

In his *Quodlibetal Questions* Aquinas observes that something is brought into actuality to the maximum degree by reason of the fact that it participates by likeness in the first and pure act – subsisting existence, or God. Each and every thing receives its perfection by participating in existence (*esse*). From this he concludes that *esse* (existence = act of being) is the perfection of every form, since a form is perfected by having existence, and it has existence when it actually exists.[52] Here as elsewhere Aquinas uses the language of participating "by likeness" in the first and pure act, or subsisting *esse*, in order to avoid any possible suggestion that participation in the divine *esse* might mean that in some way a creature is a part of God. He is aware that an unnuanced understanding of participation might lead to a pantheistic view of the universe.[53] At the same time, as just noted, the present text concludes by observing that a thing receives its perfection by participating in *esse*, and that it has *esse* when it actually exists. Here Aquinas seems to have shifted from speaking of participating in subsisting existence, or God, to participating in existence taken as the act of being that is present in the participant itself.

These two usages also seem to appear in an important text from his Disputed Question *On Spiritual Creatures:*

Everything which comes after the first being (*ens*), since it is not its *esse*, has an *esse* which is received in something by which the *esse* is limited; and thus in every creature the nature of the thing which participates *esse* is one, and the participated *esse* is something else. And since every thing participates in the First Act by assimilation insofar as it has *esse*, the participated *esse* in each thing must be related to the nature which participates (in) it as act to potency.⁵⁴

According to the last sentence, every thing participates in the First Act (God) by assimilation to the extent to which it itself enjoys *esse*. But the remainder of that sentence, like the previous one, refers to a nature that participates in the *esse* (or act of being) that is intrinsic to the creature.

This suggests that Aquinas speaks of created or caused entities or natures as participating in *esse* in three ways: (1) as participating in *esse commune* (existence in general); (2) as participating in subsisting *esse* (God); (3) as participating in the *esse* (act of being) that is intrinsically realized in the existing creature. This final usage is brought out explicitly in an early text of Aquinas's: "each thing participates in its created *esse* (*suum esse creatum*), whereby it formally exists."⁵⁵ This also suggests that considerable care is required on the part of Aquinas's readers to determine in which sense or senses he is using the term when he speaks of participating in *esse*.⁵⁶

Moreover, if Aquinas has distinguished three ways in which one may speak of caused natures or entities as participating in *esse*, one of these – participation in subsisting *esse* or God – presupposes God's existence. Hence in the order of philosophical discovery, awareness of this usage of participation will come only after he has taken up the issue of God's existence. Of the other two usages, awareness of participation in *esse commune* would seem to come first in the order of discovery. For a thing to participate in its own *esse* is a more particular application of its participating in *esse commune*. At the same time, for Aquinas to speak of such an entity as participating in its own *esse* raises another issue: his understanding of the relationship between the essence or nature of any such entity and its *esse* or act of being.

For instance, in the text cited above from the Disputed Question *On Spiritual Creatures*, he comments that no being other than God is identical with its *esse* (act of being or existence). Hence its *esse* is received by something that serves to limit that *esse* and that is not to be identified with it. As he puts it there, the nature of the creature that participates is one, and the *esse* in which it participates is something else. Moreover, the participating nature is related to the *esse* it receives and limits as potency is related to act.[57] In other words, Aquinas draws a very close connection between the metaphysics of participation and his view that, in all substantial entities other than God, there is real (that is, not merely mind-dependent) composition of nature or essence, on the one hand, and *esse* (act of being), on the other. With this we return to the second general question raised above about his theory of participation. His theory of real composition of essence and *esse* in beings other than God is indeed a necessary condition for and a part of his metaphysics of participation.[58] This is so also because, as Aquinas sees it, composition of essence and *esse* (act of being) is required to account for the limited and participated presence of *esse* in any such being.

VI. ESSENCE AND *ESSE*

Not long after the death of Aquinas in 1274, controversy broke out concerning whether essence and existence are really distinct in creatures. In fact, this issue had already been debated before Aquinas's death by Siger of Brabant. In presenting a number of different positions, Siger refers to Aquinas's view and appears to find it difficult to understand.[59] It is not surprising, therefore, to discover that even today not all Aquinas's interpreters are in total agreement concerning his views on this issue. He speaks more frequently about composition of essence and *esse* than about their real distinction. Nonetheless, at times he does refer to them as being really distinct, presumably because he realizes that if they are to enter into real composition with one another, they must to that degree be distinct from one another.[60]

It should also be noted that Aquinas's terminology varies when he refers to the principle in finite entities that participates in existence (*esse*). He also refers variously to the principle in finite beings that enters into composition with *esse*. For instance, on different occasions he refers to the participating and receiving principle as a being (*ens*), or as "that which is," or as substance, or as essence, or as form, or as a creature, or as a thing, or as nature, or simply as that which

participates.[61] In discussions concerning the relationship of this principle to the act of being (*esse*) with which it enters into composition,
his meaning will usually be faithfully expressed if we simply employ
the term "essence" to render it. It seems clear that Aquinas does
defend a composition of essence and act of being (*esse*) in all finite
substantial entities that is more than any purely mental or conceptual composition, which may, therefore, be described as real. It is
also clear that he does not regard either essence or existence as a
being in its own right. Moreover, in a number of passages he offers
argumentation to support such composition. Some of his arguments
are philosophical, and some are "theological" in the qualified sense
that they presuppose God's existence whether that is established on
philosophical grounds or as a matter of faith.[62] Here some representative philosophical texts and arguments will be considered.

De ente et essentia, *ch. 4*

This approach, often referred to as the *intellectus essentiae* argument, includes two and ultimately three stages. In DEE 4 Aquinas
intends to show how essence is realized in separate substances, that
is, the soul, intelligences, and the First Cause (God). While the simplicity of the First Cause is generally recognized, Aquinas notes that
some, such as Avicebron, defend a kind of matter–form composition
in both the human soul and in intelligences (or Christian angels).
Aquinas rejects matter–form composition of such entities as incompatible with their nature as intelligences. Even so, although there is
no matter–form composition in such entities, he claims that there is
a composition of form and *esse* and cites Prop. IX from the *Liber de
causis* in support. After defending the existence of separate substances that are distinct from God, Aquinas wishes to show that they
are not perfectly simple so as to be pure actuality and that they do
involve potentiality as well as actuality. This point is important because it indicates that if Aquinas's subsequent argumentation is to
succeed, it must establish some kind of real rather than purely conceptual composition of actuality and potentiality in such entities.[63]

In what we may take as stage 1 of the argument, Aquinas then
reasons that whatever is not included in the understanding or notion
of an essence or quiddity comes to it from without and enters into
composition with the essence. In support he notes that no essence

can be understood without those factors which are parts of the essence itself. But, he continues, every essence or quiddity can be understood without anything's being understood about its existing (*esse*). He notes that I can understand what a man is or what a phoenix is and not know whether it exists in reality. Therefore, he concludes, it is evident that *esse* is other than, that is, distinct from, essence or quiddity.[64]

If the argument ended at this point, one might raise serious questions about its validity. For instance, does it succeed in establishing a real otherness or distinction of essence and *esse* taken as intrinsic principles within all such entities, or does it show only that it is different for us to recognize what something is and to recognize that it is? Again, if *esse* is to enter into composition with essence, it seems that it must be a real intrinsic constituent of such an entity, its act of being. But as *esse* first appears in the argument, it simply refers to the fact that something exists ("every essence or quiddity can be understood without anything's being understood about its existing [*esse*]"). The transition from *esse* as expressing the fact of existing to *esse* as expressing an intrinsic act of being does not seem to be justified.[65]

Yet Aquinas immediately adds a second stage to the argumentation, perhaps because he was aware of weaknesses in the first stage. He now allows for the possibility that there is some thing whose quiddity is its very *esse* (act of being). But such a thing can only be first and unique. (It is important to note that he has not yet assumed that this unique entity does exist; he is claiming only that if it exists, it must be first and unique.)[66] To prove this he reasons that there are only three possible ways of accounting for the multiplication of something: (1) by the addition of a differentia, in the way a generic nature is multiplied in its species; (2) by the reception of a form in different instances of matter, in the way a specific nature is multiplied in different individuals; or (3) because one instance of the thing in question is unreceived (*absolutum*) and the other is received in something else. In this third way, if there were such a thing as a separated heat, it would be distinguished from heat that is not separated (that is, heat received in something else) by reason of its separation.

Aquinas quickly shows that if there is such a thing as pure and subsisting *esse*, it could not be multiplied in the first way; for then it would not be *esse* alone, but *esse* plus an added form that served to differentiate it. Nor could it be multiplied in the second way, for then it would not be merely *esse* but *esse* plus matter (*esse materiale*). He does not eliminate the third way, presumably because he accepts it. If there is such a subsisting *esse*, it will be distinguished from all other (received) instances of *esse* by reason of the fact that it alone is separate. In all other cases *esse* would be received by something else. As he puts it, it follows from this that there can be only one thing that is identical with its *esse*. The *esse* of every other thing is distinct from its quiddity, or nature, or form. Therefore, the same holds for separate intelligences. In them there is form (essence), and in addition to form there is *esse* (act of being).[67]

So far, then, Aquinas has used the hypothesis of the existence of one first being in which essence and *esse* are identical to show by contrast that in every other case, including separate intelligences, essence and *esse* are not identical. He has not yet expressly claimed or even assumed such a first being actually exists; nor has he yet shown that in all others, including separate intelligences, essence and *esse* are compounded as potentiality and actuality. This explains why he now introduces a third stage in his argumentation, a proof for God's existence.[68]

Whatever belongs to a given thing is either caused by the principles of that thing's nature (as the ability to laugh in a human being) or comes to that thing from some extrinsic principle (as light is present in air owing to the influence of the sun). But *esse* itself cannot be efficiently caused by the form or quiddity of a thing, for in that case such a thing would cause itself to exist, which Aquinas rejects as impossible. Therefore everything whose *esse* is other than its nature receives its *esse* from something else. Since what exists through something else is traced back to that which exists through itself as to its first cause, it follows that there must be some thing which is the cause of being for all other things by reason of the fact that it is *esse* (not *esse* plus something else). To reject this conclusion would force one to postulate an infinite regress of caused causes of *esse*.[69]

After concluding that an intelligence is form plus *esse* and that it receives its *esse* from the first being that is *esse* alone, Aquinas addresses the act–potency composition of separate intelligences. What receives something from another is in potency with respect to what it receives, and that which it receives is present in it as its act.

He concludes, therefore, that the quiddity or form that is an intelligence is in potency to the *esse* it receives from God, and that its *esse*
is received as act. Therefore potency and act (essence and *esse*) are
present in intelligences, even though intelligences lack matter and
form.[70] Or, as Aquinas puts this, the quiddity or essence of an intelligence "is identical with what the intelligence is, and the *esse* it
receives from God is that whereby it subsists in the nature of
things." It is clear from the context that *esse* here means the intrinsic act of being whereby such an intelligence exists. Aquinas also
finds confirmation for his position in the Boethian dictum that substances of this type are composed of *quod est* ("that which is") and
esse (the act of being).[71]

Only after completing his argumentation for God's existence does
Aquinas return by way of contrast to the essence–*esse* composition
of an intelligence so as to correlate them as potentiality and actuality. The argument for God's existence itself uses as its point of departure the otherness (distinction) of essence and *esse* in all beings
(including intelligences) other than God. The argumentation for distinction or otherness of essence and *esse* does not, therefore, presuppose prior knowledge of God's existence, even though some dispute
this reading of Aquinas's text.[72]

*Other arguments based on the uniqueness of self-
subsisting* esse

In many of these arguments Aquinas takes God's existence as already
granted and reasons from it to distinction or composition of essence
and *esse* in other beings. This is perfectly appropriate given the structure and the theological nature of the writings in which they appear.
But in at least some of these presentations the logic of the argumentation is such that it need not presuppose that God exists. Here only
arguments of the last-mentioned type will be considered.[73]

For instance, in SCG II.52, after having argued against matter–
form composition of created intellectual substances, Aquinas maintains that they are nonetheless composed of the act of being (*esse*)
and essence ("that which is"). According to the second argument,
any common nature, simply considered in itself as separate, can
only be one. This is so even though many individuals may share in
that nature. For instance, if the nature of animal could subsist in

itself, separate from all particular kinds of animal, it would not include in itself those differentiae that are proper to given species such as human being or cow. When the differentiae that constitute the species are removed, the genus remains undivided in itself. If, therefore, *esse* were common in the way a genus is, there could be only one separate and subsisting *esse*. And if, as is indeed the case, *esse* is not divided by differentiae as is a genus, but only because it is received in this or that subject, it follows with even greater reason that there can be only one instance of subsisting *esse*. Since this is God, nothing but God can be identical with its own *esse*.[74]

Even though Aquinas can and does assume in this argument that God exists (he has already offered philosophical argumentation for this in SCG I.13), the assumption is not required for the argument to be valid. The argument rests on the impossibility of there being more than one self-subsisting *esse*. If many other beings do exist, in all of them, with this single possible exception, essence and *esse* must differ.

His third argument rests on the impossibility of there being more than one completely infinite *esse*. Completely infinite *esse* embraces the total perfection of being. If such infinity were found in two different beings, there would be no way in which one might be distinguished from the other. But subsisting *esse* must be unlimited because it is not limited by any receiving principle. Therefore it is impossible for there to be any subsisting *esse* apart from the first being.[75] This argument likewise need not presuppose the existence of God. At most there can be one unlimited being. Since all others are limited, in them *esse* must be received by something other than *esse* if it is to be limited.

Similar reasoning appears in his QDSC 1.1. There he takes for granted the infinity of God, who has in himself the fullness of being. If so, God's *esse* cannot be received in any distinct nature, for it would then be limited to that nature. Therefore, God is his very *esse*. But this is true of no other being. For instance, if whiteness could exist in separation apart from every receiving subject, it could only be one. So too, there can only be one subsisting *esse*. Therefore, anything else, since it is not its *esse*, must have an *esse* that is received in something else by which that *esse* is limited. Central to this argument is Aquinas's claim that there cannot be more than one subsisting *esse*. Even though he here takes God's existence for

granted, his argument need not do so. Again it rests on the impossibility of there being more than one separate *esse*.[76]

The genus argument

Aquinas attributes his inspiration for this argument to Avicenna. He
uses it in texts throughout his career, beginning with his Commentary on the *Sentences*.[77] As he explains in QDV 27.1, ad8, if something belongs to the genus *substance*, it must be compounded, and
by real composition. Such a thing must subsist with its own *esse*,
and this *esse* must differ from the thing itself. Otherwise such a
thing would not differ from other members of the genus *substance*
either in terms of its *esse* or in terms of the quidditative content it
shares with them. Therefore everything that falls within the category substance is composed of *esse* and "that which is" (*quod est*),
that is, of the act of being and essence.[78] While this kind of argument
has the merit of showing that Aquinas intends to establish a real
composition of essence and act of being in substances other than
God, and while it does not presuppose God's existence, it seems to
move very quickly, perhaps too quickly, from a logical and conceptual distinction to an ontological and real composition and distinction of essence and act of being.[79]

Arguments based on participation

Frequently Aquinas reasons from the participated character of finite beings to the composition of essence and existence (*esse*)
within them. For instance, he offers two versions of this approach
in his Commentary on *De hebdomadibus*. There he is attempting
to show that if existence (*esse*) and "that which is" differ conceptually in simple entities, in composites they differ really. He first
reasons that existence (*esse*) itself does not participate in anything
else and does not include anything other than existence (*esse*) in its
formal meaning. Hence he concludes that existence (*esse*) itself is
not composed; therefore, it cannot be identified with a composite
thing (or essence).[80]

Such reasoning is limited to matter–form composites, but his
next approach is broader. Subsisting forms or intelligences other
than God are not perfectly simple because they are restricted to their

given kind of being. Hence no such subsisting form can be identified with existence in general (*esse commune*); each only participates in it.[81] Because of this it will be composed of its form or essence, on the one hand, and of its *esse* (act of being), on the other. This line of thinking is developed in ST Ia.75.5, ad 4. Any participated characteristic is related to what participates in it as its act. But any created subsisting form must participate in existence (*esse*) if it is to subsist. And participated *esse* is limited to the capacity of that which participates in it. Therefore only God, who is identical with his *esse*, is pure and unlimited act. Created intellectual substances are composed of potentiality and actuality, that is, of form and of participated *esse*.[82] The heart of this reasoning, in these texts and in others, is this: if something participates in a perfection, existence (*esse*) in the case at hand, it must be distinct from and enter into composition with the perfection in which it participates.[83]

Argumentation based on limitation

Although this approach is seldom employed by Aquinas as a distinct argument for composition of essence and *esse*, its underlying principle appears frequently throughout his works. In his Commentary on the *Sentences* it is offered as a distinct argument. Every creature has limited *esse*. But *esse* that is not received in something is not finite, but is unrestricted (*absolutum*). Therefore to account for the fact that it is limited, a creature's *esse* must be received in something else, and the creature must consist at least of these two, that is, of *esse* and of that which receives it.[84] The working principle – that actuality as such or, in this case, *esse*, is not self-limiting – appears in many other contexts in Aquinas's writings. For instance, he appeals to it in order to prove that God is infinite. Rather than offer explicit philosophical argumentation to justify the principle, however, Aquinas seems to regard it as evident. This may be because it easily follows from his special way of viewing the act of being, *esse*, as the actuality of all acts and the perfection of all perfections. To admit that *esse* could be self-limiting would be to suggest that limitation (imperfection) is accounted for by that which is pure perfection in and of itself (*esse*).[85]

We have now seen major parts of Aquinas's solution to the problem of the One and the Many in the order of being. Many individual beings can exist because each one of them participates in *esse commune*. No one of them is identical with it or exhausts it. If particular entities share in *esse* in limited fashion, this is because in each of them there is an essence principle that limits the *esse* it receives. Each receiving and limiting essence principle enters into real composition with the act of being (*esse*) it receives. This solution finds its fullest explanation only after God's existence has been established, for then it can also appeal to an actual rather than hypothetical participation of finite beings in self-subsisting *esse*, or God. But before turning to Aquinas's arguments for God's existence, we must consider some other aspects of his metaphysics of finite being.

VII. SUBSTANCE AND ACCIDENTS

As we have seen, Aquinas depended on Aristotle's *Metaphysics* IV 2 in developing his theory of analogical predication by reference to a first. For both Aristotle and Aquinas, substances are beings in the primary and principal sense. As we have also seen, substance is said to have a stronger claim on being than negations and privations, generation, corruption and motion, and the various accidents. This is because substance exists in its own right and *per se*.[86]

In commenting on *Metaphysics* V, Aquinas refers to first substance as the particular or individual substance of which all else is predicated. He finds Aristotle identifying four different modes of substance and, like Aristotle, quickly reduces these to two: (1) first substance, or that which serves as the ultimate subject of propositions, subsists in itself, and is distinct or separate from other things in the sense that it cannot be ontologically communicated to them; and (2) substance taken as "form" or as essence and quiddity which, for Aquinas, clearly includes substantial form and prime matter in the case of composites. He frequently recalls this distinction. For instance, in ST Ia.29.2 he writes that substance may indicate (a) the quiddity of a thing that its definition signifies (*ousia* in Greek and *essentia* in Latin) or (b) the subject or *suppositum* that subsists in the genus substance.[87]

Aquinas of course knew Aristotle's distinction in the *Categories* between substance in the primary sense (or first substance) and second substance. Tempting though it may be, one should not simply equate this distinction with that mentioned in the previous paragraph. In particular, one should not identify substance taken as quiddity or essence with second substance. In matter–form composites, substance taken as essence, or nature, or quiddity is related to substance taken as subject as formal part to concrete whole. But the concrete subject or whole includes individuating characteristics as well. Thus we cannot say "Socrates is humanity." We can, however, predicate second substance of first substance, for instance, by saying "Socrates is a man." It follows, therefore, that second substance is not to be identified with substance taken as essence, or nature, or quiddity.[88]

Although substance subsists in itself, it also stands under accidents or serves as their foundation and support.[89] In his Commentary on *Metaphysics* V, Aquinas turns to diverse modes of predication in order to derive the ten Aristotelian predicaments or categories, including substance and nine supreme kinds of accidents. He reminds us that these different modes of predication correspond to and reflect different ways in which being is realized (diverse *modi essendi*). This diversity in the order of predication follows from and depends upon diversity in the order of being. By reversing this perspective, as it were, and analyzing the diversity in the order of predication, one may uncover a corresponding diversity in the order of being.[90]

Accordingly, a predicate may be related to a subject in one of three ways. The predicate may be identical with the subject as, for instance, when one says "Socrates is an animal." For Socrates is what is said to be animal. And the term "Socrates" is said to signify first substance – the individual substance of which everything is predicated.[91]

In a second way the predicate may be derived from something that is in the subject, either in itself (absolutely), and as following upon the matter of the subject, yielding (2) quantity; or as following from its form, yielding (3) quality. If the predicate is taken from something that is in the subject only insofar as the subject is ordered to something else, category (4), relation, is given.[92]

In the third way a predicate is derived from something that is external to the subject. If that from which the predicate is taken is entirely outside the subject and does not in any way measure the subject, category (5), *habitus*, results, such as to be wearing shoes or to be clothed. If that from which the predicate is taken is realized entirely outside the subject but does measure the subject, this measurement may be in terms of time, yielding category (6), "time when." If that from which the predicate is derived measures the subject in terms of place, category (7), place where (*ubi*), results. Or if it measures the subject not only in terms of place but in terms of the way the parts of the body in place are ordered to one another, category (8), position (*situs*), is the result, for instance to be seated or to be standing.[93]

If that from which the predicate is taken is only partly external to the subject and is internal to it insofar as the subject is a principle of action, category (9), action, is given. If what the predicate is taken from is partly external but is intrinsic to the subject as that which receives the action, category (10), "to be acted upon" (*passio*), results.[94]

Both in this text and in a more-or-less parallel derivation in his Commentary on the *Physics*, Aquinas justifies ten categories. His remarks in other contexts indicate that he regards them as distinct and as irreducible to any smaller number, even though such reductions were undertaken by later medieval thinkers such as Henry of Ghent and William Ockham. For instance, while Aquinas recognizes with Aristotle that the motion involved in an action and its corresponding passion is one and the same, he regards them as two distinct categories.[95]

Throughout his career Aquinas regards substance as a receiving or material cause of the accidents that inhere in it. When dealing with proper accidents (*propria*, those that are necessarily found with an essence of a specific kind, such as a human being's ability to laugh), Aquinas also assigns other kinds of causality to the substances in which they inhere. Thus in ST Ia.77.6, ad 2, he writes that a subject causes a proper accident in three ways: (a) as a final cause; (b) in a certain way as an active or efficient cause; and (c) as a material cause. To describe this second kind of causality he sometimes refers to proper accidents as flowing from or as naturally resulting from the essences or principles of their substantial subjects.[96]

VIII. MATTER AND FORM

Aquinas recognizes an approach to matter–form composition based on generation in the unqualified sense (substantial change as distinguished from accidental change). In doing this he follows Aristotle's procedure in *Physics* I. He sets up a parallel or analogy that moves from the principles required for nonessential or accidental change to those required for substantial change. We know that the wood is different from the form of a bench or a bed, because wood is now under one form and now under another. This kind of change is accidental. But when we observe an element, such as air, becoming water, we must also conclude that something that existed under the form of air is now under the form of water. And if wood is different from the form of a bench or the form of a bed, so too the underlying subject must be different from the form of air and the form of water. This underlying subject must, therefore, be related to natural substances in the way wood is related to a bench or a bed. According to Aquinas, this underlying subject is prime matter. Form and the underlying subject are principles *per se* of what is produced according to nature. Privation (the simple absence in the underlying subject of the form to be acquired through generation) is a third principle of change, but only a principle *per accidens*.[97]

In commenting on *Metaphysics* VII 3, Aquinas observes that the investigation of matter seems to belong first and foremost to natural philosophy. In the *Metaphysics* Aristotle takes from physics what he has already determined about matter, namely that considered in itself it is "neither a quiddity (that is, not a substance), nor a quality, nor any of the other genera by which being is divided or determined."[98] Since matter is the first subject that remains under changes and motions in terms of quality, quantity, and so on, but also in terms of substance, Aquinas concludes that matter is different in essence from all substantial forms and privations. But Aquinas sees Aristotle establishing the difference of matter from all forms not by following the path of natural philosophy, but by appealing to predication, a procedure proper to logic. And logic, Aquinas notes, is closely related to metaphysics.[99]

Briefly put, there must be something of which the various forms just mentioned are predicated in such fashion that the subject of which they are predicated differs in essence from the forms that are predicated of it. Aquinas here has in mind concrete (what he calls "denominative") predication. For instance, when white is predicated of a man, the quiddity of the white differs from that of the man. It is in this concrete or denominative way that the other supreme genera are predicated of substance, and that substance is predicated of matter. Thus we can say "A man is white," but not "A man is whiteness" or "Humanity is whiteness." So too we can say "This material thing is a man," but not "Matter is a man" or "Matter is humanity." Therefore, just as substance (a man) differs in essence from accidents (white), so matter differs in essence from substantial forms. From this it follows that the ultimate subject (matter) is not a "what," that is, not a substance, nor quantity, nor anything else that falls into a given genus or category.[100] For Aquinas, as will be seen below, it is pure potentiality.

In addition to this way of establishing the matter–form distinction based on change and buttressed by an appeal to logic (through predication), Aquinas offers a more strictly metaphysical approach to the same principles. As already noted, composition of essence and *esse* is an important part of his answer to the problem of the One and the Many in the order of being. But at the level of material entities, he admits that there can be many individuals within the same class or species. He can hardly appeal to that which is common to all members of a given species to account for that whereby each member differs from every other. The form of a material entity accounts for the fact that it enjoys this kind of being rather than any other, and hence for that which it has in common with other members of its species. But to account for the fact that an individual member of a species does not exhaust that specific kind of being, Aquinas appeals to another principle within the essence of such a being. This principle limits or restricts the form or act principle within the essence of this particular subject. This other principle is prime matter. Central to Aquinas's reasoning is his view that act as such, and therefore, form as such, is not self-limiting. If we recognize limited instances of a given kind of being, we must therefore postulate a distinct limiting principle within the essence of each such limited being, that is, prime matter.[101]

This also means, of course, that in composite entities there is a twofold actuality–potentiality composition. Matter is potentiality with respect to substantial form. And a material being's composite essence is itself in potentiality with respect to the thing's act of being (*esse*).[102] It is also important to stress that for Aquinas the essence of a material being includes both prime matter and substantial form; it must not be reduced to substantial form alone. It also means that according to Aquinas, because pure intelligences or angels lack matter, they cannot be multiplied within the same species.

Each angel is a separate species in and of itself. (This particular point was contested during his lifetime and was included among the 219 propositions condemned by Bishop Stephen Tempier at Paris on March 7, 1277.)[103]

Another much-contested part of Aquinas's theory of matter and form was his view that prime matter is pure potentiality. Many thirteenth- and fourteenth-century thinkers defended the view that prime matter enjoys some degree of actuality in itself and also held that God could keep prime matter in existence without its being informed by any substantial form.[104] Even at the beginning of his career Aquinas maintained that prime matter is the ultimate subject of form and privation, and that in itself it includes neither form nor privation. Hence it has no determination or actuality in and of itself. He steadfastly defended this position throughout his career. As he sees things, even a minimum degree of actuality on the part of prime matter would compromise the essential unity of a matter–form composite. Thus near the beginning of his Commentary on *Metaphysics* VIII 1, for instance, he argues that if prime matter included any actuality in itself, when another substantial form was introduced, matter would not receive unqualified substantial being from that form, but only some kind of accidental being.[105] Consequently, he insists, prime matter cannot be maintained in existence without some substantial form, not even by divine power. As he puts this in Quodlibet III (Easter 1270), for matter to exist in actuality without some form implies a contradiction, that is, that matter is in actuality and not in actuality at the same time, which not even God can bring to pass.[106]

Aquinas's view that there is only one substantial form in each substance, including human beings, was also much contested during his lifetime and after his death. One of his major reasons for defending this view is this: if substantial form communicates substantial existence to matter and the matter–form composite, a plurality of substantial forms would result in a plurality of substantial existences and would, therefore, undermine the composite's substantial unity. If the first substantial form gave substantial existence, all other forms could contribute only accidental *esse*. As Aquinas reasons in ST Ia.76, if a human being derived the fact that it lives from one form, the fact that it is an animal from another, and the fact that it is human from still another, it would not be one in the unqualified sense.[107]

IX. THE EXISTENCE OF GOD

Aquinas is convinced that philosophical argumentation can prove that God exists. We have already seen one early version of such argumentation from his *De ente et essentia*. At the same time, he denies that God's existence is self-evident to us in this life. It can be established philosophically only by reasoning from effect to cause: by demonstration of the *fact* (*quia*) rather than by a demonstration of the reasoned fact (*propter quid*), as he explains in ST Ia.2.2.[108] He offers philosophical arguments for God's existence in many of his writings throughout his career, and all of them remain faithful to this effort to move from knowledge of an effect to knowledge of God as the cause whose existence must be admitted to account for that effect. In the DEE argumentation, the effect in question is the existence of beings whose *esse* is not identical with their essence and who are, therefore, dependent on something else for their existence. In SCG I.13, two long, complex arguments take as the effect from which they depart the fact of motion in the universe. And in ST Ia.2.3, his best-known presentation of arguments for God's existence, each of the "five ways" begins with some effect that he regards as evident to us.[109]

Thus the first way begins with something that, according to Aquinas, is evident to us on the strength of sense experience: certain things in this world are moved. But, he reasons, whatever is moved is moved by something else. To justify this he explains that to move something is to bring it from potentiality to actuality. Something cannot be brought from potentiality to actuality except by a being that is in actuality. Since nothing can be in actuality and potentiality at the same time and in the same respect, he concludes that nothing can be mover and moved at the same time (and in the same respect) or move itself. Therefore whatever is moved is moved by another. Aquinas considers, but rejects as inadequate, recourse to an infinite regress of moved movers. He concludes that one must grant the existence of some first mover that is not moved by anything else, which everyone understands to be God. Since the literature surrounding the first way and the others is vast, it cannot be pursued in detail here. Suffice it to note that Aquinas's claim that nothing can be reduced from potency to act except by a being already in act does not mean that the being in act must formally possess the motion it communicates to what is moved. It may do so, or it may simply have the power to communicate this motion; that is, it may possess this motion virtually.[110]

Aquinas grounds the second way on efficient causality and on his observation of an order of efficient causes among sensible things. He comments that it is impossible for something to be the efficient cause of itself, since it would then be prior to itself (at least in the order of nature). Again he rejects, as insufficient, recourse to an infinite series of caused efficient causes. In ordered efficient causes the first is the cause of the intermediary, and the intermediary, whether one or many, is the cause of the ultimate effect. If one denies that there is a first (uncaused) efficient cause, one must reject the intermediary causes and the ultimate effect. He concludes therefore the existence of a first efficient cause, which "all name God."[111]

The third way consists of two major steps and is based on the possible and the necessary. Step one begins with the observation that we experience things that are capable of existing and not existing since they are subject to generation and corruption. It is impossible that all things that exist are such (revised text), that is, capable of existing and not existing, because for anything that can fail to exist there is a time when it does not exist. If therefore all things are capable of not existing, at some time nothing whatsoever existed, and hence, nothing would now exist. Since not all existents are capable of existing and not existing, there must be a necessary being. Instead of ending the argument here, however, Aquinas adds step two. Every necessary (that is, incorruptible) being has a cause of its necessity from something else or it does not. One cannot regress to infinity with caused necessary beings, as he has just shown in the second way with respect to efficient causes. Therefore, he concludes, there must be a necessary being that does not depend on anything else for its necessity and that causes the necessity in all else. This being everyone calls God.[112] (For a simpler version of the argument based on possibility and necessity, see SCG I.15 and II.15.)

The fourth way is based on degrees of perfection. We find among things some that are more or less good, more or less true, and more or less noble than others. But the more and less are said of different things insofar as they approach in different degrees something that is such to the maximum degree. For instance, that is hotter which more closely approaches the maximally hot. Therefore there is something that is truest and best and noblest and, therefore, being to the maximum degree. Aquinas cites *Metaphysics* II in support, to the effect that those things that are true to the maximum degree are also being to the maximum degree. Here he is evidently thinking of truth of being (ontological truth) rather than of truth of a proposition (logical truth). But instead of ending the argument here, he continues. That which is said to be maximally such in a given genus is the cause of everything else in that genus. Therefore there is something that is the cause of being (*esse*) and of goodness and of every other perfection for all other beings, and this we call God.[113] While this is evidently a more Platonic approach to God's existence, it is interesting to find Aquinas citing what we might call more Platonic passages from Aristotle in support. Readers who are less sympathetic to the Platonic approach may have difficulty with the first part of this argument. A more satisfactory, if still Platonic, argument based on participation may be found in Aquinas's Commentary on St. John's Gospel.[114]

The fifth way is based on the evidence for governance that Aquinas discerns among natural bodies. He notes that certain things that lack knowledge, that is, natural bodies, act for the sake of an end. This is clear, he argues, from the fact that they always, or at least usually, act in the same way so as to obtain that which is best. Hence this cannot be accounted for by chance; rather it is by intention that they reach their end. But things that lack knowledge cannot tend to an end unless they are directed by some knowing and intelligent being, just as an arrow is directed by an archer. Therefore, there is some intelligent being by which all natural things are ordered to their end, and this we call God. This argument should not be regarded as based on order and design, therefore, but as based on final causality. It is not the overall order and design of the universe that serves as its point of departure, but finality within natural bodies.[115]

Since Aquinas has here offered five arguments, did he regard it as evident that they all conclude to one and the same being, or God? While he evidently thinks that they do, it is important to note that he reserves a subsequent article (ST Ia.11.3) for the issue of divine unicity. If we compare the five ways with the argument in DEE 4, the latter has the merit of explicitly and immediately establishing the uniqueness of that being whose essence and *esse* are identical. There in stage two the point has already been made that there can only be one such being. This argument also takes as its point of departure a more metaphysical starting point, otherness of essence and *esse* in all entities, with one possible exception. But the five ways have the advantage that one needs less philosophical sophistication to recognize their respective points of departure.

X. NAMING GOD

In beginning ST Ia.3 Aquinas comments that once one knows *that* something exists, it remains to determine *how* it is, so as to know *what* it is. But in the case of God we cannot know what he is, but what he is not. Consequently, Aquinas devotes ST Ia.3–11 to determine *how* God is *not*, by denying of him all that is inappropriate. In ST Ia.12 he seeks to determine how God can be known by us, and in 13 he takes up the issue of the divine names. Here and many places elsewhere Aquinas maintains that we can know that God is, and what he is not, but not what he is. In other words, quidditative knowledge of God is not possible for human beings in this life, either as a result of philosophical investigation or as based on divine revelation.[116]

This position does not prevent Aquinas from acknowledging that some of the names we apply to God are predicated of him substantially (ST Ia.13.2) and properly (13.3). This means that as regards what such names (those of pure perfections) signify, they are properly said of God. But as regards the way in which they signify (*modus significandi*), they are not properly said of God; they retain a mode of signifying that pertains to creatures.[117]

In ST Ia.13.5 Aquinas rejects univocal predication of any names of God and creatures. He refuses to acknowledge that all names are predicated of God and creatures in purely equivocal fashion, and instead defends analogical predication of certain names, that is, names of pure perfections. Here, as in most of his mature discussions of this issue, he rejects the analogy of many to one and opts for the analogy of one to another. This means that when such a name is applied to a creature and to God, it is said analogically of God because of the relationship the creature bears to God as its principle and cause. Underlying Aquinas's defense of analogical predication of such names of God is his conviction that, no matter how great the diversity between creatures and God, in some way every effect is like its cause. This likeness between a creature viewed as an effect and God, its uncaused cause, is the ontological justification for the analogical predication of the divine names.[118]

NOTES

1 In BDT 5.4: "which has as its subject being considered as being"; In M Prooemium: "the subject of this science is being in general."

2 For a full discussion of the different kinds of objects of the three theoretical sciences (physics, mathematics, metaphysics) as expressed in terms of their degree of freedom from and dependency upon matter and motion, see In BDT 5.1. On *ens mobile* as the subject of natural philosophy or physics, see In Ph I.1.3. On mathematics as studying *ens quantum*, see In M IV.1.532.

3 For Aristotle, see in particular *Metaphysics* VI 1, 1026a29–32. For some recent discussions of this issue in Aristotle, see Owens 1978, pp. xiii–xxvii, 35–67; Owens 1982; Mansion 1956a and b; and Dumoulin 1986, pp. 107–74.

4 For Avicenna, see Avicenna 1977, Bk I, cc. 1–2, pp. 4–13. For Averroes, see Averroes 1562–1574, Vol. 4: *Commentary on the Physics*, Bk I, com. 83, ff. 47rb–48va. While Averroes accepts Aristotle's description of metaphysics as the science of being as being, he notes that this means substance and in fact substance in its highest instance, that substance which is the first form and final end which moves both as first form and as final cause. See Vol. 8: *Commentary on the Metaphysics*, Bk IV, com. 1, ff. 64rb–va, com. 2, ff. 65rb–66rb; Bk XII, com. 5, f. 293rb. For a metaphysical argument for God's existence, see Aquinas's DEE 4, analyzed below. Aquinas also seems to allow for a demonstration in physics of a first mover that, at least at the end of his Commentary on the *Physics*, he identifies with God (see In Ph VIII.23.1172).

5 See In BDT 5.4; In M Prooemium. For discussion see Zimmermann 1965, pp. 159–80. In ST IaIIae.66.5, ad 4, Aquinas writes that *ens commune* is the proper effect of the highest cause, God. This precludes including God under *ens commune*, for he would then cause himself. Aquinas explicitly refuses to include God under *esse commune* in his Commentary on the *Divine Names*. See In DDN 5.2.660.

6 See In BDT 5.4; ST Ia.1.1–8; SCG I.3–6. For his discussion of these three designations (metaphysics, first philosophy, divine science) see In BDT

5.1 and In M Prooemium. For discussion of the different reasons he offers in these texts (one early and one late) for describing this science as first philosophy, see Wippel 1984b, ch. 3, pp. 55–67 ("First Philosophy According to Thomas Aquinas").

7 In BDT 2.3. Cf. SCG I.7.

8 In BDT 2.3

9 SCG II.4 Note that this entire chapter develops differences between the ways in which the philosopher and the believer study created reality, that is, as it is in itself, and as it represents the divine reality and is in some way ordered to God. Weisheipl dates SCG from 1259–1264 and notes that the earliest possible date for Bk II is 1261. (See Weisheipl 1983, pp. 359–60.) He places In BDT in 1252–1259 (see p. 381 as corrected on p. 482), and In M at 1269–1272 (p. 379). Hence Aquinas's position concerning this issue remained consistent.

10 QDV 1.1. For Avicenna see *Liber de philosophia prima* I, c. 5, pp. 31–32. For other texts in Aquinas, see QDV 21.1; In BDT 1.3, obj. 3; In M I.2.46; ST IaIIae.55.4, ad 1. See also ST IaIIae.94.2, where he again seems to have in mind the process of resolution (analysis) to which he had referred in QDV 1.1: "What comes first to our apprehension is being, an understanding of which is included in anything else anyone apprehends." For a brief discussion of the processes of synthesis (composition) and analysis (resolution) in other contexts, especially In BDT 6.1, see Wippel 1984b, pp. 61–67. For a helpful collection and discussion of texts dealing with resolution, see Tavuzzi 1991; but the author's claim that "the very possibility of Aquinas's science of metaphysics presupposes a prior demonstration of the existence of God and the intellectual seizure of God as *Ipsum Esse Subsistens* as the *terminus* of metaphysical resolution *secundum rem*" (p. 225) is dubious at best. For some other interpreters who recognize the need to distinguish between a primitive and a metaphysical notion of being in Aquinas, see Renard 1956, p. 73; Krapiec 1956; Klubertanz 1963, pp. 45–52; and Schmidt 1960, pp. 377–80.

11 On these two operations of the intellect, see In BDT 5.3: "The first operation has to do with the very nature of a thing. . . . The second operation, however, has to do with the very *esse* of the thing." As used here *esse* seemsd to refer to the thing's actual existence. On Aquinas's discussion of the verb "is" as predicated sometimes in its own right ("Socrates is") and sometimes only as joined to the principal predicate in order to connect it with a subject ("Socrates is white"), see his In PH II.2. Cf. ST Ia.3.4, ad 2, where he writes that *esse* may signify the act of existing (*actum essendi*), or it may signify the composition of a proposition produced when the mind joins a predicate to a subject. For other

texts where he writes that the intellect's first operation (simple apprehension) is directed to a thing's quiddity, while the second (composition
or division–judgment) is directed to its *esse*, see In Sent I.19.5.1, ad 7;
I.38.1.3. For discussion see Gilson 1952, pp. 190–204; and Owens 1980a,
pp. 20–33. For rejection of the view that *esse* when taken as a thing's act
of existence is grasped through judgment, see Régis 1959, pp. 322–33
(which should be compared with his critical review of Gilson's *Being
and Some Philosophers*, reprinted in the latter at pp. 217–21). On the
complexity of the notion of being, see In BDH 2.23–24. See also ST
IaIIae.26.4.

12 In BDT 5.1; 5.3.

13 In BDT 5.1; 5.3. See also MacDonald's Chapter 6, herein.

14 In BDT 5.1; 5.3 (on *separatio*); 5.4 (on the two ways in which things may
not depend on matter). For discussion of all of this see Wippel 1984c.
Additional references are given there.

15 For discussion of the pertinent texts, including some difficult passages
from In M, see ibid., pp. 83–104. For additions to the secondary literature see Jordan 1986, pp. 149–63; Leroy 1984 and Leroy 1948.

16 In Ph I.6.39. On Parmenides cf. In M I.9.138–39.

17 See Fabro 1961, pp. 510–13, 535. For usage of this terminology and
division of his own book accordingly, see the helpful study, Montagnes
1963. For other useful studies of analogy in Aquinas, see Lyttkens 1952;
McInerny 1961 and 1968; and Klubertanz 1960.

18 See Section X below.

19 DPN, which Weisheipl dates at 1252–1256 (1983, p. 387).

20 DPN. For the Aristotle text, see 1003a33–36.

21 DPN. For the Averroes text, see *In IV Met.*, com. 2, ed. cit., Vol. 8, f.
65va. For a comparison of these two texts, see Montagnes 1963, pp. 178–
80. See also Aquinas, In M IV.1.537–539.

22 DPN. On the point that being is intrinsically realized both in substance
and in accidents, see QDV 1.1.

23 In M IV.1.540–543.

24 See In M IV.1.535. Cf. In M XI.3.2197; ST Ia.13.5.

25 See SCG I.34.

26 QDP 7.7. See QDV 2.11. According to an analogy of proportionality,
instead of predicating a name such as "intelligent" of a creature and God
because God causes intelligence in the creature, one would reason that
as human understanding is related to the human intellect, so is divine
understanding related to the divine intellect. This justifies our saying
that God understands or is intelligent. For discussion of this brief shift in
position in the year 1256 (the time of QDV 2), see Montagnes 1963, pp.
70–93.

27 QDV 1.1. Note especially: "But in this connection some [names] are said to add to being insofar as they express a mode of being itself that is not expressed by the name 'being'."

28 Ibid.

29 Ibid. "for there are various degrees (*gradus*) of being (*entitas*); the various modes of being (*modi essendi*) are derived on the basis of these degrees, and the various genera [or categories] of things are derived on the basis of these modes."

30 Aquinas's recognition of a hierarchy of being is already evident throughout much of his very early DEE (especially 2–5) and in his relatively late DSS (especially 8). DSS dates from 1271–1273, according to Weisheipl 1983, p. 388. For some confirmation of the need for analogical predication of "being" of individual substances, see In Sent I.35.1.4: "and therefore whenever the form signified by a name is the act of being itself (*esse*), [that form] cannot be associated [with the name] univocally, for which reason the noun "being" (*ens*) likewise is not predicated univocally." Cf. Fabro 1950, pp. 170–71.

31 Aquinas knew of Parmenides's position through Aristotle, and he defended the reality of nonbeing in a qualified or relative sense in his own efforts to defend multiplicity within the order of being. See In M I.9.138 and In Ph I.14.121 (on Parmenides). For texts where he develops the notion of relative nonbeing, see Wippel 1985.

32 In BDH 2.

33 For a fuller discussion and for secondary literature, see Wippel 1987a. Especially important are the following studies: Geiger 1953; Fabro 1950 and 1961; and Clarke 1952a and 1952b.

34 In BDH 2.25.

35 Ibid.

36 Ibid. It should be noted that in reaching this conclusion, Aquinas is also supporting a Boethian axiom on which he is directly commenting, to the effect that "that which is" can participate in something, but *esse* cannot.

37 See In BDH 2.29 and 23.

38 See In BDH 2.32. On the one truly simple being which is subsisting *esse*, see In BDH 2.36.

39 There has been considerable difference of opinion among twentieth-century scholars both about the meaning of *esse* in the Boethian text itself and about the way Aquinas interprets it in his Commentary. For references and for a critical review of many of these interpretations, see McInerny 1990, pp. 161–98.

40 See SCG II.52; QDP 7.2, ad 4; ST Ia.3.4, ad 1.

41 In addition to SCG II.52, see SCG I.26 for the second reason Aquinas

offers to account for the error some have made in identifying God with the *esse* of all things.

42 See In DDN 5.2.658–659. Aquinas here finds the author showing that *ipsum esse* is common to all things because, as he explains, "nothing can be described as an existent unless it has *esse.*"

43 In BDH 2.34.

44 In BDH 2.24.

45 ST Ia.45.5, ad 1.

46 On Aquinas's philosophical argumentation for God's existence, see Section IX below.

47 In DDN 5.1.631.

48 In DDN 5.2.660. In n. 658 Aquinas explains that here Dionysius is showing that God is the cause of *esse commune* itself. He thereby shows that *esse* is common to all things (see n. 42 above) and how *esse commune* stands in relation to God.

49 See n. 47 above.

50 "If something is found to be present in something by participation, it must be caused in it by that to which it belongs essentially. . . . It follows therefore that all things other than God are not identical with their *esse*, but participate in *esse*. It is necessary therefore that all things which are distinguished by reason of diverse participation in *esse* so as to exist more or less perfectly be caused by one first being, which exists most perfectly" (ST Ia.44.1). See ST Ia.3.4 on divine simplicity.

51 Ibid. For the Aristotle text, see *Metaphysics* II 1, 993b24–31.

52 QQ 12.5.1. From this Aquinas completes his response to the question originally asked: "Is an angel's existence an accident of the angel?" He replies that the substantial existence (*esse*) of a thing is not an accident, but the actuality of an existing form.

53 Cf. In DDN 2.3.158. There he contrasts the communication of the divine essence to the three divine persons in the Trinity with the communication of a likeness of the divine essence to creatures through creation.

54 QDSC 1.1.

55 In Sent I.29.5.2.

56 See Dümpelmann 1969, pp. 24ff., 34–35.

57 Cited in n. 54 above.

58 This is especially true if one recognizes the importance of participation by composition for Aquinas's explanation of participation in *esse*. For discussion of this along with Fabro's emphasis on the same, see Wippel 1987a, pp. 152–58.

59 See Siger de Brabant 1981, *Introductio*, q. 7, pp. 44–45 (Munich Ms.); and Siger de Brabant 1983, *Introductio*, q. 7, pp. 32–33 (Cambridge Ms.), *Introductio*, 2, p. 398 (Paris Ms.).

60 In addition to the text from In BDH cited in n. 38 above, see In Sent
    I.13.1.3; 19.2.2; and QDV 27.1, ad 8 (to be discussed below). While the
    last of these texts refers to a real composition of *esse* and *quod est* (that
    which is) rather than a real distinction, it makes the same point; if two
    principles are really compounded with one another rather than purely
    mentally, this must be because they are really distinct from one another.
61 See, for instance, his usage of *ens* and *id quod est* (In BDH, cited above in
    nn. 36, 37, 38); *substantia* (QQ 3.8.1); *forma* (In BDH, cited above in n.
    43); *natura, res* (QDSC, cited above in n. 54); and *essentia* (DEE 4,
    analyzed below; QDV 21.5).
62 For some twentieth-century thinkers who have denied that Aquinas
    defended any kind of "real" distinction between essence and *esse*, see M.
    Chossat, "Dieu," *Dictionnaire de théologie catholique,* Vol. 4, pt. 1, col.
    1180; and F. Cunningham in an earlier series of articles which find their
    ultimate expression in Cunningham 1988. For authors who disagree
    with this reading while allowing for some terminological variation in
    Aquinas and in their interpretations, see Fabro 1939 and Fabro 1950, pp.
    212–44; Sweeney 1963; Owens 1965, pp. 19–22; and Wippel 1984b, chs.
    5 and 6.
63 "... but they have an admixture of potentiality."
64 "Whatever is not included in the notion of an essence or quiddity comes
    to it from without and enters into composition with the essence, be-
    cause no essence can be understood without those factors which are
    parts of the essence. But every essence or quiddity can be understood
    without anything being understood about its existing (*esse*): I can under-
    stand what a man is or what a phoenix is and not know whether it exists
    in reality. Therefore it is evident that *esse* is other than essence or
    quiddity."
65 For this second criticism see Van Steenberghen 1980, p. 41.
66 "Unless perhaps there is some thing whose quiddity is its very *esse*, and
    this thing can only be one and first."
67 "Wherefore it follows that such a thing which is identical with its own
    esse can only be one; therefore in every other thing, its *esse* and its
    quiddity or nature or form must be other."
68 This is the major point of disagreement between my interpretation and
    that proposed by J. Owens (see n. 72 below). As I read the text, its proof
    that essence and *esse* are really distinct does not presuppose prior knowl-
    edge of the argument for God's existence.
69 Note the key presupposition for the argument for God's existence – the
    distinction between nature or essence and *esse*: "Therefore it is neces-
    sary that every such thing whose *esse* is other than its nature receive [its]
    esse from something else."

70 Note in particular: "therefore the very quiddity or form which is an intelligence must be in potency with respect to the *esse* it receives from God, and that *esse* is received as act."

71 Ibid.

72 For different interpretations of this see Owens 1965, 1981, and 1986; Wippel 1979 and 1984a; MacDonald 1984; and Patt 1988.

73 Arguments of this kind are of concern here because this presentation follows the philosophical order in presenting Aquinas's metaphysical thought. See n. 9 above.

74 SCG II.52 attempts to show that in created intellectual substances there is some composition by reason of the fact that "in them *esse* and *quod est* are not identical."

75 Ibid. Note in particular: "Subsisting *esse* must be infinite because it is not limited (*terminatur*) by anything which receives it."

76 Note that the text then continues with the passage cited above in n. 54. For other texts see In Ph VIII.21.1153, and DSS 8. For discussion see Wippel 1984b, pp. 148–49.

77 In Sent. I.8.4.2. For later versions see SCG I.25; QDP 7.3; ST Ia.3.5. For discussion see Wippel 1984b, pp. 134–39.

78 In this article Aquinas asks whether grace is something positive that is created in the human soul. After arguing that it is, he must meet the eighth argument against this view – nothing can be in a genus unless it is compounded; grace is not compounded; therefore, it is not in a genus and is not created. In replying he maintains that what falls directly in the genus *substance* is indeed compounded in a real composition of *esse* and *quod est*, and presents our argument. Such does not hold for things in the categories of accident.

79 For discussion of this see Wippel 1984b, pp. 138–39.

80 In BDH 2.32. Cf. n. 38 above.

81 Ibid., n. 34. "nevertheless because every such form determines *esse*, no such form is identical with *esse* itself, but has *esse*. . . . [A]n immaterial subsisting form, since it is a certain thing which is determined with respect to species, is not identical with existence in general, but participates in it."

82 "But in intellectual substances there is a composition . . . of form and of participated *esse*."

83 Cf. the text from QDSC cited in n. 54 above.

84 In Sent. I.8.5.1, s.c. While this argument appears in the article's *sed contra*, it is clear from the context and from Aquinas's reply in the corpus that he accepts it.

85 See QDP 7.2, ad 9. "this which I call *esse* is the most perfect of all: which is evident from the fact that act is always more perfect than potency.

Any designated form is not understood [to be] in actuality except by reason of the fact that it is held to exist. . . . Therefore it is evident that this which I call *esse* is the actuality of all acts, and because of this, it is the perfection of all perfections." For Aquinas's use of this to prove that God is infinite, see In Sent I. 43.1.1; ST Ia.7.1; CT 18.

86 In M IV.1.540–543.

87 In M V.1.898 (on first substance); nn. 903–905 (on reducing the four modes of substance to two). Note Aquinas's remark in ST Ia.29.2, ad 3: "Wherefore in things composed of matter and form, essence signifies not form alone nor matter alone but the composite of common matter and common form insofar as they are principles of the species."

88 See QDP 9.1. After noting that in matter–form composites essence is not entirely identical with substance taken as subject, Aquinas comments that in the case of simple substances (such as angels) essence and (substance taken as) subject are identical in reality, although they may be distinguished conceptually (*ratione*).

89 Ibid.

90 In M V.1.890.

91 In M V.1.891.

92 In M V.1.892.

93 Ibid.

94 For discussion see Wippel 1987c, pp. 18–23.

95 For the derivation from the Commentary on the *Physics*, see In Ph III.5.322. See n. 323 on action and passion as distinct categories. For discussion see Wippel 1987c, pp. 25–28, and pp. 32–34 on Aquinas's view that the categories are ten and irreducible.

96 "it must be said that a subject is a cause of its proper accident – a final cause, and in a certain way an active cause, and also a material cause, insofar as it receives the accident." He goes on to explain that the essence of the soul is the cause of all its powers as an end and as an active principle, and that it is a receiving principle for some of them, for example, intellect and will, which inhere in the soul alone rather than in the composite of body and soul. Cf. ST Ia.77.5. For fuller discussion see Wippel 1987b.

97 In Ph I.13.118. On the principles *per se* and *per accidens* of change, see n. 112. Cf. Aristotle, *Physics* I 7, 191a3–12.

98 In M VII.2.1285. For the Aristotle text, see *Metaphysics* VII 3, 1029a20–21.

99 In M VII.2.1286–1287.

100 In M VII.2.1287–1289. For discussion see Doig 1972, pp. 317–19. Cf. p. 280, n. 1. For the importance Aquinas assigns to denominative or concrete predication, see n. 1289: "Therefore concrete or denominative

predication shows that just as substance is essentially different from accidents, so is matter essentially distinct from substantial forms."

101 See In BDH 2.24: "because a substantial or accidental form, which of its essence (*ratione*) is common, is limited (*determinatur*) to this or to that subject." Cf. ST Ia.11.3, obj. 1; QDSC 1: "for prime matter receives a form by limiting (*contrahendo*) it to individual existence (*esse*)." Also see loc. cit., ad 2: "There is one [limitation of form] insofar as the form of the species is limited to an individual; and this limitation is by means of matter." Also see In Sent I.43.1.1; CT 18, where, while arguing for the divine infinity, Aquinas writes: "No act is found to be limited except by a potentiality which receives it: for we find that forms are limited according to the potentiality of matter." On the non-Aristotelian character of Aquinas's view that unreceived act (or form) is unlimited, see Clarke 1952, pp. 169–72, 178–83.

102 See, for instance, QDSC 1.

103 See, for instance, DEE 4; SCG II.93; ST Ia.50.4. For Bishop Tempier's condemnation see Denifle and Chatelain 1889, I, pp. 543–61: prop. 81. Cf. prop. 96. For background see Wippel 1977 and Hissette 1977. On propositions 81 and 96 see Hissette 1977, pp. 82–87 (propositions 42 and 43 according to the Mandonnet numbering that he follows). In brief, those opposed to the position in question saw in it a limitation on divine omnipotence.

104 For example, John Pecham, Richard of Middleton, William of Ware, John Duns Scotus, and William Ockham as discussed in Wolter 1965, pp. 131–34. For this in Henry of Ghent, see Macken 1979.

105 See, for instance, In Sent I.39.2.2, ad 4; QDV 8.6; SCG I.17; QDP 1.1, ad 7; ST Ia.5.3, ad 3; 48.3; 115.1, ad 2; and In M VIII.1.1689.

106 QQ 3.1.1. According to Aquinas, to say that God cannot bring to pass something that is self-contradictory is not to restrict divine omnipotence.

107 See ST Ia.76.3 (first argument against plurality of souls in human beings); and 76.4. Cf. QDSC 1, ad 9; 3; QDA 9; 11.

108 For his denial that God's existence is self-evident (*per se notum*) to us, see ST Ia.2.1. For his criticism of Anselm's *Proslogion* argumentation, see ST Ia.2.1, ad 2.

109 For a detailed study of Aquinas's different arguments for God's existence based on a chronological examination of his writings, see Van Steenberghen 1980.

110 For much of this literature see ibid., pp. 358–66. Also see Kenny 1980b, for a critical presentation; and Owens 1980c, chs. 6–11. In criticizing the application of act-potency reasoning to the first way, Kenny fails to distinguish between virtual and formal possession of what an agent

communicates (see pp. 21–22). For interesting discussions of the principle that whatever is moved is moved by something else, see Kenny 1980, pp. 26–33; and Weisheipl 1965. Also see Weisheipl 1985, chs. II and V; and the detailed study by Hassing (1991).

111 While both this argument and that offered in DEE 4 are based on efficient causality, there is a fundamental difference. This argument takes as its point of departure exercises of efficient causation that are directly evident to sense experience. The argument in DEE takes as its point of departure a sophisticated metaphysical conclusion: the distinction of essence and *esse* in beings, including spiritual beings, other than God.

112 I have followed a variant in the Leonine text and read "Impossibile est autem omnia quae sunt, talia esse" instead of "Impossibile est autem omnia quae sunt talia, semper esse." As Aquinas understands the term "possibile" here, he has in mind things subject to generation and corruption. On the variant reading see, for instance, Van Steenberghen 1980, pp. 188–89. For other discussions of this argument, see Owens 1980b; Knasas 1980, pp. 488–89; and Kenny 1980b, pp. 55–57.

113 For the Aristotle text, see *Metaphysics* II 1, 993b30–31. For fuller discussion of Aquinas's views on truth of being and truth of a proposition, see Wippel 1989 and Wippel 1990, especially pp. 543–49.

114 See *Lectura super evangelium Johannis*, Busa ed., Vol. 6, p. 227. Here the argument is presented as that of the Platonists and is based on participation. All that which is (something) by participation is reduced to that which is such of its essence, as to that which is first and supreme. Since all existents participate in *esse*, there must be something at the peak of all things that is *esse* of its essence. For discussion see Fabro 1954, esp. pp. 79–90. Also see Van Steenberghen 1980, p. 280.

115 For Aquinas's effort elsewhere to show that every agent acts on account of an end, see SCG III.2. Also see Klubertanz 1959, esp. pp. 104–5.

116 ST Ia.3 (Introduction): "But because concerning God we cannot know what he is, but what he is not, about God we cannot consider how he is, but rather how he is not." Cf. ST Ia.12.12, ad 1: "In reply to the first argument it must be said that [human reason] cannot arrive at a simple form so as to know of it what it is." Also see SCG 1.30: "Concerning God we cannot grasp what he is, but what he is not, and how other things stand in relation to him." For discussion and additional texts and secondary literature see Wippel 1984b, Ch. IX.

117 See ST Ia.13.1, ad 2; SCG I.30; Wippel 1984b, pp. 224–26 (on the distinction between the *res significata* and the *modus significandi*).

118 For the distinction between the analogy of many to one and the analogy of one to another, see Section IV above. Also see SCG I.34; QDP 7.7. For discussion see Montagnes 1963, pp. 65–81. On the similarity of an

effect and its cause no matter how great the dissimilarity between them, see SCG I.29 (and Aquinas's appeal to this in I.33 to reject purely equivocal predication of names of God and creatures); QDP 7.7, ad 5; ad 6 ad contra; ST Ia.13.5: "And thus, whatever is said of God and of creatures is said in so far as there is some ordering of the creature to God as to its principle and cause, in which all the perfections of things preexist in surpassing fashion."

5 Philosophy of mind

This chapter is concerned first with Aquinas's account of what the mind is and how it relates to the body and then with his account of what the mind does and how it does it – the metaphysical and the psychological sides of his philosophy of mind.[1]

I. SOUL AS THE FIRST PRINCIPLE OF LIFE

The central subject of Aquinas's philosophy of mind is what he calls rational soul (*anima rationalis*) far more often than he calls it mind (*mens*). This apparently trivial fact about his terminology has theoretical implications.[2] Aquinas's philosophy of mind can be understood only in the context of his more general theory of soul, which naturally makes use of many features of his metaphysics.

Obviously, Aquinas is not a materialist. God – subsistent being itself, the absolutely fundamental element of Aquinas's metaphysics[3] – is, of course, in no way material. But even some creatures are entirely independent of matter, which Aquinas thinks of as exclusively corporeal.[4] The fundamental division in his broad classification of created things is between the corporeal – such as stars, trees, and cats – and the incorporeal (or spiritual) – for example, angels. (Aquinas sometimes calls spiritual creatures "separated substances" because of their incorporeality.) But this exhaustive division seems to be not perfectly exclusive, because human beings must be classified as not only corporeal but also spiritual in a certain respect. They have this uniquely problematic status among creatures in virtue of the peculiar character of the human soul.

Simply having a soul is not enough to give a creature a spiritual component, since Aquinas uses "soul" generically in a way that

128

even many materialists could tolerate. Nobody objects to dividing physical things into animate and inanimate, and Aquinas's generic use of *anima* treats the term as if it were merely a noun of convenience associated with "animate" (*animata*): "In order to inquire into the nature of the [human] soul, we have to presuppose that 'soul' (*anima*) is what we call the first principle of life in things that live among us; for we call living things 'animate' [or 'ensouled'], but things that are devoid of life 'inanimate' [or "not ensouled"]" (ST Ia.75.1c).⁵ So trees and cats, no less than we, have souls, although in Aquinas's view neither plants nor nonhuman animals are in any respect spiritual creatures. Still, he emphatically denies that even the merely nutritive soul of a plant or the nutritive + sensory soul of a beast can be simply identified with any of the living thing's bodily parts. He finds a basis for ruling out that possibility in what he uses as soul's defining formula: "the first principle of life."

From Aristotle Aquinas learned of pre-Socratic materialists who had simply identified souls as bodies – bodily parts of living things. He sees those philosophers as having begun, quite properly, by considering what is most apparent about life: the presence in living things of certain distinctive activities, which, because they naturally imply life (*vita*) at some level or other, are called "vital" – for example, growth or cognition. But in his view those ancient reductive materialists, "claiming that bodies alone are real things, and that what is not a body is nothing at all" (ST Ia.75.1c), confused the shorter-range project of identifying material sources or partial explanations (*principia*) of one or another vital activity with the search for the soul behind *all* of them, the *first* principle, the *ultimate* intrinsic source or explanation of all of an animate thing's vital activities and its mode of existence.

The confusion in pre-Socratic materialism can be shown in many ways, Aquinas thinks. In SCG II.65 he offers several arguments with that aim, but none of those is as strong as the anti-reductionist argument he presents later, in ST Ia.75.1c, against the possibility of reducing an animate being's soul to any of its bodily parts.

In this argument he invites us to consider a particular vital activity, such as visual perception. Of course, eyes must be included in a correct explanation of vision – and, he might have said, skin in the explanation of touch, roots or stomachs in explanations of growth, and so on. That is, vital activities typically do have bodies among their principles. And since a principle of a particular *vital* activity may indeed be considered a principle of *life* (although only in that particular respect and to an appropriately restricted extent), it may be granted that some bodies – such as a living animal's normal eyes – are principles of life. It is in that special, limited sense that the ancient materialists were on the right track. But no one, Aquinas thinks, would call an eye (or a root, or a stomach) a *soul*. So, he says, *some* principles of life clearly are bodies, but those that are aren't souls.

Of course, there are other kinds of bodies – stones, for instance – that are not only not principles of life but even naturally lifeless, and so *no* body considered just as a body has life *essentially*. But a *first intrinsic principle* of life (which imbues everything else in an animate body with life) must have life essentially. If it did not, its having life would be explained on the basis of something else intrinsic to that living body, and it would not be that body's *first* principle of life. Therefore, *no* soul, no *first* principle of life, is a body. If a soul is in any respect corporeal – in its essential dependence on some bodily organ, for instance – it will not be in virtue of its corporeality that it animates the thing whose soul it is.

Furthermore, any vegetable or animal body has the life it has only in virtue of being a body organized in a way that confers on it natural potentialities for being in particular sorts of states. And a body is organized in this or that way and has these or those natural potentialities only because of a certain principle that is called the body's *actus*, the substantial form that makes it actually be such a vegetable or animal body.[6] Therefore, the *first* principle of life in a living body, its soul, is no bodily part of that body, but rather its form, one of the two metaphysical parts of the composite of matter and form that absolutely every body is.

This argument, which Aquinas applies to the explanation of life in absolutely any living corporeal thing, is not effective against every sort of materialism. Materialists who tolerate Aquinas's generic concept of soul and who understand soul not simply as a body but as a function of a body or as the effect of a configuration of physical components, can also tolerate the critical line taken in this anti-reductionist argument, however they might react to its conclusion identifying soul with form. Only when Aquinas presents his account of the *human* soul in particular does he take a position entirely incompatible with materialist theories of living things.

II. THE PECULIAR CHARACTER OF THE HUMAN SOUL

In a theory that recognizes the soul of a plant as a merely nutritive first intrinsic principle of life, and the soul of a nonhuman animal as a nutritive + sensory principle of that sort, it comes as no surprise that the soul of a human being is to be analyzed as nutritive + sensory + rational. Aquinas thinks of the human soul not as three nested, co-operating substantial forms, however, but as the single form that gives a human being its specifically human mode of existence, including potentialities and functions, from its genetic makeup on up to its most creative talents.[7] And so he will often simply identify the human soul as the rational soul, an identification made entirely appropriate by the fact that *rational* is the differentia of the human species in the genus *animal*. A consequence of this identification is his frequent designation of the entire substantial form of a human being by its distinctive aspect of rationality,[8] as in this passage: "It is necessary to say that that which is the principle of intellective activity, what we call the soul of a human being, is an incorporeal, subsistent principle" (ST Ia.75.2c).[9] Here he reveals not only what distinguishes human beings from all other animals but also what makes the human soul peculiar: its status as "subsistent," a necessary condition for its existing apart from the body whose form it is.

We have already seen Aquinas arguing that no soul considered as the ultimate (or first) intrinsic principle of a corporeal creature's vital activities can be identified with anything corporeal. And since he here expressly identifies the soul of a human being with the principle of the distinctively human vital activity of intellection, we could have anticipated his claim that that principle must be incorporeal. But now he is concerned not merely with what such a principle could not be but also with "*that which is* the principle." He is going beyond the primarily negative conclusion of his generic anti-reductionist argument to make a further, affirmative claim about the nature of the form that *is* to be identified as the human soul; and both the negative and the affirmative parts of this thesis are theoretically dictated ("It is necessary to say"). The human soul, just because it is distinctively the principle of intellective activity, not only must not be identified as corporeal, it must be described as *subsistent.* For that reason he cannot simply rely on the result of the anti-reductionist argument, which has to do generally with any living being's first principle of life and which entails nothing regarding such a principle's subsistence. Instead he must develop a new incorporeality argument that is specific for the principle of intellective activity, the distinctively human faculty of intellect, the cognitive faculty of the rational soul.

This new argument rests on two highly theoretical claims: (A) "through intellect the human being can have cognition of the natures of all bodies"; and (B) "any [faculty] that can have cognition of certain things cannot have any of those things in its own nature" (ST Ia.75.2c).

Claim (A) has an implausible ring to it, but the implausibility is reduced by a careful reading, which shows that Aquinas intends it as a claim about a *general* human *capacity* in respect of the *natures* of all bodies.[10] Although there seems to be no possibility of *proving* (A),[11] the plausibility of its universality has certainly been enhanced since Aquinas's day by the spectacular development of the natural sciences, the paradigms of systematic intellective cognition of the natures of bodies.

Claim (B) means something like this: to be a cognitive faculty is to be essentially in a state of receptive *potentiality* relative to certain types of things, the faculty's proper objects – such as sounds, for the faculty of hearing. So if the faculty itself has such a type of thing in it *actually* – such as a ringing in the ears – it forfeits at least some of the natural receptive potentiality that made it a cognitive faculty in the first place.[12] Coating someone's tongue with something bitter will diminish and distort her sense of taste;[13] just because it is a corporeal organ of cognition, the tongue can be made to forfeit a cognitional potentiality in this way as a consequence of acquiring an accidental physical quality. "So if the *intellective* principle had in itself the nature of *any* body, it would not be capable of cognizing *all* bodies. But *every* body has *some* determinate nature, and so it is impossible that the intellective principle be a body" (ST Ia.75.2c).[14] Moreover, even a normal, unaltered tongue, simply in virtue of being a body itself, lacks the power of cognizing at least one body that might otherwise be included among its proper objects: it can't taste itself. On the other hand, as the very existence of philosophical psychology shows, "our intellect does have cognition of itself."[15]

Since any normal corporeal organ of (sensory) cognition must, simply as corporeal, be incapable of cognizing *some* corporeal objects and can, as a consequence of physical alteration, be rendered incapable of cognizing still more, it follows, given the universality of claim (A), that the intellective principle not only cannot *be* but also cannot directly *use* any corporeal organ in performing its distinctive operation. Of course, our cognition of any particular body itself is sensory, and so our cognition of anything associated with bodies, including their natures, depends ultimately on sensory cognition. So one's intellect does depend *for its data* on the operation of the corporeal organs of one's other faculties, but in processing those data it does not use any body at all in the direct, essential way visual cognition uses the eye: "as the organ by means of which that sort of activity is carried out" (ST Ia.75.2, ad 3).[16]

According to Aquinas, the *subsistence* of the human soul follows from this strong thesis of its incorporeality. The vital activity of intellective cognition, which distinguishes the human soul from all other terrestrial souls, is one that it performs "on its own (*per se*), in which the body does not share," not even to the extent of supplying an organ for the activity.[17] But nothing can operate on its own in this strong sense except something "that subsists on its own." A glowing coal, which does subsist on its own, can warm something else; but heat, an accidental form whose real existence is utterly dependent on its occurring in some matter, is just for that reason incapable of warming anything on its own. The human soul, therefore, is "something incorporeal *and* subsistent" (ST Ia.75.2c).

III. THE HUMAN SOUL AS BOTH A SUBSISTENT ENTITY AND A SUBSTANTIAL FORM

Aquinas's subsistence thesis, which clearly is incompatible with materialism of any sort, brings with it both an advantage and a difficulty for his theory of the soul. On the positive side, it establishes a necessary condition of immortality: if the distinctively human, personal aspect of the human animal is something incorporeal and subsistent, biological death need not be the death of the person.

The human soul's subsistence on its own is the philosophical basis for a reasoned account of personal immortality.[18] The difficulty the subsistence thesis poses for Aquinas's theory is its threat to the unity of the human being. A human being is defined as a rational animal; an animal is defined as a living, sensitive, *corporeal* being; and these definitions are essential to Aquinas's general, fundamentally Aristotelian account of nature. Aristotle himself ensures the coherence of this portion of the account in his explanation of the human soul as the substantial form of the human body, an explanation that Aquinas wholeheartedly adopts, as we have seen. The subsistence thesis, however, especially as employed in support of immortality, threatens to leave the human being *identified* with the human soul, looking like an incorporeal, subsistent entity that is temporarily and rather casually associated with a body – looking like Plato's rather than Aristotle's human being.[19]

To avoid this outcome, Aquinas must offer a more precise account of the soul's subsistence, attempting to make it compatible with the account of the soul as a form. He takes up this challenge repeatedly,[20] sometimes explicitly addressing the issue of the compatibility of the two claims that (E) the soul is a subsistent entity and that (F) the soul is a form.

Perhaps the fullest discussion of this sort is in the first question of his *Disputed Questions on the Soul* (QDA): "Can the human soul be both a form and a real particular (*hoc aliquid*)?" The eighteen opening arguments (the "Objections") support a negative reply on the basis of a very creditable array of considerations against Aquinas's affirmative position.[21]

Aquinas's opening move in dispelling the apparent incompatibility of (E) and (F) is his introduction of a distinction regarding the Aristotelian technical notion of a real particular (*hoc aliquid*), a notion more precise and even more familiar to his contemporaries than that of a subsistent entity. "*Strictly* speaking," he says, *hoc aliquid* applies to "an individual in the category of substance [that is,] a primary substance." Something is an individual in the category of substance, strictly speaking, if and only if (1) it is "not in something else as its subject" (the way heat is in the glowing coal) and so "can subsist on its own"; and (2) it is "something complete in some species and genus of substance," something that occupies a place of its own in the natural order of things. A human being's hand, for instance, belongs to her not as her color does but as a part belongs to a whole, and so it can subsist on its own (although unnaturally, and as a hand only in a manner of speaking). But, of course, it is only the whole human being that is complete in the genus *animal* and the species *rational animal*. Since a human hand has no place of its own in the genera and species of substance, it satisfies (1) but not (2) and so counts as a *hoc aliquid* only broadly speaking.

Having set the stage with this distinction, followed by rejections of variously unsatisfactory ancient theories of the soul, Aquinas presents his own view. Like the human hand, the human soul is in the human being not as heat is in a coal but as a part is in a whole, and so it is "capable of subsisting on its own" – that is, it satisfies (1). As for (2), the soul's status is subtler and loftier than the hand's. Like the hand, the soul on its own cannot satisfy (2). But, quite unlike the hand or any other bodily part of the rational animal, the human soul "as the [substantial] form of the body has the role of *fulfilling* or *completing* (*perficiens*) the human species" – that is, the soul is not only the *rationality* but, indeed, the full *rational animality* of the human body, specifying that corporeal thing as a human being. Without the soul that body is a corpse, which can be called a human body only equivocally. Although the soul itself has no place of its own among individuals sorted out in the species and genera of substance, it is what gives the human being its unique place in that system, what enables this or that human being to satisfy (2), and so it is more nearly a *hoc aliquid* than any bodily part could be.[22] Still, we can best appreciate the peculiar status Aquinas establishes for the human soul not by focusing on its claims to the designation of *hoc aliquid*, but rather by seeing just how he combines (E) and (F): by showing that neither of those apparently conflicting claims regarding the human soul can be correctly understood without taking the other into account.

Beginning with what is most accessible to us, as he prefers always to do, Aquinas reasons from the vital activities of a human being to the peculiar character of its first principle of life and its mode of existence:

And so we can in this way come to know the human soul's mode of existence, on the basis of its activity. For insofar as it has an activity [viz., intellective cognition] that transcends material things, its existence, too, is raised above the body and does not depend on it. On the other hand, insofar as it is naturally suited to acquire immaterial cognition from what is material, the fulfilment of its nature clearly cannot occur without union with the body; for something is complete in its nature only if it has [in itself] the things that are required for the activity that is proper to its nature. Therefore, since the human soul, insofar as it is united to the body as a form, also has its existence raised above the body and does not depend on it, it is clear that the soul is established on the borderline between corporeal and separate [i.e., purely spiritual] substances.   (QDA 1c)[23]

The borderline status of the human soul is not merely picturesque. The distinctively human vital activity is intellective and thus spiritual rather than corporeal, since intellect neither is nor directly uses a corporeal organ. But intellection involves sensation, which is necessarily corporeal in its organs and operations; and "involves" here means more than merely "is added to" or even "depends on." For, as we have seen, the proper objects of intellect come to it only via the senses, but the human sensory soul, properly understood, is just an aspect of the rational soul. And so the soul's involvement with the body is not a case of a spiritual creature's using a body as a person might use a lamp. The union of soul and body may more accurately be thought of as a human soul's *constituting* some matter *as* a living human body, something like the way a quantity of electricity (which needs no bulb or wire to *exist*) constitutes some matter as a lighted lamp.

IV. INTELLECT – PHILOSOPHICAL AND THEOLOGICAL ASPECTS OF AQUINAS'S ACCOUNT

Aquinas's account of what the mind does and how it does it divides naturally into his theories of intellect and of will, the cognitive and appetitive faculties of the rational soul. I begin by focusing on intellect.[24]

Aquinas's philosophy of mind is like most other parts of his work in its interweaving of philosophical and theological strands. Among the foundations of his theory of human cognition are a few basic theological doctrines (which he elucidated and supported with philosophical analysis and argumentation): God, the creator, is omniscient, omnipotent, and perfectly good; and part of God's purpose in creating is the manifestation of himself to rational creatures.[25] Aquinas's theism is so thoroughly informed by reason that when he combines such doctrines with theories, he seems always to be guided by the expectation that the theology and the philosophy will turn out to be mutually confirming, neither overriding the other, as in this characteristic account of body and mind: "The immediate purpose of the human body is the rational soul and its operations, since matter is for the sake of the form, and instruments are for the sake of the agent's activities. I maintain, therefore, that God designed the human body in the pattern best suited to that form and those activities" (ST Ia.91.3c).

Sensory cognition is, as we have seen, indispensable to the cognitive activity distinctive of the rational soul; and so the senses, too, he says, "have been given to human beings not only in order to get the necessities of life, but also to acquire cognition" (ST Ia.91.3, ad 3).[26] Consequently the *human* animal, unlike all the others, is called not *sensory* but rather *rational* substance "because sensation is less than [rationality], which is proper to a human being." Still, just because of sensation's indispensable contribution to intellect's operations, sensing "is more excellently suited to a human being than to other animals" (ST Ia.108.5c).[27] After all, the *rational* soul is identified as a human being's single substantial form, informing *all* its faculties. Theological considerations again fall into place: since it is the human rational soul, not the human body or its senses, in respect of which human beings are made in the image of God,[28] it is entirely reasonable that *its* cognitive faculty in particular should manifest special excellence; and since the human intellect depends on the human senses, the creator who leaves his image in the intellect can hardly leave the senses less than superbly suited for cognitive service to intellect.[29]

Picking up the philosophical strand, even Aquinas's comments on "All human beings desire to know" and the rest of the opening passage of Aristotle's *Metaphysics* contain all the elements needed for an argument on natural grounds that would, in turn, confirm his theological observations. For example, "the proper activity of a human being considered just as a human being is to think and understand, for it is in this respect that a human being differs from all others. That is why a human being's desire is naturally inclined to thinking and understanding and, as a consequence, to acquiring organized knowledge. . . . [But] a natural desire cannot occur in vain" (In M I.1.3–4).[30] Therefore, we might fairly conclude, nature, including human cognitive faculties, must be organized in such a way as to enable human beings in general to satisfy their natural desire to know (allowing for wide individual, accidental differences). And since the object of a thing's natural desire is that thing's natural good, it is not surprising to find Aquinas often alluding to the Aristotelian observation that truth is intellect's natural good, the very thing to which a perfectly good God would guarantee intellect's access generally.[31]

V. INTELLECT – AQUINAS'S DIRECT REALISM

The guaranteed access is utterly direct, to the point of formal identity between the extra-mental object and the actually cognizing faculty in its cognizing of that object (although Aquinas's terminology can be initially misleading on this score):

What is cognized intellectively is in the one who has the intellective cognition by means of its likeness. And it is in this sense that we say that what is actually cognized intellectively *is* the intellect actualized (*intellectum in actu est intellectus in actu*), insofar as a likeness of the thing that is cognized is [on such an occasion] the form of the intellect, in the way that a likeness of the sense-perceptible thing is the form of a sense actualized [on an occasion of sense perception].   (ST Ia.85.2, ad 1)[32]

The fact that these strong claims of formal identity are expressed in terms of "likenesses" might suggest that the foundations of Aquinas's theory of intellection contain a dubious mixture of direct realism and representationalism. Dispelling that impression depends on getting a clearer view of Aquinas's account of the data of cognition, their transmission, and their transformation.

"Intellect's operation arises from sensation" (ST Ia.78.4, ad 4).[33] Corporeal things make physical impressions on the corporeal organs of "the external senses," which have both "proper objects" (colors for sight, sounds for hearing, and so on) and "common objects" (shapes for sight and touch, and so forth). The internalized sensory impressions, the "sensory species," are transmitted to "internal senses," which store the sensory species and process them in various ways.[34] Our principal concern with the internal senses now is with one of the roles of the one Aquinas calls "phantasia": producing and preserving the sensory data that are indispensable for intellect's use, the "phantasms."[35] In intellect itself Aquinas distinguishes two Aristotelian "powers": "agent [i.e., essentially active or productive] intellect," which acts on the phantasms in a way that produces "intelligible species," which constitute the primary contents of the mind, stored in "possible [i.e., essentially receptive] intellect."[36]

The likenesses that are identified as sensory species and phantasms may be literally "likenesses": images – realizations of the material forms (colors, sounds, textures, etc.) of external objects in different matter, the matter of the external/internal sensory apparatus of the human body.[37] And, in keeping with the formal-identity theory, the sensory species, at least, are likenesses that lose none of the detail present in the external senses themselves (which, of course, vary in sensitivity among individuals and from one time to another in the same individual):[38] "A sense organ is affected by a sense-perceptible thing, because to sense is to undergo something. For that reason the sense-perceptible thing, which is the agent [in sensation], makes the organ be actually as the sense-perceptible thing is, since the organ is in a state of potentiality to this [result]" (In DA II.23.547). The likeness essential to sensory cognition, then, in no way compromises direct realism; at this level the relationship is causal, rather than representational in a distinctive, stronger sense.[39]

It is natural for us to have cognition of complex, hylomorphic things, Aquinas thinks,

in virtue of the fact that our soul, through which we have cognition, is the form of some matter [i.e., is itself a component in a hylomorphic composite]. But the soul has two cognitive powers. One is the act of a corporeal organ, and it is natural for it to have cognition of things as they exist in individuating matter, which is why sense has cognition of individuals only. But the soul's other cognitive power is intellect, which is not the act of any corporeal organ. And so through intellect it is natural for us to have cognition of natures. Natures, of course, do not have existence except in individuating matter.[40] It is natural for us to have cognition of them, however, not as they are in individuating matter but as they are abstracted from it by intellect's consideration. Thus in intellection we can have cognition of such things in universality, which is beyond the faculty of sense.   (ST Ia.12.4c).

It is easy to read this account as if it left intellective cognition quite detached from extra-mental reality, but, as we will see, intellect, too, has access to individuals.

Phantasms are likenesses of particular material things re-realized in physical configurations of the organ of phantasia, which Aquinas located in the brain.[41] Although the forms presented in the phantasms have been stripped of their original matter, the phantasm-likeness is particularized by its details, the external object's original individuating matter being "represented" by features of the phantasm. Phantasms themselves, then, are not proper objects of intellective cognition, although they are indispensable to it.

Intellect can have cognition of the natures of corporeal things, which are among its proper objects, only after it performs an abstraction whose raw material is phantasms and whose product is "intelligible species."[42] Aquinas sees this abstraction of the universal from its particular(s) as required by an Aristotelian principle he accepts: "Things have to do with intellect to the extent to which they can be separated from matter" (De anima III 4, 429b21); and the extent to which phantasia's phantasms are separated from the external object's original matter by no means exhausts our capacity for abstraction. But, of course, nothing could provide intellective cognition of the nature of a *material* thing unless, even in the degree of abstraction appropriate to intellection, it included the abstracted *concept* of the thing's material component.[43] So, since the real complex substances outside the mind are themselves concrete hylomorphic individuals, to have cognition that depends on "abstracting the form from the individuating matter, which the phantasms represent, is to have cognition of that which is in individuating matter, but not *as* it is in such matter" (ST Ia.85.1c).[44]

Nevertheless, abstraction does not entail any decrease in veridicality:

if we consider a color and its characteristics without at all considering the apple that has the color, or even [if we] express verbally what we have intellective cognition of in that way, there will be no falsity of opinion or of speech. For the apple has no part in the nature (ratio) of the color, and so nothing prevents our having intellective cognition of the color without any such cognition of the apple. . . . For there is no falsity in the fact that the intellect's way of having intellective cognition [of a thing] is different from the thing's way of existing.   (ST Ia.85.1, ad 1)[45]

Just as the apple's color can be cognitively considered veridically independent of any consideration of the apple, so

> those things that pertain to the specific nature (*ratio speciei*) of any material thing – a stone, a man, a horse – can be [veridically] considered without the individuating principles that have no part in the specific nature. And that is what abstracting the universal from a particular, or the intelligible species from phantasms, amounts to – viz., considering the specific nature (*natura speciei*) without considering the individuating principles that are represented by phantasms. (ibid.).[46]

The intelligible species are purely conceptual, noneidetic, thoroughly abstract entities occurring only in possible intellect – like one's *concept* of triangularity or one's *understanding* of the Pythagorean theorem rather than like even abstract geometric imagery.[47]

It is important to see that these intelligible species themselves are not proper objects of intellective cognition any more than phantasms are; direct realism could hardly be sustained if either of those entities internal to the human being were identified as a proper object of ordinary, non-reflexive cognition. Aquinas does recognize, however, that intelligible species serve as the immediate objects of a kind of abstract thinking he seems to call "considering":[48] "Our intellect both abstracts intelligible species *from* phantasms, insofar as it considers the natures of things universally, and yet also has intellective cognition of them [i.e., those natures] *in* the phantasms, since without attending to the phantasms it cannot have intellective cognition of even those things whose [intelligible] species it abstracts" (ST Ia.85.1, ad 5). In tandem with phantasms, intelligible species are intellect's means of access to the proper objects of intellective cognition.[49] And intellect's proper objects include the corporeal natures themselves, which exist only outside the mind, in material individuals.[50]

The abstractedness, the universality, of intelligible species may suggest that for Aquinas intellective cognition takes place in an ivory tower, walled off from concern with or even access to real concrete particulars. And his talk of intellect's need to "attend to" the phantasms in order to have any cognition at all may sound like enjoining intellect to look out the window occasionally, to get in touch with reality.[51] But his identification of this proper object of intellection as "the quiddity or nature *existing in corporeal mat-*

ter"[52] shows that although abstraction does remove the nature from the particularizing circumstances that still accompany it in the phantasm, and although certain sorts of abstract thinking are performed on it only in that stripped-down condition, still, using the intelligible species in intellective cognition of the external world requires examining the corporeal nature in its natural setting. Attending to the phantasms, then, is not something intellect has to do over and over again, but is, rather, its essential cognitive *orientation*. A physicist can't *understand* heat without abstracting its nature from individuating conditions, but neither can she understand *heat* without being aware that what she has acquired understanding of is a feature of external, individuated, corporeal matter. As for actual individual instances, can anyone have intellective cognition of this very heat in this particular glowing coal? Yes and no. The uniquely individuated heat now emanating from it can be an object only of sensory cognition, but intellect can know an individual *through* its nature, can know that what is being felt here and now is intense *heat*, that what is being seen here and now is *red-orange*, and so on. Only sense (assisted by "the memorative power," an internal sense) can recognize Socrates, but only intellect (orientated via phantasms) can describe him.[53]

VII. INTELLECT – ITS OBJECTS, OPERATIONS, AND RANGE

The proper object of intellect under consideration here Aquinas sometimes designates by terms more technical than "nature" – most importantly, "what-it-is-to-be-such-a-thing" (*quod quid est*, his vesion of Aristotle's *to ti esti*) and the closely related "quiddity" (or whatness) of a thing.[54] Understandably, he counts intellect's cognition of its proper object as the *first* operation of intellect even though, as we've seen, agent intellect's abstracting of intelligible species is a necessary precondition of the cognition of the quiddities of things.[55]

Apparently, then, intellect's "first operation" consists in the formation (by agent intellect in possible intellect) of concepts of external objects – just what might have been expected. But since the proper objects of the first operation are identified as the quiddities, the essential natures, of things, this account is especially liable to misinterpretation. For the science of nature, no matter how highly developed, also has the quiddities of things as its objects, and Aquinas is under no illusions about the difficulty of achieving scientific knowledge.[56] His account of intellect's first operation depends on our recognizing that a child's first acquisition of the concept of a star differs only in degree from the most recondite advance in astronomy's understanding of the nature of a star.[57] Quiddities, the proper objects of intellect's first operation *and*, in just the same respect, the objects of the culminating cognition of nature may helpfully be thought of, then, as proper objects of both inchoate and culminating (alpha and omega) intellective cognition.

Aquinas's account is open to misinterpretation here in part because of an ambiguity in his characterizations of the first operation.[58] Sometimes he describes it in terms of the proper object in general, leading one to think of it simply as any cognition of quiddities, deserving the designation "first" in virtue of the primacy of its object. In this sense "the first operation" covers the whole range of the cognition of quiddities, from alpha to omega and from abstract consideration to concrete cognition. But Aquinas also describes the first operation in terms of only the initial stage of the cognition of quiddities, the first acquisition (and not also the deepening and refining) of the answer to "What's that?," the pre-theoretic alpha cognition. This narrower description of the first operation provides a clear contrast with his standard description of intellect's "*second* operation" as the making of (affirmative and negative) judgments, affirming by propositionally "compounding" with each other concepts acquired in the first operation, denying by "dividing" them from each other. But at every stage past initial acquisition, the cognition of quiddities will partially depend on this second operation, and on reasoning as well:[59] "the human intellect does not immediately, in its first apprehension, acquire a complete cognition of the thing. Instead, it first apprehends *something* about it – viz., its quiddity, which is a first and proper object of intellect; and *then* it acquires intellective cognition of the properties, accidents, and dispositions associated with the thing's essence. In doing so it has to compound one apprehended aspect with, or divide one from, another and proceed from one composition or division to another, which is reasoning" (ST Ia.85.5c).[60] The resultant full-blown intellective cognition may be either theoretical or applied.

Philosophy of mind is obviously relevant to epistemology in its account of intellect and just as obviously relevant to ethics in its account of will. Aquinas's epistemology is found mostly within his account of intellect, especially in the part he devotes to acts of intellect.[61] He was far more concerned with moral than with epistemological issues, however, and his ethics is so fully developed that he integrates his extended, systematic treatment of acts of will into it rather than including it in his philosophy of mind.[62] For that reason this chapter has less to say about Aquinas's theory of will than about his theory of intellect.

As a faculty of terrestrial creatures, will, the other faculty of the rational soul, is as distinctively human as intellect and is, Aquinas argues, a necessary concomitant of intellect.[63] But will's metaphysical provenance is much more primitive than intellect's and utterly universal. Absolutely every form, Aquinas maintains, has some sort of tendency or *inclination* essentially associated with it: "on the basis of its form, fire, for instance, is inclined toward a higher place, and toward generating its like" (ST Ia.80.1c); and so every hylomorphic thing, even if inanimate, has at least one natural inclination.

Inclination is the genus of appetite. Animate things that lack cognitive faculties, and even inanimate things, have necessitated, one-track inclinations, sometimes called "natural appetites" (for example, gravitational attraction). Living beings with merely nutritive souls have no cognition at all, but they do have natural appetites beyond those associated with inanimate bodies (such as phototropism in green plants). At the level of animal life there is sensory cognition, and with cognition come accidental goals, dependent on what happens to be presented to the animal's senses as desirable, or good for it: "an animal can seek (*appetere*) things it apprehends, not only the things it is inclined toward on the basis of its natural form" (ST Ia.80.1c). It has not only natural but also *sensory* appetite, which Aquinas often calls "sensuality," "the appetite that *follows* sensory cognition" naturally (ST Ia.81.1c).

Appetite is the genus of will. The human soul of course involves natural appetites (for instance, for food of *some* sort), but its sensory and intellective modes of cognition bring with them sensory appetites, or passions (such as, for food of *this* sort) and *rational* appetite, or volition (for food low in cholesterol, for instance).[64]

IX. SENSUALITY AND RATIONAL CONTROL

The appetitive power associated with sensory cognition is one we share with nonhuman animals – a cluster of inclinations (passions) to which we are subject (passive) by nature. In twentieth-century English we would probably label them instincts, urges, drives, emotions. Aquinas, following an Aristotelian line, thinks of sensuality as sorted into two complementary appetites or powers: the *concupiscible* – the inclination to seek the suitable and flee the harmful (pursuit/avoidance instincts) – and the *irascible* – the inclination to resist and overcome whatever deters one's access to the suitable or promotes the harmful (competition/aggression/defense instincts). Distinct sets of passions (or emotions) are associated with each of these powers: with concupiscible: joy and sadness, love and hate, desire and repugnance; with irascible: daring and fear, hope and despair, anger.[65]

For philosophy of mind and for ethics, the important issue is the manner and extent of the rational faculties' control of sensuality, a control without which the unity of the human soul is threatened and Aquinas's virtue-centered morality is impossible. We can see that will exercises some control of the relevant sort, because a human being, as long as he or she is not aberrantly behaving like a nonrational animal, "is not immediately moved in accordance with the irascible and concupiscible appetite but waits for the command of will, which is the higher appetite" (ST Ia.81.3c). The kind of control exercised by a *cognitive* rational faculty (standardly identified in this role as practical reason, strictly speaking, rather than intellect), is less obvious and particularly interesting in view of Aquinas's account of intellective cognition. Some aspects of the sensory soul are beyond reason's control. Since reason itself has no control over the presence or absence of external things, it cannot completely control the external senses, at least as regards initial sensations. On the other hand, sensuality and the internal senses are not immediately dependent on external things, "and so they are subject to reason's command" (ST Ia.81.3, ad 3). As anyone can find out by introspection, passions can be stirred up or calmed down by applying certain intellectively cognized universal considerations to the particular occasions or objects of the passions, and reason exercises just that sort of control. But because to do so reason must deal with sensory faculties, its medium of control is phantasms, which it manipulates and even creates by controlling the imaginative power.[66] Broadly speaking, then, rational control reverses the flow chart associated with intellective cognition.

Morality would be a lot easier than it is if that were the whole story, but, as everyone knows, passions are rebellious. Elaborating an Aristotelian theme (*Politics* I 2), Aquinas observes that the soul's rule over the (normal) body is "despotic": in a normal body, any bodily part that can be moved by an act of will is moved immediately when and as will commands. By contrast, the rational faculties rule sensuality "politically." The powers and passions that are the intended subjects of this rational governance are also moved by imagination and sense, and so are no slaves to reason. "That is why we experience the irascible or the concupiscible fighting against reason when we sense or imagine something pleasant that reason forbids, or something unpleasant that reason commands" (ST Ia.81.3, ad 2).

X. VOLITION AND CHOICE, NECESSITATION AND FREEDOM

Like every other form, the substantial form of the human being has an essential inclination. Rational animals seek their well-being, or happiness (*beatitudo*), as naturally and necessarily as flames rise up. And so, Aquinas maintains, will necessarily seeks happiness. The moral implications of that claim and his reasons for making it are not at issue here, nor can his account of human freedom be thoroughly examined here; but we must consider their relevance to his conceptions of will and of the relationship between will and intellect.[67]

In an attempt to inject some precision into his account of the relationship between necessitation and volition, Aquinas distinguishes four kinds of necessitation corresponding to the Aristotelian causes, acknowledging that one kind, but *only* one kind, is entirely incompatible with volition – the necessitation of *coercion* (corresponding to efficient causation) or "violence, which is contrary to the thing's inclination." And since coercion is the only sort of necessitation entirely absent from will's orientation toward happiness, any appearance of incompatibility between that natural human inclination and the exercise of genuine volition by human beings can in theory by explained away (ST Ia.82.1c). But since Aquinas takes the familiar view that "we are in control of our actions to the extent to which we can choose this one or that one," he follows Aristotle in acknowledging that our "seeking the ultimate end is not one of the things we are in control of" (ST Ia.82.1, ad 3).[68] Moreover, since our happiness is the naturally necessitated ultimate end, considerations of it govern all volition, as intellect's grasp of necessary first principles governs all cognition.[69] Our only choices concern ways and means of achieving our happiness, since "there are *particular* goods that do not have a *necessary* connection with happiness" (ST Ia.82.2c); but when we do choose, we always choose what strikes us as somehow contributing to our happiness.

Do we, then, make *free* choices? *Are* we really in control of our actions? Aquinas answers those questions affirmatively and emphatically: "The very fact that the human being is rational necessitates its being characterized by free decision (*liberum arbitrium*)" (ST Ia.83.1c).[70] And yet there are grounds for uncertainty about his understanding of human freedom, among which is an apparent change in his distinction between sensuality and will.

As we have seen, sense apprehends particulars and intellect apprehends universals, but that difference between the two modes of human cognition seems offhand not to mark a significant difference between their associated appetitive faculties, sensuality and will. Many would base the distinction between them on the perception that will, unlike sensuality, is characterized by self-determination. As Aquinas himself says, rather early in his career, "Will is distinguished from sensory appetite not directly on the basis of following the one sort of apprehension or the other but rather on the basis of determining its own inclination or having its inclination determined by something else" (QDV 22.4, ad 1). Later, however, Aquinas appears to drop self-determination as the differentia, with the result that his more mature theory of will can look like a version of compatibilism, acceptive of will's being other-determined: "An appetitive power is a passive power that is naturally suited to be moved by what is apprehended" (ST Ia.80.2c), and "intellectively cognized good moves will" (ST Ia.82.3, ad 2). He explains that an apprehended thing that moves an appetitive power is "an unmoved mover" (because it moves by *final* causation), while the appetitive power it moves (will, let's say) is "a moved mover" – for example, will, *moved* by the intellectively apprehended good thing, *moves* the person toward it.[71] And in that same context his only explicit basis for distinguishing between the sensory and rational appetites is, indeed, just the difference between their objects of apprehension.[72]

Aquinas's apparent abandonment of self-determination as the differentia of will is a significant change, but it does not bring determinism or compatibilism with it. The pertinent difference between sensory and intellective apprehension is that sense, as cognizant of particulars only, presents sensuality with one object, which moves it "determinately"; rational cognition, on the other hand, cognizant of universals, "gathers several things together," thus presenting will with an array of particular goods of one sort, "and so the intellective appetite, will, can be moved by many things and not [just] by one, necessitatedly" (ST Ia.82.2, ad 3).[73] Moreover, since what intellect apprehends as good it presents to will as an *end* (subordinate to happiness), moving will only in the manner of a *final* cause, intellect does *not* coerce will's choice. Will, on the other hand, naturally orientated toward what is good for a human being, "moves intellect and all the powers of the soul" *coercively*, in the manner of an *efficient* cause, just as "a king who aims at the whole kingdom's common good moves the various governors of the provinces by his command" (ST Ia.82.4c).

So will's choice regarding particular goods collectively presented to it by intellect is free in a sense Aquinas takes to be both necessary and sufficient for his theoretical and practical purposes, and its freedom is greatly enhanced by its coercive power over intellect, enabling it to direct intellect's attention to other things or to other aspects of the object intellect presents to it. But the fact that Aquinas's account of choice presents choice as essentially and extensively involving the cognitive as well as the appetitive faculty of the rational soul leads him to ascribe choice to both reason and will in different respects: "the act [of choice] by which will tends toward something proposed [to it by reason] as good is *materially* an act of will but *formally* an act of reason because it is directed toward its end by reason" (ST IaIIae.13.1c). Because "choice is completed in a kind of movement of the soul toward the good that is chosen," and because will is the agent of movement of that kind, choice "is clearly an act of the appetitive power" (ibid.).

NOTES

1 Aquinas bases his philosophy of mind on Aristotle's, of which T. H. Irwin provides an excellent, concise, critical account in Irwin 1991.

2 In Aquinas's relatively infrequent use of "mind" it is typically a synonym for "intellect" (*intellectus*), which is his name for just the *cognitive* faculty distinctive of the rational soul and not also its distinctive *appetitive* faculty, will. See, e.g., ST Ia.75.2c, where he says that this principle (or source, or faculty) of cognition "is called mind, or intellect." But, like most other philosophers, he sometimes also uses these terms very broadly – e.g. "the human soul, which is called intellect, or mind" (ibid.). Compare n. 8 below.

3 See Wippel's Chapter 4, this volume.

4 In this respect he differs significantly from many of his medieval predecessors and contemporaries, who were *universal* hylomorphists, analyzing *all* creatures as composites of form and matter, at the expense of accepting spiritual matter and the doctrine of the plurality of substantial forms. These issues and many others relevant to the subjects of this chapter are explained in well-documented discussions in Pegis 1983.

5 Notice that he intends his claim to cover only terrestrial, biologically living beings, those "that live among us," not every being that can be said to be living – such as God or angels. And he must intend to emphasize the "in" when he describes soul as the first principle of life in terrestrial beings, since he of course takes God to be unconditionally (and extrinsically) the first principle of life for creatures.

6 *Actus* is an important technical term for Aquinas and other medieval philosophers. It means both action and actuality, in a way that may be clarified by such observations as these: A thing *acts* only if and only to the extent to which it *actually* and not just potentially exists and is a thing of such and such a sort. Consequently, whatever it is in virtue of which the thing acts in a certain way = that in virtue of which it actually is a thing of that certain (appropriate) sort. Therefore, that in virtue of which *primarily* the thing acts (the primary intrinsic source or first principle of its characteristic action) = *the substantial form* of the thing. Compare ST Ia.76.1c and n. 7 below.

7. Among Aquinas's statements of opposition to the doctrine of the plurality of substantial forms, this one is perhaps his fullest succinct presentation: "The difference between a substantial form and an accidental form

is that an accidental form does not bring about an actual being considered absolutely (*non facit ens actu simpliciter*), but rather its being actually *such*, or *so much* – for example, large, white, or something else of that sort – while a substantial form does bring about an actual being considered absolutely. That is why an accidental form comes to a subject that is already an actual being, while a substantial form comes not to a subject that is already an actual being but to one that is so only potentially – viz., to prime matter. It is clear on this basis that it is impossible for there to be more than one substantial form of one thing, since the first [such form] would bring about the thing's being actual considered absolutely, and all the others would come to a subject that is already actual: for they would not bring about its actual being considered absolutely but [only its being] in a certain respect" (In DA II.1.224). For his application of this position to the case of the human soul in particular, see, e.g., ST Ia.76.3, 76.4, 77.6.

8 Many of Aquinas's 643 uses of the term *anima rationalis* occur in discussions of the distinctively rational faculties of intellect and will, but he also often uses that designation for the human soul in *all* its aspects. (The precise number of these uses, like countless other details regarding Aquinas's writings, is available in the multivolume Busa 1974–80, a staggeringly impressive resource for research in Aquinas. Each of the 643 entries under "**anima** + rationalis," for instance, consists in a quoted passage, supplying enough context to enable the reader to identify the nature of the discussion.)

9 Of course a human being's soul is the principle of such vital activities as the person's nutrition and sensation, too, but it is in its role as the principle of intellection (and volition) that we recognize it as "the soul of a *human* being," and it is in that respect that Aquinas needs to consider the soul in order to construct his argument for incorporeal subsistence.

10 The natures of corporeal things are not the only objects proper to intellective cognition, among which Aquinas also includes, for instance, mathematical entities. But corporeal natures constitute the overwhelming majority of intellect's proper objects, and for purposes of this discussion it is convenient to focus exclusively on them. Their importance is reflected in the fact that Aquinas develops his most detailed account of intellection in connection with the cognition of corporeal natures.

11 For Aquinas's arguments supporting claim (A) see, e.g., ST Ia.84.

12 Cf. ST Ia.75.1, ad 2. Aquinas's favorite example in support of (B) is the pupil of the eye, which lacks all color. But the pupil of the eye as the organ of vision is receptive of shapes as well as of colors, despite its having a precise shape. Similarly, the skin neither lacks texture nor is

insensitive to its own texture, and yet textures are among its proper objects.

13 Aquinas says that such a person will be unable to taste anything sweet; everything will taste bitter to her. Shouldn't he have said that she will be unable to taste anything *bitter?* or that things that taste bitter to people whose tongues are functioning normally will be *tasteless* (sensorily uncognizable) to her? Developing the example along that line seems not only more accurate but also more precisely supportive of the point he wants to make. (As for sweet things, it seems he ought to have said that they might taste at least *differently* bitter to the subject.)

14 Although there is a sense in which bodies are objects of intellective cognition, it is important to notice that its *immediate, proper* objects are not bodies themselves but "the *natures* of bodies" or, as Aquinas often puts it, their *quiddities* (or essences) (see, e.g., ST Ia.84.7c). As the proper objects of intellect, these natures or quiddities of bodies must be *abstracted* from the data supplied by the senses. Corporeal (material) organs are, simply in virtue of their materiality, receptors of material data only and so restricted to particular material objects. Materiality itself, in the faculty or in its objects, is an obstacle to intellective cognition. See, e.g., DEE 4; SCG II.51.

15 ST Ia.87.1c; see also 87.2–4. Aquinas insists that philosophy of mind must stem from a consideration of what we have direct access to, the activity of intellection: we have universal cognition of our intellect "insofar as we consider the nature of the human mind on the basis of intellect's *activity*" (ibid.).

16 Cf. the parallel discussion in In DA III.7.680 ff.: "our intellect is naturally suited to have intellective cognition of all sense objects . . . [I]t is capable of cognizing not only one kind of sense objects (like sight or hearing), or only one kind of common or proper accidental sensible qualities, but, instead, universally, of [cognizing] sensible nature entirely. Thus, just as sight is devoid of a certain kind of sense object, so intellect must be devoid of sensible nature entirely."

17 The plausibility of this argument for the human soul's status as a subsistent entity obviously depends on the strength of the claim that in its distinctive operation it must act altogether independently. In this argument Aquinas, following Aristotle's lead (*De anima* III 4, 429a24–27), claims only its independence from corporeal things, leaving open the theoretical possibility that it might be operationally dependent on some *spiritual* creature other than itself. Avicenna and Averroes had put forward different theories of the human soul that presented it as dependent in just that way. Aquinas's many attacks on their theories

were motivated expressly by various other considerations, but a defense of his argument for subsistence alone could have called for their refutation. (For Avicenna's and Averroes's theories and Aquinas's attacks on them, see, e.g., SCG II.59–62, 73, 75, 78; ST Ia.76.2; QDSC 9, 10; QDA 3; DUI *passim*.) Their position, sometimes called "monopsychism," was one thesis of the "Latin Averroism" Aquinas argued against; on the controversy generally see Van Steenberghen 1980b. See also MacDonald's Chapter 6 (this volume), Section VII.

18 For Aquinas's arguments for the incorruptibility of the human soul, see, e.g., SCG II.79–81; QQ 10.3.2; ST Ia.75.2, 6; QDA 14. Herbert McCabe helpfully relates the issue of immortality to the rest of Aquinas's philosophy of mind in McCabe 1969, where he presents an exposition of the argument developed in ST and QDA.

19 Aquinas often argues expressly against what he takes to be Plato's conception of the human being. See, e.g., DEE 2; SCG II.57; QDA 1; ST Ia.75.4; QDSC 2.

20 For example, In Sent II.1.2.4, 17.2.1; SCG II.56–59, 68–70; QDP 3.9, 3.11; ST Ia.76.1; QDSC 2; QDA 1, 2, 14; DUI 3; In DA III.7.; CT 80, 87.

21 The Objections in QDA 1 may be sorted into, first, the "If (E), not (F)" type, which includes Objs. 1, 3–7, 9, and 10. The second type concludes "If (F), not (E)" and includes only Obj. 12; the third concludes, more broadly, "Not both (E) and (F)" and includes Objs. 2, 8, and 18. So these first three types are all arguments for the incompatibility of (E) and (F), without clearly favoring either as the account of the soul; but the remaining Objections do seem to be affirming or denying (E) or (F) in one way or another. The fourth type concludes "Not (E)": Obj. 11; the fifth, "Not (F)": Obj. 15. The sixth, a stronger form of the first type, concludes "Since (E), not (F)" or uses (E) as a premiss to conclude "Not (F)" and so might be characterized as Platonist; it includes Objs. 13, 14, 16, and 17. But the two "Contrary Arguments" (*sed contra*) immediately following the Objections are designed to show that there are, nevertheless, compelling reasons for thinking that the truth must be (E) *and* (F). The first of them argues along this line. A thing belongs to a certain species in virtue of the thing's "proper form," and a thing belongs to the human species in virtue of its rational soul, so, (F) the rational soul is the proper form of a human being. But intellective cognition is the specifying activity of the rational soul, and it is carried out by the human soul *on its own*. And whatever operates entirely on its own must be an entity that subsists on its own. So, (E) the human soul is a subsistent entity. Therefore, (E) and (F).

22 ST Ia.75.2, ad 1, presents a weaker, less detailed version of this argument.

23 Compare the more detailed parallel argument in QDSC 2.

24 For a sophisticated but accessible exposition and appraisal of this part of

Aquinas's philosophy of mind, see Kenny 1980a, Chapter 3, "Mind" (pp. 61–81).

25 See, e.g., ST Ia.2–26 on God's existence and nature, and 44–46 on God's production of creatures.

26 See also ST IaIIae.31.6c; IIIa.11.2, ad 3.

27 See also ST Ia.91.3, ad 3; In DA II.6.301; QDM 5.5; QDA 8.

28 See, e.g., ST Ia.3.1, ad 2; 93.2c; 93.6c.

29 Furthermore, the beatific vision, the transcendent culmination of cognition and the creator's intended perfection of human existence, is defined as an act of the perfected human *intellect*, released from its terrestrial dependence on the senses (see, e.g., ST Ia.12, esp. 12.1; IaIIae.3.8c; Suppl. 92.1c [In Sent IV.49.2.1]; SCG III.51).

30 I use "think and understand" here to translate *intelligere*, which I translate more often as "have intellective cognition"; and I use "to acquiring organized knowledge" here to translate *ad sciendum*.

31 "[J]ust as *true* is intellect's *good*, so *false* is what is *bad* for it, as is said in *Ethics* VI [2, 1139a27–31]" (ST Ia.94.4c); see also In PH I.3.7; In NE VI.2.1130; In M VI.4.1231; ST IIaIIae.60.4, ad 2. I discuss the epistemological implications of this "theistic reliabilism" in Kretzmann 1992. See also Jenkins 1991.

32 See Geach's stimulating account of this direct realism in Anscombe and Geach 1961.

33 Aquinas finds this principle in Aristotle, *Metaphysics* I 1 and *Posterior Analytics* II 19, 100a3–14; cf. ST Ia.84.6, s.c.

34 Although sensory species themselves are realized in the anatomical matter of the percipient's sensory apparatus, the internalization process of sensory cognition detaches the corresponding sense-perceptible aspects of external things from their *original* matter: "a form perceptible by sense is in the thing outside the soul in one way, and it is in another way in the soul, which takes up the forms of sense-perceptible things without the matter – e.g., the color of gold without the gold" (ST Ia.84.1c). On the internal senses see, e.g., ST Ia.78.4.

35 Aquinas sometimes uses the Latin word *imaginatio* for this faculty, but he seems to prefer Aristotle's Greek word *phantasia*, at least when he is discussing cognition. Since the internal sense in question is in several respects more broadly conceived than imagination as we tend to think of imagination, it seems better to follow Aquinas's lead and retain the foreign word as a technical term. For Aquinas's account of phantasia, see, e.g., ST Ia.84.6; 84.7; 85.1, s.c. & ad 3; 85.2, ad 3; SCG II.80 & 81.1618. The Aristotelian source of the producing and preserving role for phantasia is *De anima* III 3, 427a16–429a9; see Aquinas's commentary (In DA) *ad loc.*

36 On this distinction of intellective powers, see, e.g., QDV 10.6c: "[W]hen

our mind is considered in relation to sense-perceptible things that exist outside the soul, it is found to be related to them in two ways. [1] It is related to them in one way as *actuality to potentiality* – insofar as things outside the soul are potentially intelligible and the mind itself is actually intelligible. It is in *this* respect that we say that in the mind there is *agent* intellect, which makes things actually intelligible. [2] It is related to them in the other way as *potentiality to actuality* – insofar as the determinate forms of things, which exist actually in things outside the soul, are in our mind only potentially. It is in *this* respect that we say that in our soul there is *possible* intellect, which has the function of receiving the forms abstracted from sense-perceptible things and made actually intelligible by the light of agent intellect." Also QDV 10.6, ad 7: "In the reception in which possible intellect acquires [abstracted, intelligible] species of things from phantasms, the phantasms play the role of a secondary, instrumental agent, while agent intellect plays the role of the primary, principal agent. And so the effect of the action is left in possible intellect in accordance with the condition of both agents and not in accordance with the condition of one or the other alone. That is why possible intellect receives forms as *actually intelligible* in virtue of *agent intellect*, but as *likenesses of determinate things* on the basis of a cognition of the *phantasms*. And so the actually intelligible forms exist neither in themselves, nor in phantasia, nor in agent intellect, but only in possible intellect."

37 Although Aquinas expresses himself in ways that at least permit the interpretation of the sensory species as literally images (visual, aural, etc.), an interpretation of them as encodings of some sort, involving no iconic resemblance, is also possible and seems not only more plausible but also in some respects better suited to his account generally.

38 Full-fledged formal identity and its consequent veridicality do not extend to phantasia (and its phantasms), because it is not purely passive, even though it is classified as an internal *sense:* "Two operations are found in the sensory part of the soul. One occurs only by way of a change effected in it, and the operation of sense in this respect is completed by having a change effected in it by a sense-perceptible thing. The other operation is *formation*, which occurs when the *imaginative* power [phantasia] *forms for itself* an image (*idolum*) of a thing that is absent, or even of a thing that has never been seen" (ST Ia.85.2, ad 3). The discussion in this chapter ignores difficulties associated with nonveridical phantasms.

39 Of course, effects are by their very nature potentially representative of their causes. Sense itself has no cognition of the nature of the relationship or the degree of conformity between sensory species and external

objects: "For although sight has the likeness of the visible thing, it has no cognition of the relationship there is between the thing seen and the sense's apprehension of it" (ST Ia.16.2c).

40 Aquinas takes this to be the single, most important respect in which Aristotelianism differs from Platonism and alludes to it very often; hence the "of course."

41 See, e.g., In M V.14.693. Kenny 1969 is helpful in sorting out these matters.

42 See, e.g., ST Ia.13.9c; 57.1, ad 3; 57.2, ad 1; and esp. 85.1 *passim.*

43 "Natural entities, however, are intellectively cognized on the basis of abstraction from individuating matter," representations of which are components of phantasms, "but not from sense-perceptible matter entirely. For a human being is intellectively cognized as composed of flesh and bones, but on the basis of an abstraction from *this* flesh and *these* bones. And that is why it is not intellect, but sense, or imagination, that has *direct* cognition of individuals" (In DA III.8.716).

44 See also, e.g., ST Ia.85.1, s.c.; In BDT 5; 6; and esp. In DA III.8.716, quoted in n. 43 above.

45 See also, e.g., ST Ia.13.12c, 50.2c; In DDN 7.3.724: "all cognition is in accord with the mode [of existence and operation] of that by which something is cognized."

46 See also, e.g., In DA III.8.717, 10.731.

47 Intelligible species may be either *concepts* (of) or *thoughts* (that). See, e.g., ST IaIIae.55.1c. On the non-eidetic character of intelligible species, see, e.g., ST Ia.85.1, ad 3: "But by the power of agent intellect a kind of likeness results in possible intellect as a result of agent intellect's converting [i.e., abstracting] operation on the phantasms. This likeness [the intelligible species] is indeed representative of the things of which those are the phantasms, but *representative of them only as regards their specific nature.* And it is in *this* way that intelligible species are said to be abstracted from phantasms, *not* in such a way that some form, numerically one and the same as the form that was in the phantasms before, occurs in possible intellect later (as a physical object is taken from one place and carried to another)."

48 Notice the prominence of the verb "consider" in the two passages quoted just above. On "consideration" (*consideratio*) see ST IIaIIae.53.4, 180.4.

49 See, e.g., ST Ia.85.2c & ad 2.

50 Aquinas thinks this feature of intellective cognition is apparent even etymologically: "The name 'intellect' derives from the fact that it has cognition of the *intimate* characteristics of a thing; for '*intelligere*' [to have intellective cognition] is by way of saying '*intus legere*' [to read penetratingly]. Sense and imagination have cognition of external acci-

dents only; intellect alone succeeds in reaching a thing's essence" (QDV 1.12c).

51 The Latin is *convertere se ad*, with the easily misinterpreted literal sense of "turn itself back toward," "turn around to." That literal sense has a kind of diagrammatic correctness, if we think of a flow chart for the transmission of data from external senses through phantasia to intellect; but it also suggests an effortful deviation on intellect's part, and that is precisely wrong.

Aquinas's insistent claim that "when our intellect has intellective cognition it must always attend to phantasms" (ST Ia.84.7c) is easily misinterpreted. His principal theoretical evidence for it is brought out, I think, in his many observations that (a) intellect can *consider* only abstract universal natures, but (b) universal natures as the proper objects of intellective *cognition* exist only in corporeal particulars, and (c) corporeal particulars are *presented* to intellect only in phantasms. See, e.g., ST Ia.84.7c and n. 53 below. This evidence is obscured if the two observations he presents near the beginning of ST Ia.84.7c as readily accessible indications (*indices*) of intellect's dependence on phantasms are given the implausible status of Aquinas's "two proofs of this thesis" (Kenny 1969, p. 289).

52 ST Ia.84.7c; see also, e.g., 84.8c, 85.1c, 85.5c & ad 3, 85.6c, 85.8c, 86.2c, 87.3c, 88.1c, and 88.3c.

53 "Now it belongs to the essence (*ratio*) of this nature [i.e., this proper object of intellective cognition] that it exist in some individual, which is not without corporeal matter – e.g., it belongs to the essence of the nature of stone that it be in this [or that] stone, and to the essence of the nature of horse that it be in this [or that] horse, and so on. That is why the nature of stone, or of any material thing whatever, cannot be cognized completely and truly except insofar as it is cognized as existing in a particular. A particular, however, we apprehend through sense and imagination. And so in order for intellect to have actual intellective cognition of its proper object it is necessary that it attend to the phantasms so that it may observe (*speculetur*) the universal nature existing in the particular" (ST Ia.84.7c).

54 For some details on the terminology, see Kretzmann 1992. Aquinas offers some helpful introductory remarks in In DA III.8.705–706 and 712–713 : "the quiddities of things are other than the things only *per accidens*. For example, the quiddity of a white man is not the same as a white man, because the quiddity of a white man contains within itself only what pertains to the species *human being*, but what I call a white man has within itself more than what pertains to the human species. . . . [I]n connection with all things that have a form in matter the thing and

its what-it-is-to-be-such-a-thing are not entirely the same: Socrates is not his humanness. . . . [I]ntellect has cognition of both [the universal and the individual], but in different ways. For it has cognition of the nature of the species, or of what-it-is-to-be-such-a-thing, by directly extending itself into it; it has cognition of the individual itself, however, by a kind of reflection, insofar as it returns to the phantasms from which the intelligible species are abstracted."

55 See, e.g., In Sent I.19.5.7, ad 7.

56 See, e.g., In DA I.1.15: "the essential principles of things are unknown to us"; In Sym Ap, preface: "our cognition is so feeble that no philosopher has ever been able to investigate completely the nature of a fly"; also QDV 4.1, ad 8; 6.1, ad 8; 10.1c & ad 6; QDSC 11, ad 3; SCG I.3.18; ST IaIIae.8.1c; In PA I.4.43; II.13.533.

57 See, e.g., In DA III.8.718: "what intellect has cognition of is the quiddity that is in things. . . . For it is obvious that the sciences are about the things intellect has cognition of"; SCG III.56.2328: "The proper object of intellect is what-it-is-to-be-such-a-thing, the substance of a thing. . . . Therefore, whatever is in a thing that cannot be cognized through the cognition of its substance must be unknown to intellect."

58 Another source of misinterpretation is Aquinas's apparent claim of infallibility for intellection: "Intellection regarding the quiddity of a thing is always true, as is a sensation regarding its proper object"; see, e.g., ST Ia.58.5c, 85.6c; In PH I.2.20, 3.31. This issue, which has more to do with epistemology than with philosophy of mind, is considered at length in Kretzmann 1992. See also MacDonald's Chapter 6, herein.

59 Cf. Section VII of MacDonald's Chapter 6. As abstraction precedes the first operation, so reasoning, the use of the second operation's propositions in inferences, follows the second. In at least one place Aquinas expressly identifies reasoning (ratiocinatio) as the third operation – not of intellect, but of reason, which may sometimes be thought of as intellect in motion (In PA I.1.4). See also, e.g., In Joh 1.1.26; In Sent III.23.1.2.

60 See also, e.g., In Sent III.35.2.2ac; SCG III.58.2836; ST Ia.14.6c; 58.5c; 75.5c; 85.3c & ad 3; 85.4, ad 3.

61 See MacDonald's Chapter 6.

62 See McInerny's Chapter 7, this volume. In ST Aquinas's discussion of acts of intellect is concentrated in Ia.84–89, part of his treatise on the nature of a human being (Ia.75–102), while his discussion of acts of will, only adumbrated in Ia.82–83, constitutes a large and important part (IaIIae.6–21) of his extended treatment of morality (IaIIae and IIaIIae). In his QDA, one of the most important sources for his philosophy of mind, will is not discussed at all.

63 See, e.g., ST Ia.19.1c.

64 This introduction of Aquinas's concept of will is based mainly on ST Ia.80.1; for a similar account, different in some important respects, see the earlier QDV 22.4.

65 For an introduction to this material, see, e.g., ST Ia.81.2. Like other features of Aquinas's account of appetitive powers, his theory of the passions is developed as part of his treatise on ethics: ST IaIIae.22–48.

66 See, e.g., ST Ia.81.3, ad 3; and QDV 25.4c: "since one and the same thing can be considered under various conditions, being made [thereby] either attractive or repulsive, reason presents a thing to sensuality, by means of imagination, under the guise of the pleasurable or the painful, in accord with the way it seems to reason"; also QDV 25.4, ad 4 & ad 5.

67 For the moral implications, see McInerny's Chapter 7. Lonergan 1971 contains a very well-informed, stimulating study of Aquinas's account of human freedom; and for a very helpful discussion of relevant issues, see Stump 1990.

68 See *Nicomachean Ethics* III 3, 1111b 26–29; 6, 1113a15.

69 ST Ia.82.1c; 82.2c; following Aristotle, *Physics* II 9, 200a15–34.

70 Aquinas's standard term for choice in his analysis of human action (in ST IaIIae.6–17) is *electio*. When he discusses what seems closest to a twentieth-century conception of free choice, he uses the term *liberum arbitrium*. But for more than one reason it seems worth preserving the terminological difference by translating *arbitrium* in this context as "decision." See, e.g., ST Ia.83.3, ad 2: "Judgment (*iudicium*) is, so to speak, the conclusion and determination of deliberation. But deliberation is determined primarily, of course, by reason's pronouncement (*sententia*) and secondarily by appetite's acceptance [of that pronouncement]. That is why the Philosopher says in *Ethics* III[5, 1113a9–12] that 'judging on the basis of deliberation, we desire in accordance with deliberation'. And in this way choice (*electio*) itself is called a kind of judgment, on the basis of which it is named free decision (*liberum arbitrium*)." This assimilation of choice to judgment via decision is an indication of the intimate relationship between will and reason on which Aquinas's conception of freedom is based. See also n. 73 below.

71 In this connection Aquinas cites Aristotle: *De anima* III 10, 433a13–26; *Metaphysics* XII 7, 1072a26–30.

72 "Therefore, because what is apprehended by intellect is different in kind from what is apprehended by sense, it follows that the intellective appetite is a power different from the sensory appetite" (ST Ia.80.2c). Not all the difficulties in Aquinas's apparently evolving theory of will can be even mentioned in this chapter. His most complete, unified discussion of relevant topics is probably the single article of QDM 6.

73 See also ST IaIIae.17.1, ad 2: "The root of freedom considered as the

subject [of freedom] is will; considered as its *cause,* however, [the root of freedom] is reason. For will can be led (*ferri*) freely to various things just because reason can have various conceptions of what is good. And so philosophers define free decision (*liberum arbitrium*) as the free judgment of reason (*liberum de ratione iudicium*), as if [to indicate that] reason is freedom's cause."

I am grateful to Scott MacDonald and to my co-editor for helpful comments on an earlier draft of this chapter.

6 Theory of knowledge

Aquinas does not build his philosophical system around a theory of knowledge. In fact the reverse is true: he builds his epistemology on the basis provided by other parts of his system, in particular, his metaphysics and psychology. To examine what we can recognize as a distinct and systematic theory of knowledge, then, we need to extract his strictly epistemological claims from the metaphysical and psychological discussions in which they are embedded.[1]

I. COGNITION

Cognition is Aquinas's fundamental epistemic category. He endorses the Aristotelian view that the soul is potentially all things, and he holds that cognition involves its actually becoming a given thing or, as he sometimes puts it, its being assimilated to that thing in a certain way.[2] As Aquinas sees it, the development of this notion of cognition as the soul's assimilation to the objects cognized requires him to deal with two sorts of issues. First, he needs a metaphysical account of the two relata: the human soul and the object of human cognition. Here he draws primarily on his Aristotelian hylomorphism. On the one hand, the soul is the substantial form of the body, that by virtue of which human beings are substances with a characteristic form of life or set of potentialities that distinguishes them as a species.[3] The objects of cognition, on the other hand, are primarily the particular corporeal substances to which we have access through sense perception.[4] In accordance with his metaphysics, Aquinas explains that a cognizer is assimilated to an object of cognition when the form that is particularized in that object – such as a stone – comes to exist in the cognizer's soul.[5]

160

Second, Aquinas sees himself as needing to account for the soul's capacity for being assimilated to objects in this way. The account he provides is primarily psychological, identifying the sorts of powers the soul must possess and the processes it must engage in if cognitive assimilation of the kind he has identified is to be possible.[6] As animals, human beings possess a sensory cognitive power that gives them cognitive access to the particular corporeal substances and accidents that inhabit the external world. Moreover, if human beings are to cognize universals, they must have intellective cognitive powers by virtue of which they are able to transform the enmattered, particularized forms existing in sensible objects into what Aquinas calls intelligible species.[7] In intellective cognition the cognizer is assimilated to the object of cognition by being informed by the intelligible species of the object – that is, as a result of the object's form (which, insofar as it exists in the object, is particular and merely potentially intelligible) coming to exist in the intellective soul (a mode of existing in which the form is universal and actually intelligible).

This much of the psychological story of cognition provides a rudimentary account of how we can be cognitively assimilated to what Aquinas thinks of as the simple elements of reality, substances and their accidents. In intellective cognition we possess various substantial and accidental forms, what Aquinas calls the natures or quiddities of things, insofar as they are abstracted from their enmattered conditions in the particular corporeal substances with which we have sensory contact. But the simple elements in reality exist together in complexes – particular accidents inhere in particular substances – and so, if it is to be assimilated to reality, the soul must not only possess the forms of the simple elements of reality but also manipulate them to form complexes isomorphic with reality (subject-predicate propositions). On Aquinas's view, intellect is the power by virtue of which we can be assimilated in this way to reality, and by virtue of intellect's activity of understanding (*intellectus*) we can both grasp the natures of things and use them as constituents of propositions (Aquinas calls the latter activity compounding and dividing).[8]

Moreover, Aquinas holds that cognition is not restricted to the sort of intake of information made possible by sense perception and understanding. Human beings are also able to acquire cognition of new things by reasoning discursively on the basis of things already cognized. By virtue of its distinct activity of reasoning (*ratio, ratiocinatio*), intellect enables us to infer certain propositions from other propositions.[9]

Aquinas's strictly epistemological views are to be found within this broad metaphysically and psychologically oriented account of cognition. In accordance with this account, his epistemology breaks naturally into two parts: one dealing with the prior, data-gathering stage of the process, and one dealing with its latter, inferential stage. Aquinas subsumes the account of the data-gathering stage under his philosophical psychology, where he draws heavily on Aristotle's *De anima*.[10] He develops his account of the inferential stage as a part of his logic, following Aristotle's lead in *Posterior Analytics*.[11]

II. KNOWLEDGE

Cognition, Aquinas's basic epistemic concept, is clearly not itself knowledge, for he allows that we can have false cognition.[12] Moreover, he seems to allow not only that our relatively sophisticated conceptual and propositional assimilation of reality can constitute cognition but that our more primitive sorts of assimilation – our possession of raw sensory data, for example – can constitute cognition as well. On Aquinas's account, then, cognition is broader than knowledge.

Commentators have sometimes taken Aquinas's notion of *scientia* to explicate his concept of knowledge.[13] He conceives of *scientia* as a species of cognition, defining it as complete and certain cognition of truth. But *scientia* is not only narrower than cognition, it is also narrower than knowledge, as we shall see. In my view, Aquinas has no term that corresponds precisely with the English word "knowledge," but I think the general view of cognition sketched here identifies a space in his framework corresponding to our notion of knowledge.[14]

Aquinas holds that the intellective power, unlike the other cognitive powers of the human soul, is self-reflexive with respect to its activities.[15] That is to say, the intellect can take its own activities, including its acts of cognition, as objects of thought and judgment. As a result, a creature with intellect has the capacity not only for being cognitively conformed to reality but also for considering whether or not its cognitions in fact conform to reality – that is, for engaging in a sort of second-order cognition requiring both a first-order cognition and cognition of that first-order cognition's conformity to reality. Since Aquinas thinks of truth as consisting primarily in the adequation or conformity of cognition (or thought) to reality, he calls the second-order judgment (that a given cognition conforms to reality) cognition of *the truth* of what is cognized.[16] By virtue of possessing intellect, human beings have the self-reflexive capacity for cognizing the truth of their cognitions.

The epistemological significance of this capacity for self-reflexive cognition is that self-reflexive cognition makes it possible for human beings not only to accept or hold propositions but also to have grounds or reasons for holding them. Reflective consideration of whether or not a proposition conforms to reality is essential to evaluating and governing our own judgments and thought processes. We might say that, on Aquinas's view, the self-reflexive capacity of intellect makes human beings the sort of creature for whom epistemic justification can be an issue.[17]

Thus, Aquinas's notion of cognition of the truth of what is cognized opens a space in his conceptual framework for questions about epistemic justification; and his discussions of particular kinds of knowledge, including *scientia*, can be viewed primarily as attempts to identify and explicate different kinds and degrees of epistemic justification.[18] These accounts specify and evaluate the various kinds of epistemic grounds we can have for judging that our cognitions conform to reality, that is, the grounds by virtue of which we can cognize the truth of our cognitions.

III. *SCIENTIA* AND INFERENTIAL JUSTIFICATION

Aquinas conceives of *scientia* as the paradigm for knowledge. Near the beginning of his Commentary on *Posterior Analytics* he tells us that the common view about what *scientia* is holds that to have *scientia* with respect to something is to have *complete and certain* cognition of its truth.[19] *Scientia* is knowledge paradigmatically because complete and certain cognition of the truth of a given proposition constitutes impeccable justification – a kind and degree of justification that guarantees the proposition's truth.

Aquinas takes this view of *scientia* to be the starting point for philosophical analysis. It tells us in a general way what *scientia* is, whereas what we want from a philosophical theory is a specification of that general account, which will tell us precisely what having complete and certain cognition consists in. Aquinas's Aristotelian analysis is a theory of demonstration: the proper object of *scientia* is the conclusion of a demonstrative syllogism (Aquinas begins by defining the demonstrative syllogism as a syllogism productive of *scientia*), and so to have *scientia* with respect to some proposition *P* is to hold *P* on the basis of a demonstrative syllogism, that is, to hold *P* where one's epistemic grounds for *P* are the premisses of the syllogism and the fact that *P* is entailed by those premisses.[20]

Hence, to have *scientia* with respect to some proposition *P* is to hold *P* with a certain sort of inferential justification. Now Aquinas holds that because the sort of justification essential to *scientia* is inferential, it is also derivative. *Scientia* acquires its positive epistemic status from the premisses of the demonstrative syllogism and the nature of the syllogistic inference.[21]

[Aristotle] says that because we believe (*credimus*) a thing that has been concluded and have *scientia* (*scimus*) with respect to it by virtue of the fact that we possess a demonstrative syllogism, and we possess this insofar as we have *scientia* with respect to the demonstrative syllogism (*in quantum scimus syllogismum demonstrativum*), it is necessary not only that we antecedently cognize the first principles of the conclusion but also that we cognize them more than the conclusion.   (In PA I.6.2)

Aquinas goes on immediately to offer his own explanation and defense of this Aristotelian argument:

That on account of which a given thing is [such and such] is itself [such and such] to a greater degree. . . . But we have *scientia* (*scimus*) with respect to conclusions and believe them on account of the principles, therefore we have *scientia* with respect to principles to a greater degree than we have it with respect to conclusions and we believe the former to a greater degree than we believe the latter. Now with respect to this argument one should notice that a cause is always stronger (*potior*) than its effect.

(In PA I.6.3–4)

In this passage Aquinas is constrained by Aristotle's text to use *scientia* in a sense broader than the technical sense he marks out for that term in his surrounding commentary and elsewhere.[22] He claims here that we have *scientia* not only with respect to the conclusions of a demonstration but also with respect to its principles (or premisses). His point, however, is clear: if one is epistemically justified in holding a proposition on the basis of a demonstrative syllogism, then one must be justified to a greater degree in holding the premisses of the demonstration. Since the positive epistemic status of the demonstration's conclusion depends on the positive epistemic status of its premisses, the epistemic status of the premisses must be greater or stronger than the epistemic status of the conclusion.

The principle of inferential justification and the general causal principle Aquinas derives it from might seem implausibly strong. Why must a cause be *greater* than its effect in the relevant respect? Similarly, why should it be impossible for one's inferential justification for holding a proposition to attain the level of justification one has for the premisses of the inference? (I cannot take up the causal principle here, but I will return to this worry as it applies specifically to the principle of inferential justification.)[23]

If we think of propositions whose positive epistemic status is the source of the positive epistemic status of some other proposition as being *epistemically prior* to that other proposition, then we can attribute to Aquinas the view that for a person who has *scientia* with respect to a given proposition (and so holds it as the conclusion of a demonstration), the premisses of the demonstration must be epistemically prior to the demonstration's conclusion.[24] His account of *scientia* as a sort of inferential justification, then, leaves us in need of an understanding of the nature of this epistemic priority. If the justification characteristic of *scientia* is derivative, what is the nature of the justification from which it derives?

IV. *SCIENTIA* AND FOUNDATIONALISM

Aquinas allows that when we have *scientia* (in the strict sense) with respect to some proposition *P*, it is possible that we hold some of the premisses of the demonstrations on the basis of which we hold *P* on the basis of still other demonstrative syllogisms of which they are, in turn, the conclusions. But he denies that all premisses in demonstrations producing *scientia* can be held on the basis of still other demonstrations. Some propositions must have their positive epistemic status not by virtue of an inference (*per demonstrationem*), but non-inferentially, by virtue of themselves (*per se*).[25] Propositions that are known by virtue of themselves (*per se nota*) are Aquinas's epistemic first principles, the foundations of *scientia*.

Aquinas offers two sorts of argument for his view that *scientia* requires foundations. The first, a version of the Aristotelian argument that has become the best known argument for epistemological foundationalism, proceeds by attacking rival accounts of justification, concluding that inferential justification is possible only if there is non-inferential justification. This argument is essentially negative, supporting a kind of foundationalism by default, as it were, and leaving open the skeptical possibility that there is no inferential justification. Aquinas's positive characterization of the nature of non-inferential justification constitutes his second sort of defense of foundationalism. (The first sort of argument is considered in this section, the second in the next.)

Aquinas identifies the positions opposing his own as those committed to the view that (A) all epistemic justification is inferential. Moreover, since he thinks it clear that one cannot be justified in holding a proposition on the basis of an inference from propositions one is unjustified in holding, he assumes that his epistemological rivals share with him a commitment to a principle of inferential justification according to which (B) one can be inferentially justified in holding a proposition only if one is justified in holding some other proposition(s).[26] Following Aristotle, Aquinas identifies two distinct positions built on (A) and (B).

The first position – the skeptical alternative – uses (A) and (B) as the starting point for a skeptical argument. The principle of inferential justification (B) entails that (1) if some person S is inferentially justified in holding a given proposition P, then S is justified in holding some other proposition Q. But (A) entails that (2) S's justification for holding Q can only be inferential. Hence (by (B)), (3) if S is justified in holding Q, S must be justified in holding some other proposition R. Now (4) this regress of justification is either infinite or stops at some propositions that S is not justified in holding. (5) If it stops at propositions S is not justified in holding, then (by (B)) S is not justified in holding any of the propositions inferred (directly or indirectly) from them. But (6) if the regress of justification goes on *ad infinitum*, then if S is to be justified in holding P, S must get through infinitely many distinct inferences involving infinitely many distinct propositions. But (7) it is impossible to get through infinitely many inferences involving infinitely many propositions.[27] Therefore

(8) it is impossible for S to be justified in holding P (or for any person to be justified in holding any proposition).[28]

The second position endorses (A) and (B) but tries to avoid the first position's skeptical conclusion by allowing what Aquinas calls circular demonstration. According to this view, the regress of inferential justification can be infinite without being vicious if it circles back on itself. For example, S might be inferentially justified in holding P on the basis of Q, Q on the basis of R, and R on the basis of P, at which point the chain of inferences begins to repeat itself. This sort of regress of justification will be infinite (since the return to P does not end the search for justification but merely starts us out again on the same path) but, unlike a non-circularly infinite chain, it needn't contain infinitely many distinct inferences. This position, then, argues for the falsity of premiss (6) of the skeptical argument. It shares with the skeptical position a commitment to (A) and (B), but holds with them that (C) inferential justification is (ultimately) circular.

Aquinas rejects both of these positions.[29] In reply to the second position, he appeals to the asymmetry of the relation of epistemic support. He argues that if our justification for holding some proposition P is dependent on our justification for holding another proposition Q, then for us Q is epistemically prior to and more fundamental than P. But if we are inferentially justified in holding P on the basis of Q and inferentially justified in holding Q on the basis of P, then from an epistemic point of view, P is for us *both* prior to and posterior to Q, which is impossible. His second argument appeals to the vacuousness of circular reasoning as a source of justification. If we are justified in holding P by virtue of inferring it from Q, and if we are justified in holding Q by virtue of inferring it from P, then it seems that we have essentially done nothing more than infer P from itself, and it seems absurd to suppose that we can acquire justification for holding P by inferring it from itself when we are not justified in holding P by itself. The absurdity is apparent when the circle contains only two propositions, and making the circle bigger does not remove the absurdity. Aquinas concludes that the notion of circular inferential justification is absurd and that one cannot defend the possibility of inferential justification by appeal to it.

His reply to the skeptical alternative is more concessive. He grants that, assuming (A) and (B), the skeptical argument is sound: if we assume that all justification is inferential, then we are indeed committed to a vicious regress of justification and the skeptical conclusion that there can be no justification.[30] His reply to the argument consists in simply pointing out that we need not make the relevant assumption. If we assume instead that some justification is non-inferential, that is, if we accept a kind of foundationalism, then we can avoid the skeptical conclusion.

Aquinas's view, then, is that *scientia* requires foundations. Having *scientia* with respect to some proposition *P* requires one to be inferentially justified in holding *P* on the basis of a demonstrative syllogism or chain of demonstrative syllogisms whose ultimate premises one is non-inferentially justified in holding.

Suppose that someone who has a demonstration [for a given conclusion] syllogizes on the basis of demonstrable (or mediate) premises. That person either possesses a demonstration for these premises or he does not. If he does not, then he does not have *scientia* with respect to the premises, and so does not have *scientia* with respect to the conclusion that he holds on account of the premises either. But if he possesses a demonstration for the premises, he will arrive at some premises that are immediate and indemonstrable, since in the case of demonstrations one cannot go on *ad infinitum*. . . . And so it must be that demonstration proceeds from immediate premises either directly or indirectly through other mediating [propositions] (*per aliqua media*).   (In PA 1.4.14)

What reason can Aquinas give us for preferring to the skeptic's assumption that all justification is inferential his own supposition that there is *scientia* and the sort of non-inferential justification required for it? I think part of the answer is to be found in his positive account of non-inferential justification. If that account is independently defensible, then we will have good reason for thinking that there is non-inferential justification, and Aquinas's modest reply to the skeptical argument will be sufficient.

V. IMMEDIATE PROPOSITIONS AND EPISTEMIC FOUNDATIONS

In the text just quoted and throughout the opening chapters of In PA, Aquinas prefers to call the propositions that constitute *scientia*'s foundations *immediate* propositions. That designation highlights their place in the theory of demonstration he is developing.

Therefore, if one asks how one possesses *scientia* of immediate propositions, [Aristotle] replies that there is *scientia* of them, [too]; indeed cognition of them is a kind of source of all *scientia* (for cognition of conclusions – which are, strictly speaking, the objects of *scientia* – derives from cognition of the premisses). But as far as immediate premisses are concerned, there is not simply *scientia*; in addition to *scientia*, immediate premisses are cognized by virtue of cognition of the premisses' own terms and not by virtue of some middle term external [to the premiss]. For once one has *scientia* of what a whole is and what a part is, one cognizes that every whole is greater than its part. This is because in propositions of this sort . . . the predicate belongs to the account of the subject (*praedicatum est de ratione subiecti*). And so it is reasonable that cognition of these premisses is the cause of cognition of the conclusions because what is by virtue of itself (*per se*) is always the cause of what is by virtue of something else (*per aliud*).   (In PA 1.7.8)

A demonstration is a species of syllogism, and a categorical syllogism's conclusion follows validly from its premisses when and only when the conclusion's subject and predicate (the syllogism's extreme terms) must be related in the way the conclusion asserts, provided that those terms are each related to some third term (the syllogism's middle term) in the way that the syllogism's two premisses assert. The conclusion of a valid syllogism, then, is a mediate proposition insofar as its predicate is shown to be related in the appropriate way to its subject by virtue of some third, middle term external to the conclusion itself. To say that the theory of demonstration's foundational premisses are immediate propositions is to say that they are not themselves conclusions of demonstrations; they are indemonstrable.

Aquinas's logic and epistemology rest here on his metaphysical realism. He holds that there are real natures of naturally occurring substances and accidents and that these real natures can provide the content for universal categorical propositions. Genuine kind terms refer to real natures, and real definitions explicate these natures by identifying a kind's genus and specifying differentia (which are also real natures). Thus, 'human being' refers to the real nature *human being*, the real definition of which is *rational animal*.[31] When Aquinas says that an immediate proposition is one in which the predicate belongs to the account (or definition – *ratio*) of the subject, he means that the real nature referred to by the predicate term is an element in the real definition of the subject, that the predicate term names the subject's genus or specifying differentia (for example, *A human being is an animal*).[32] Which propositions are immediate, then, depends solely on what real natures there are and what relations hold among them, that is, on the basic structure of the world, and not on the psychology or belief-structure of any given epistemic subject. Propositions are immediate by virtue of expressing what might be called metaphysically immediate relationships or facts, the relationships that hold between natures and their essential constituents.[33]

This metaphysical picture allows us to see the kind of objectivist requirement Aquinas incorporates into the theory of demonstration. When he claims that the first principles of demonstration must be immediate and indemonstrable, he is claiming that they must express metaphysically immediate propositions and not just propositions that are epistemically basic and unprovable for some particular epistemic subject. That a given proposition *P* happens to be indemonstrable *for some person S* because there are no other propositions in *S*'s belief-structure on the basis of which *S* would be justified in holding *P* is no guarantee that *P* is, on Aquinas's view, an immediate, indemonstrable proposition.[34] The structure of demonstration, then, is isomorphic with the metaphysical structure of reality: immediate, indemonstrable propositions express metaphysically immediate facts, whereas mediate, demonstrable propositions express metaphysically mediate facts.[35]

Moreover, Aquinas holds that because fully developed demonstrations are isomorphic with reality, the premisses in a demonstration can be thought of as giving the *cause* of the conclusion. *Causa* in these contexts might better be rendered by "explanation," since the sort of causation he has in mind is not restricted to, and in fact typically is not, efficient causation. The premisses in a demonstration give the explanation of the conclusion in the sense that they cite the underlying and metaphysically more basic facts in virtue of which the conclusion is true; they provide what we might think of as a theoretically deep explanation.[36] For example, that a figure of a certain sort has the sum of its interior angles equal to two right angles is both demonstrated and explained by appeal to the facts that figures of that sort are triangles and triangles have the sum of their interior angles equal to two right angles. That triangles have the sum of their interior angles equal to two right angles is paradigmatically an immediate proposition, and it provides a paradigmatically formal-causal explanation of the fact that a particular sort of figure has interior angles equal to two right angles: figures of that sort have interior angles equal to two right angles because they are triangles, and triangles, by their very nature, are figures having the sum of their interior angles equal to two right angles.[37]

This metaphysical picture explains how immediate propositions express metaphysical foundations and how they fill the role of epistemic foundations. First, by virtue of being predications in which the predicate belongs to the account of the subject, they are essential predications and, as such, universally and necessarily true. Second, Aquinas holds that the facts expressed by immediate propositions are such that when we are acquainted with them, we cannot fail to see their necessity; that is, we cannot conceive of the falsity of those propositions.[38] To be acquainted with them is thereby to be non-inferentially justified in holding the immediate propositions that express them. Aquinas often says that propositions of this sort are such that once one conceives their terms, one is aware of the propositions' truth. This is because, for him, conceiving the terms of an immediate proposition consists in attaining an explicit understanding of the real natures named by those terms. Thus, conceiving the subject of the proposition "A human being is an animal" requires having an explicit real definition for human beings, that is, conceiving of human beings *as* essentially rational animals. Aquinas's view is that one cannot explicitly be aware that being a human being essentially consists in being a rational animal and at the same time fail to be aware that a human being is an animal. To conceive the subject and the predicate of an immediate proposition is thereby to be directly aware of the proposition's necessary truth.[39]

Non-inferential justification, then, consists in one's being directly aware of the immediate facts that ground a proposition's necessary truth. When one sees that a proposition expresses an immediate fact of this sort, one cannot doubt its truth (since one cannot conceive of its being false) or be mistaken in holding it.[40] Aquinas says that in these cases immediate propositions are evident to us.

When Aquinas is focusing on the epistemological rather than the logical or metaphysical status of immediate propositions, he describes them as cognized (*cognita*) or known (*nota*) by virtue of themselves (*per se*). He might better have said that they are cogniz*able* or know*able* by virtue of themselves since he holds that a proposition's being immediate is no guarantee that it will be known by any human being.

[A]ny proposition whatever whose predicate is in the account of the subject is, considered in itself (*quantum est in se*), immediate and known by virtue of itself (*per se nota*). Now the terms of certain [of these] propositions are such that everyone is aware of them (*in notitia omnium*). . . . Thus, it must be that propositions of this sort are held to be known by virtue of themselves not only considered in themselves but also, as it were, with respect to everyone (*quoad omnes*). (For example: that one and the same thing cannot both be and not be, that a whole is greater than its part, and the like.) But there are some immediate propositions the terms of which not everyone is aware of (*non sunt apud omnes noti*). Thus, although the predicate [in these propositions] does belong to the account of the subject, nevertheless it is not necessary that propositions of this sort be granted by everyone because not everyone is aware of (*nota*) the definition of the subject. (For example: "All right angles are equal.")   (In PA I.5.7)

Immediate propositions, then, are capable of being known by virtue of themselves and are, therefore, proper objects of non-derivative knowledge. But their actually being known by virtue of themselves requires that one be acquainted with the facts expressed by those propositions, which requires that one conceive the terms of those propositions. Aquinas distinguishes between immediate propositions whose terms are common or grasped by everyone, which he calls common principles or common conceptions of the mind, and those whose terms are conceived by only some people.[41]

On Aquinas's view, then, we have non-inferential justification for holding immediate propositions whose terms we conceive. Our non-inferential justification for holding them consists in our being directly aware of the necessity of the facts they express. Now, it seems that he supposes that we have phenomenological evidence for the existence of non-inferential justification of this sort. We have seen that he holds that there are immediate propositions whose terms are conceived by everyone, and so each of us will have experience of direct acquaintance with metaphysically immediate necessary facts, facts expressed by propositions that cannot be false and that we cannot conceive to be false.[42] This implicit phenomenological appeal constitutes grounds for his foundationalism that are independent of his rejection of rival epistemological theories: our experience of being

non-inferentially justified in holding certain propositions is sufficient reason for thinking that there is non-inferential justification.

So Aquinas claims that to have *scientia* with respect to some
proposition *P* is to hold *P* on the basis of a demonstration the ultimate premises of which are propositions we are non-inferentially
justified in holding. These first principles will be (a) immediate, (b)
universal, and (c) necessary, and with respect to the demonstrative
conclusions they entail, they will be (d) epistemically prior, and
express facts that are both (e) metaphysically prior and (f) explanatory. Seeing these features of his account puts us in position to see
how this demonstrative theory of *scientia* might be taken to explicate the conception of *scientia* with which Aquinas began his discussion, the conception of *scientia* as complete and certain cognition.
On the one hand, our having *scientia* with respect to a proposition *P*
is characterized by certainty by virtue of our holding *P* on the basis
of valid syllogistic inferences whose ultimate premises are necessarily true propositions whose falsity is inconceivable to us. Inferences
of this sort from premises of this sort establish the necessary truth
(and hence, objective certainty) of their conclusions and thereby provide us with paradigmatically compelling evidence for (and hence,
subjective certainty with respect to) those conclusions.[43] On the
other hand, our having *scientia* with respect to *P* constitutes complete cognition of *P*, because to hold *P* on the basis of demonstration
is to have located *P* in a wider explanatory structure or theory that
accurately maps objective reality.

We can also see now how Aquinas's first principles fit with his
strong principle of inferential justification. We have seen that he
holds that, in the case of *scientia*, being inferentially justified in
holding *P* requires being not merely justified but *more* justified in
holding the propositions from which one infers *P*. Our justification
for holding propositions we see to be immediate is characterized by
absolute certainty: we cannot conceive the possibility of the falsity
of propositions we grasp in that way. This sort of certainty grounded
solely in our direct awareness of the necessary truth of an immediate
proposition can plausibly be thought of as constitutive of *more* justification than the sort of certainty whose basis is an inference involving two or more distinct propositions.[44] The former sort of justification is an appropriate source for the latter sort.

VI. QUALIFYING AND EXTENDING *SCIENTIA*

Critics have often pointed out the narrowness of Aquinas's account of *scientia*. It seems that only *a priori* truths of axiomatic systems such as logic and mathematics could satisfy its strict conditions. (The critics claim that it is no accident that most of Aristotle's and Aquinas's examples come from geometry.) But many objections of this sort rest on mistaken assumptions about Aquinas's view. This section presents three features of his epistemology that show it to be more subtle and resilient than many critics have allowed.

Scientia *as paradigm*

The charge that Aquinas's account has only extremely narrow application overlooks his own explicit provisions for extending it beyond those narrow bounds. His general strategy is to take the conditions on *scientia* we have seen him develop not as strictly necessary conditions, but rather as conditions that are *fully* satisfied only by the paradigm case, although they are satisfied to some extent by cases that fall short of the paradigm. (In the discussions we have looked at he often specifies that he is talking about having *scientia* unqualifiedly [*scire simpliciter*].)[45] Unqualified or strict *scientia* will satisfy the conditions we have set out. But our cognition of the truth of what we cognize admits of degrees culminating in completeness and certainty, and our justification for holding a given proposition can approach the paradigm without attaining it. Aquinas, then, can admit that paradigmatic *scientia* can be attained only in *a priori* disciplines such as logic or geometry, while allowing that we can correctly be said to have *scientia* (though not paradigmatic *scientia*) with respect to many other sorts of propositions.[46] I will mention two ways in which he makes room in his account for what we might think of as secondary *scientia*; each of the two ways involves the extension or loosening of one of the criteria for strict or paradigmatic *scientia*.

1. The first way constitutes an attempt to accommodate the strict account of *scientia* to the perspective of human epistemic subjects. Aquinas holds that as corporeal creatures, human beings have cognitive access to the world through the bodily senses. Human cognition must start from and rely on sense perception; we acquire propositions

about sensible objects first and find them psychologically easiest to assent to. For this reason, many propositions of this sort can be thought of as epistemically prior *for us.* "Now in us sensory cognition is prior to intellective cognition because in us intellective cognition arises from sense perception. Thus, with respect to us, the particular is both prior to and better known (*notius*) than the universal" (In PA I.4.16).[47] Aquinas constructs a sort of non-paradigmatic *scientia* on these distinguishing characteristics of our epistemic situation.[48]

Propositions about particular sensible objects, then, are sometimes better known to us even though by nature or considered in themselves they are not better known. As such, they can constitute immediate propositions *for us* and function as epistemic first principles grounding what is *for us* (though not unqualifiedly) *scientia*. Of course the fact that these sorts of propositions fall short of the sort of metaphysical priority, universality, and necessity characteristic of paradigmatic first principles leaves open the possibility of our being mistaken about them. But this is just to say that the sort of *scientia* they ground is not paradigmatically complete and certain cognition but only approximates it to some degree.

Now because in some cases the metaphysically posterior facts (the effects) are epistemically more accessible to us than facts that are metaphysically prior and, from an objective point of view, explanatory (the causes), Aquinas is willing to extend the condition that the premises of demonstration producing *scientia* give the cause of the conclusion. He allows that in some cases we can have (non-paradigmatic) *scientia* with respect to metaphysically prior propositions that we hold on the basis of metaphysically posterior ones. In cases of this sort, then, we may infer the cause from the effect (on the basis of necessary causal principles) rather than the effect from the cause. Aquinas calls demonstrations of this sort *factual* demonstrations (*demonstrationes quia*) because they establish that something is the case without providing a theoretically deep explanation of it of the sort metaphysically prior facts would provide. By contrast, he calls demonstrations the premises of which give the cause or explanation of the conclusion *explanatory* demonstrations (*demonstrationes propter quid*).[49] Paradigmatic *scientia* requires explanatory demonstration, but merely factual demonstrations give us *scientia* of a sort.[50]

His favorite examples of such cases are propositions of natural science and theology. In these cases our epistemic starting points reflect the limitations imposed by our corporeal nature rather than the natural order of the world. In natural science, for example, we must start from the sensory accidents of corporeal objects, since these are most accessible to us, and only subsequently acquire facts about the real natures of those objects. Facts about the real natures of corporeal objects are, absolutely speaking, prior to and explain facts about their accidental features, but these metaphysically prior facts are, at least initially, hidden from us.[51]

Similarly, Aquinas holds that our corporeal natures limit the sort of epistemic bases we can have for *scientia* with respect to propositions about divine matters. We could have paradigmatic *scientia* with respect to propositions about God only if we could base those propositions via paradigmatic demonstrations on immediate propositions about God's real nature. Of course human cognitive limitations preclude our conceiving God's nature as it is in itself.[52] Aquinas allows, however, that we can be justified in holding propositions about God on the basis of demonstrations that begin ultimately from propositions about God's effects (creatures) that are evident to sense perception. On his view, we can be said to have *scientia* with respect to propositions we hold on these grounds despite the fact that our justification for them falls short of providing us with the sort of deep and complete theoretical justification provided by explanatory demonstrations. We can have this sort of non-paradigmatic *scientia*, for example, with respect to propositions that assert God's existence and attribute to him certain attributes.[53]

2. A second way in which Aquinas allows for non-paradigmatic forms of *scientia* involves accommodating the paradigm of *scientia* to objects that fall short of being absolutely necessary. He holds that because of their particularity and materiality, the objects of natural science – corporeal substances in the realm of nature – admit of contingency. He allows that we can have *scientia* with respect to them, however, to the extent that we can render them universal. He tells us, for example, that a particular lunar eclipse can be viewed as universal and necessary with respect to its cause "because it never fails that there is a lunar eclipse when the earth is interposed directly between the sun and moon" (In PA I.16.8). Similarly, we can have *scientia* with respect to what he calls for-the-most-part truths – propositions expressing states of affairs that will result from the natural tendencies of

things provided that external causal factors do not interfere – by constructing demonstrations specifying that some condition obtains or by ruling out the obtaining of conditions that would impede the relevant natural tendencies. Where there is causal or conditional natural necessity, then, we can have *scientia* of a sort, even if not paradigmatic *scientia*.

Moreover, he even allows that generalizations and probabilistic propositions can be the object of *scientia* despite the fact that they are not, strictly speaking, universal and necessary. He holds that we can have demonstrations of for-the-most-part truths that begin from premisses that are also for-the-most-part truths.

[N]evertheless demonstrations of this sort do not provide one with *scientia* that what is concluded is true unqualifiedly but only in a certain respect, namely, that it is true for the most part. The premisses that one uses [in demonstrations of this sort] have truth in this way, too. Thus, in respect of the certitude of the demonstration, cases of *scientia* of this sort fall short of cases of *scientia* that have to do with things that are necessary absolutely speaking. (In PA II.12.5)[54]

This passage seems clearly to allow for what we might call probabilistic *scientia*.[55]

Hence, Aquinas holds that the paradigm of justification, attainable in certain purely formal, a priori disciplines, guarantees the truth of cognition by virtue of grounding it in the universality and necessity of the objects cognized and the infallibility of our access to them.[56] But he allows kinds and degrees of justification that only approximate that necessity and infallibility. It is a mistake, then, to suppose that his epistemology is coextensive with his account of strict *scientia*, but he does take strict *scientia*, as he conceives of it, as the paradigm of epistemic justification and the model by which other sorts of justification are to be understood and against which they are to be measured. In that sense the account of *scientia* is not merely a part of his theory of knowledge, but its cornerstone.

Aquinas's taking paradigmatic *scientia* as the model for understanding epistemic justification generally leads him to devote less attention than we might like to the account of derivative, non-paradigmatic varieties of justification. For the most part he marks no precise boundaries between different kinds of non-paradigmatic justification and specifies no exact criteria for determining whether or not a given case of non-paradigmatic justification approximates the paradigm nearly enough to ground rational acceptance or knowledge.

Difficult first principles

Aquinas's requirement that *scientia* be grounded in propositions that are known by virtue of themselves (*per se nota*) has been misunderstood as requiring that the foundations of *scientia* must be propositions that are self-evident in such a way that they are clearly and obviously true to any normal adult or competent language user.[57] Critics quite rightly point out that on this way of reading the requirement, only the simplest truths of logic and arithmetic are plausible candidates for the foundations of Aquinas's *scientia*, since for virtually any proposition (including analytic and necessary propositions) one can find ordinary people who not only fail to find it *obviously* true but even reject it.

I have just argued that Aquinas allows for non-paradigmatic *scientia* that can take as its foundations propositions that are not immediate propositions absolutely speaking. But leaving this point aside, we have seen that Aquinas's conception of immediate propositions and our epistemic relation to them is richer and more sophisticated than this misinterpretation allows. As we have seen, on his account immediate propositions needn't be intelligible, let alone obvious, to everyone. One is directly aware of the necessary truth of an immediate proposition only when one conceives the natures of the subject and predicate. Moreover, Aquinas holds that it is difficult to attain a complete conception of certain things. It follows that direct awareness of the necessary truth of immediate propositions about certain things will be difficult to attain. Propositions of this sort, then, can be epistemic foundations absolutely speaking despite their being opaque to some, or even many, normal people.

A closely related objection to Aquinas's foundationalism charges that one who holds it is self-referentially inconsistent.[58] On Aquinas's account, a person can be (paradigmatically) justified in holding a given proposition only if either of two conditions is met: (1) the proposition is known by virtue of itself for that person or (2) the person holds it ultimately on the basis of propositions that are known by virtue of themselves for that person. Call this thesis *T*. Now, according to *T*, one is (paradigmatically) justified in holding *T* itself only if either (1) or (2) is met. But *T* is clearly not self-evident (after all, many epistemologists have rejected this sort of account). Moreover, it is difficult to see how it could be derived from propositions that are self-evident. So, even if *T* is true, we cannot be (paradigmatically) justified in accepting it.

At most, this argument would constitute an objection to Aquinas's account of strict *scientia*, since thesis *T* characterizes only that part of his theory of knowledge. But the objection fails in any case for two reasons. First, Aquinas denies that the fact that many have rejected some proposition shows that the proposition cannot be known by virtue of itself. So the fact that *T* is controversial does nothing to show that condition (1) has not been met. Second, Aquinas in fact claims to be justified in holding *T* by virtue of condition (2). We have seen him maintain that the components of *T* are instances of general metaphysical principles, namely, that anything that is *F* must be *F* either by virtue of itself or by virtue of something else that is sufficient in relevant respects to have brought about its being *F*, and that it cannot be the case that all things that are *F* are derivatively *F* (are *F* by virtue of something else). Aquinas derives *T* straightforwardly from these principles and takes basic metaphysical principles of this sort, his versions of principles of sufficient reason, to be immediate propositions knowable by virtue of themselves.[59] Of course, one might object at this point that these metaphysical principles themselves are not obviously self-evident. But, as we have seen, given his view of what it is for a proposition to be knowable by virtue of itself, this complaint by itself cannot convict Aquinas of any inconsistency or incoherence.

Non-demonstrative justification

The high profile Aquinas gives to his account of *scientia* has led some to suppose mistakenly that that account exhausts his theory of knowledge when, in fact, it is only one part of it. Aquinas recognizes a sort of justification acquired neither from direct awareness of immediate propositions (understanding) nor from demonstration (*scientia*), but from what he calls dialectical or probable (*probabilis, persuasoria*) reasoning.[60] Dialectical reasoning is distinguished by its producing conclusions that are not certain but merely probable. Probable arguments are not restricted to deriving conclusions from immediate propositions by means of valid syllogistic forms: they may rely on premisses that are not necessary and certain but possess some positive epistemic status (propositions held by most people, on good authority, on inductive grounds, etc.) and make use of broadly inductive argument forms.

Aquinas clearly thinks that dialectical reasoning can provide epistemic justification and that we possess this sort of justification for many of the propositions we are justified in holding. "In a process of reasoning not accompanied by utter certitude one finds degrees by which it approaches more or less to complete certitude. Indeed sometimes by virtue of a process of this sort belief (fides) or opinion is produced on account of the probability of the propositions from which it proceeds, even if scientia is not produced" (In PA Prologue).[61] In this passage Aquinas marks out an epistemic propositional attitude distinct from understanding and scientia – belief or opinion – which constitutes our epistemic stance toward propositions we take to be contingent.[62] To perceive a proposition as contingent is to perceive that one's grounds for it do not guarantee its truth, that is, to have less than complete and certain cognition of its truth. He does not, however, develop for this epistemic attitude or the probable reasoning on which it is based the sort of systematic account he provides for scientia.[63]

Thus, when Aquinas's views commit him to denying that we have scientia with respect to some proposition or when he claims that we have no demonstration for that proposition, he should not be read as thereby denying that we know it or are justified in holding it. Although he does deny, for example, that we can have scientia with respect to many of the propositions of Christian doctrine, he nevertheless thinks that we are justified in holding them on the basis of (among other things) their deriving from a reasonable authority.[64] Similarly, we should not reject his theory of knowledge on the grounds that his account of scientia is too narrow to constitute a complete epistemology.

VII. COGNITION OF REAL NATURES

As we have seen, Aquinas's account of non-inferential justification appeals to the notion of our conceiving the subjects and predicates of immediate propositions, and Aquinas thinks of these subjects and predicates as real natures. His theory of knowledge, then, leads him to a discussion of our cognitive relations to these entities, entities he thinks of as the logically simple elements out of which complex (propositional) knowledge is built.

Although our cognition of natures or quiddities is a necessary condition of our cognizing the immediate propositions that are epistemic first principles, Aquinas's account of that sort of cognition is not strictly epistemological. This is because the question of truth does not arise for this sort of cognition since its objects are not propositions, which are the proper bearers of truth values. Thus, when he begins his discussion of the notoriously difficult final chapter of *Posterior Analytics* by pointing out that it will be useful to know "how one cognizes first principles" (In PA II.20.2), he is introducing not a discussion of what *justifies* us in holding first, immediate principles, but a discussion of the causal mechanisms or psychological processes that give rise to certain kinds of psychological states or dispositions.[65]

His answer to the genetic question of how we come to have cognition of first principles is that we have certain cognitive powers (including sense perception, memory, and an agent and possible intellect) that make it possible for us to have cognition of the natures or quiddities of things, the universals that are the constituents of categorical propositions.[66] (The details of his account of the nature and functioning of these cognitive powers go beyond epistemology into psychology and even physiology, and so cannot be spelled out here.)[67] But in general Aquinas thinks of the account as a solution to an ancient, essentially epistemological puzzle.

The puzzle, which Plato inherited from the pre-Socratics and made famous, is how human beings, whose senses provide access to a world of irreducibly particular corporeal objects, can have cognition of universals. We might think of the puzzle as drawing our attention to an epistemological gap between human cognizers dependent on sense perception and cognition of universals. Aquinas sees all the main epistemological positions with which he is acquainted as motivated by this basic puzzle. He divides these views into three main groups.[68] Two groups embrace the puzzle and concede that the gap is unbridgeable: sense perception, by its very nature, is incapable of putting us in cognitive touch with universals, and so the objects of our universal cognition must be extrasensory. According to these two groups, if we are to have cognition of universals, we must have cognitive access to intelligible objects apart from sense perception.

Aquinas distinguishes between these two groups on the basis of their views about the nature of this source of universal cognition. The first group holds that the sources of universal cognition are *wholly extrinsic* to the soul. Aquinas puts in this group both a kind of Platonism, according to which the intelligible objects are separate (immaterial, independently existing) forms in which the human intellect participates, and a kind of Muslim Neoplatonism, according to which separate intelligences (immaterial, independently existing intellective souls) impress intelligible forms on the human intellect. The second group maintains that the sources of universal cognition are *wholly intrinsic* to the soul. Those who, inspired by Plato, hold that universals are innate in the soul, although the soul's innate cognition of them has been darkened by the soul's union with the body, fall into this group, as do those who maintain that the presence of sensible objects is the occasion, although not the cause, of the soul's constructing intelligible forms for itself *ex nihilo*, as it were.

The third group, the Aristotelians, cannot appeal to a kind of extra-sensory access to independent universals, for they hold that all human cognition arises from sense perception. This Aristotelian empiricism is based on the view that human beings are by nature unified corporeal substances whose natural form of access to the world is through the bodily senses.[69] If they are to avoid skepticism, then, the Aristotelians must resolve the puzzle and bridge the epistemological gap. Aquinas presents his theory of intellective abstraction as the solution. He views his position as a kind of middle ground between the other two positions, holding that the sources of universal cognition are partly extrinsic and partly intrinsic to the soul. His empiricism identifies an external source: cognition of universals, like all human cognition, originates from sense perception, and so from the external world of material particulars. But he acknowledges that something is required on the side of the soul, namely, a cognitive capacity (in particular an agent intellect) that manipulates sensory data to produce intelligible universals. We cognize the universal real natures that constitute the subject and predicate of epistemic first principles when we possess actually intelligible species or forms abstracted by this mechanism from the material conditions that render them merely potentially intelligible.

Leaving aside the details of the theory of abstraction, Aquinas summarizes his general position in this commentary on the concluding paragraphs of *Posterior Analytics:*

> It is clear that, strictly speaking and *per se,* one senses a particular. Nevertheless, in a certain respect sense perception is of the universal itself, for it cognizes Callias not only insofar as he is Callias but also insofar as he is this particular human being. Similarly, it cognizes Socrates insofar as he is this particular human being. Thus it is that by virtue of this sort of antecedent sensory reception, the intellective soul can consider *human being* in both. (If sense perception were such that it apprehended only what belongs to particularity and in no way apprehended with it the universal nature in the particular, it would not be possible for cognition of the universal to be caused in us by sensory apprehension.) . . . Therefore, because we receive cognition of universals from particulars, [Aristotle] concludes that it is clear that one cognizes first universal principles by means of induction, for in this way, namely, by a process of induction, sense perception produces the universal in the soul (*facit universale intus in anima*), insofar as all the particulars are considered. (In PA II.20.14)

Two features of this passage require comment. First, we must not confuse the first *universal* principles that Aquinas speaks of in this passage with the first *immediate* principles that ground his theory of demonstration. These first universal principles are not propositions but the universal natures to which the terms of immediate propositions refer; they are the principles (or fundamental elements) not of demonstrations but of propositions.[70] Second, when Aquinas says that we cognize these universal principles by means of induction, he is not making a point about our epistemic justification for holding them. He does not mean that we are inferentially justified in holding these universal principles on the basis of an inductive generalization. For one thing, these universal principles are not propositions, and only propositions can be justified by inductive inference. For another, Aquinas frequently uses the term "induction," as he does here, simply to describe the process of going through individual cases. In this passage his point is that the process of reflecting on and comparing particular cases *causes* the intellect to grasp the universal contained in the particulars, not that the process of examining the particular cases gives rise to an inductive generalization about some universal nature.[71]

Aquinas's discussion of human cognitive functioning sometimes gives the impression that he takes the attainment of intellective cognition of universals to be a relatively simple and virtually automatic accomplishment. But that impression is misleading. The passage just quoted and other occasional remarks suggest that Aquinas thinks that, at least in some cases, the process can be lengthy and laborious. The fact that our apprehension of a universal requires induction, that is, repeated encounters with the relevant sensible particulars, and accumulated experience (experimentum) indicates that the process of intellective abstraction can be deliberate, reflective, and progressive.[72] Our initial encounters with sensible objects might give us only rudimentary, shadowy, or vague cognition of their real natures, cognition that can be developed and refined with further experience. Given these remarks, it seems best to think of the abstracting activity of the agent intellect not as a sort of mysterious instantaneous production of a universal form out of the data provided to it by sensation, but as a gradual, perhaps arduous, intellectual process.[73]

This conception of our cognition of universal natures as progressive and developmental fits nicely with Aquinas's view of the existence of immediate propositions that are not known to everyone. Intellective cognition of universals is not always easy and straightforward. When it is difficult, not everyone will have attained cognition of those universals, and so not everyone will know the immediate propositions in which those universal natures are elements.

It seems, then, that Aquinas's account of our cognition of universals, like his account of scientia, focuses on the paradigm case, the case in which the psychological apparatus functions perfectly. Our actual cognition of universal real natures, however, will approach the paradigm in different ways and degrees. As in the case of scientia, Aquinas thinks that the paradigm is easier to achieve with respect to some objects than it is with respect to others. He holds, on the one hand, that universal mathematical natures are more readily accessible to us than the natures of other sorts of things, but, on the other, he is not at all sanguine about our ability to attain intellective cognition of the real natures of corporeal substances.[74] Thus, when Aquinas claims that we possess cognitive capacities that account for our ability to cognize universals and describes the causal mechanism by which those capacities achieve their result, we need not take him to be claiming that every instance of our cognition of the real natures of things satisfies the conditions he has laid out.

VIII. EPISTEMOLOGICAL OPTIMISM

For the modern reader, it is a striking feature of Aquinas's various epistemological discussions that they seldom explicitly address skeptical worries. The account of universal cognition discussed in the previous section is a typical example. His strategy throughout the development of that account is to argue that cognition of the real natures of corporeal objects is possible only if the soul has certain kinds of powers and engages in certain kinds of cognitive activities. He simply assumes that we do in fact have cognition of that sort.[75] Why is Aquinas unconcerned with skeptical worries that seem to us both clear and pressing?

It has often been suggested that Aquinas's thoroughly theological world view caused him not to take possibilities of this sort seriously, since they would entail that creatures created by God are for the most part radically mistaken about the nature of the world. There is surely some truth to the claim that Aquinas's theological commitments dictate to some extent the issues he finds most interesting and important. But we should like to know not just what caused Aquinas's lack of concern about skepticism, but what justification he has (if any) for ignoring it.

Some recent commentators have argued that, despite appearances, Aquinas is an externalist about justification and knowledge and that his externalism explains his lack of concern about skepticism.[76] If Aquinas held a sort of externalist reliabilism according to which one's being justified in holding some proposition P consists in one's holding P as the result of the proper functioning of a reliable belief-forming mechanism – a condition the satisfaction of which one needn't have access to or be aware of – then we could understand why skeptical worries have no force for him. For the most part modern externalist epistemologies have abandoned the attempt to refute the skeptic. They assume that our epistemic faculties are essentially in order and ask what sort of analysis of knowledge can account for our having it. Moreover, Aquinas's account of human cognitive functioning clearly includes an account of what he takes to be a reliable belief-forming mechanism.

This view is untenable as an interpretation of Aquinas, however, for he quite explicitly commits himself to a strong version of internalism with regard to paradigmatic knowledge and justification. As we have seen in many of the passages quoted in this chapter, Aquinas consistently and repeatedly makes it a requirement of justification that the person *possess* or have access to the grounds constitutive of his justification. A person who does not possess a demonstration cannot be said to have *scientia* (In PA I.6.2); one who does not possess the demonstration for a demonstrable premiss cannot be said to have *scientia* with respect to a conclusion derived from that premiss (In PA I.4.14); one must believe the proposition that justifies one in holding some other proposition to a greater degree than one believes the latter proposition (In PA I.6.4); we cannot be said to have *scientia* with respect to the propositions of faith because the demonstrations for them are not accessible to us (ST IIaIIae.1.5); one must be aware that an immediate proposition is immediate and necessary, otherwise one will have only opinion with respect to it (In PA I.44.8–9).[77]

Apart from this compelling textual evidence, there are two central features of Aquinas's epistemology that mark it as clearly internalist. First, as we have seen, Aquinas holds that the cognitive power distinguishing human beings from other animals, namely, intellect, makes them genuine knowers precisely because it is a self-reflexive power that allows them to have not only cognitions but also cognition of the truth of their cognitions. That is to say, it is absolutely central to Aquinas's epistemology that human beings have cognitive access to their own acts of cognition and their grounds for judging that some of them correspond with reality.[78] Second, Aquinas's main epistemological positions are virtually unstatable without appeal to his own metaphor of intellective vision, a paradigmatically internalist metaphor. Understanding and *scientia* make certain propositions *evident* to us, and their objects are things that are seen (*visa*) to be true.[79] Aquinas's elevation of this essentially metaphorical vocabulary to virtually technical status is testimony to the thoroughly internalistic nature of his theory of knowledge.

Moreover, Aquinas's explicit commitment to the reliability of our cognitive faculties has no tendency to show that his view is reliabilist or externalist. The reliabilist must hold not only that our belief-forming mechanisms are reliable but also that our justification for holding a given proposition *consists in* our belief's having been caused by a mechanism of that sort. The passages I have just cited show quite clearly that Aquinas rejects this second claim. In fact most internalists have held that our cognitive faculties are reliable, and some of them, Aquinas and Descartes among them, have offered internalist arguments for that view. They have thought that in order to be justified in holding that our cognitive faculties are reliable, we must have internalist reasons for thinking that they are. Descartes famously tries to construct arguments satisfying the requirements of his paradigmatically internalist foundationalism to show first that God exists and is no deceiver, and then that our cognitive faculties are reliable when they are properly governed. It seems to me clear that Aquinas's own grounds for thinking our faculties reliable are similar to Descartes's. If asked what justifies him in thinking our faculties reliable, he would surely reply not by claiming that his belief in our cognitive reliability is itself caused by a reliable belief-forming mechanism but by pointing us to his philosophical theology and its foundationalist arguments for the existence of a good creator of human cognizers and by appealing to cases in which we have certain and infallible cognition of truth.

Aquinas's apparent confidence that skepticism is false may well derive from his certainty that *global* skepticism is false. Our direct acquaintance with the necessary truth of certain immediate propositions constitutes indubitable and infallible access to those truths, and so with respect to those propositions and the propositions we derive from them via strict demonstrations, skepticism is provably false. Aquinas may suppose that given this certification of the intellect's ability to grasp truth in particular cases, we are justified in supposing that our cognitive faculties generally give us access to reality, at least in the absence of compelling reasons for thinking otherwise. We do not have the sort of direct guarantee of the correctness of all faculties and processes that we have for some, but the direct guarantee we do have for some gives us good reason to trust the others. Now Aquinas nowhere explicitly develops an argument of this sort, but it is the sort of line he could be expected to have recognized in and taken over from Augustine. Augustine's explicit reply to skepticism effectively ends with the establishment of the falsity of global skepticism, presumably because Augustine thinks that that conclusion shifts the burden of proof to the shoulders of the skeptic.[80] Moreover, his frequent phenomenological appeals to our experience of having complete and certain cognition of truth suggests that he takes these cases as providing evidence for a more general optimism.

But despite its general realist and anti-skeptical orientation, Aquinas's epistemology should not be characterized as particularly optimistic. On his view, human beings are limited cognitive beings with restricted access to reality. He acknowledges that what they can know about the structure of nature and the realm of immaterial beings is incomplete in both depth and breadth. The fact that his theory of knowledge focuses on the paradigms, describing the complete and successful functioning of human cognitive powers, can cause us to overlook the fact that he thinks it is often quite difficult for us to attain the paradigm.

NOTES

1   I will deal only with Aquinas's views about human knowledge, leaving aside the special issues raised by the possibility of incorporeal epistemic subjects such as God and separate intelligences.

2   ST Ia.17.3; see also ST Ia.12.4; 76.2, ad 4; 84.2, ad 2.

3   ST Ia.75–76.

4   ST Ia.84; QDV 10.6. For more on Aquinas's "empiricism," see section VII below.

5   ST Ia.75.5; 84.1; 85.2. The example of the stone derives from Aristotle (De anima III 8).

6   Aquinas develops this account throughout his treatise on the soul: ST Ia.75–79 and 84–86. See also Kretzmann's Chapter 5, herein.

7   Aquinas holds that matter is the principle of individuation for composite entities, and so any material object or object existing in matter is particular.

8   In PA Prologue; QDV 1.3; ST Ia.16.2, 85.5; In PH Prologue.

9   In PA Prologue; ST Ia.79.8; QDV 15.1.

10   ST Ia.75–79, 84–86; QDV 10.4–6; In DA.

11   See primarily In PA; In BDT. But see also his summary presentations of this part of the account in ST Ia.1–2, IIaIIae. 1–2, and QDV 14.

12   For instance, ST Ia.17.3. Hence, Ross is wrong to equate cognition and knowledge (Ross 1984), and most English translations of Aquinas, which translate cognitio as "knowledge" and cognoscere as "know," are misleading in this respect.

13   For Aquinas, who follows Posterior Analytics closely in these matters,

scientia can designate a kind of mental state or disposition – what we might call a propositional attitude. But it can also designate a set of propositions organized by subject matter and in accordance with the member propositions' logical and epistemic properties and relations – what we might call an organized body of knowledge, a theory, or a science. This chapter is concerned only with what he has to say about the first, namely, *scientia* considered as a kind of propositional attitude.

14 Aquinas commonly uses three different abstract nouns – *cognitio, scientia,* and *notitia* (and their verbal and participial cognates) – all of which are in the neighborhood of the English "knowledge" (and its cognates). For Aquinas, however, the three are not synonymous. In order to avoid confusion, I will retain the Latin *scientia* (*scire* = to have *scientia*) and render *cognitio* (*cognoscere*) as "cognition" ("cognize"). I will translate none of his epistemic terms as "knowledge" (and its cognates), with the exception of the past participle *nota* (= known). I will provide the Latin on those occasions.

15 QDV 1.9; In PH I.3; ST Ia.17.3, 87.3.

16 For the account of truth as adequation, see QDV 1.1–2, In PH I.2–3. For the notion of cognition of truth, see QDV 1.9, In PH I.3, and ST Ia.16.2.

17 See In PA Prologue. By reasoning analogous to this, Aquinas holds that the self-reflexive capacity of intellect is the necessary ground for practical reasoning and moral responsibility (See MacDonald 1991b).

18 In In PA Prologue, for example, Aquinas describes *Posterior Analytics* as intended to help us evaluate and govern demonstrative reasoning. Governance of this sort is possible for us only if we can reflectively apply standards to our processes of reasoning and the cognitions to which they give rise.

19 In PA I.4.5.

20 In PA I.4.9. Aquinas appeals to this demonstrative conception of epistemic justification in passages in which he is explicitly distinguishing *scientia* from other epistemic propositional attitudes. See, for instance, ST IIaIIae.1.4, where he identifies *scientia* as intellectual assent to a proposition on the basis of something else that is cognized (*per aliud cognitum, sicut patet de conclusionibus, quarum est scientia*). See also QDV 14.1 and In BDT 2.2, ad 4, where he claims that the discursive reasoning (represented in a demonstration) precedes and produces (*facit*) assent to the conclusion, which is *scientia*. I take it that the sort of posteriority and dependence that Aquinas identifies as essential to the intellectual assent that is *scientia* is not (merely) causal but epistemic.

21 Aquinas's account focuses almost exclusively on the nature of the premises, ignoring questions about the nature of syllogistic inference. Of course he takes questions of this sort to be the proper subject matter

of *Prior Analytics* and so no doubt feels justified in treating them as settled for the purposes of discussion of *Posterior Analytics*.

22 See In PA I.7.8 (quoted in section V below). See also In PA I.4; In BDT 2.2; QDV 14.9; ST Ia.1.2; and ST IIaIIae.1.4; 9.1, ad 1.

23 For discussion of the causal principle in general and its role in Aquinas's cosmological proofs for God's existence, see MacDonald 1991a.

24 Aquinas states this principle of epistemic priority in different ways in different passages. Sometimes he says that the principles of demonstration must be *better known* than the conclusion; sometimes he says that the principles must be *more certain* than the conclusion.

25 In PA 1.7.5–8.

26 As we have seen, Aquinas's own version of this principle requires that one be justified *to a greater degree* in holding the premisses of the inference, but he explicitly waives this strengthening qualification for the sake of the argument. See In PA I.7.2.

27 In PA I.7.3.

28 I have supplied premiss (6) since the validity of Aquinas's inference from (7) to (8) requires it.

29 In PA I.7–8.

30 "In this [the skeptics] argue correctly, for we cannot cognize the posterior [propositions] when we lack knowledge of the primary ones (*ignoratis primis*)" (In PA I.7.3).

31 For Aquinas, then, definitions are not primarily linguistic entities. Moreover, he holds that they are not propositional in structure (they do not predicate anything of anything). The proposition "A human being is a rational animal" is not itself a definition; its predicate expresses the definition of the subject. See In PA I.19.5; II.2.11.

32 Aquinas allows for certain variations, identifying three sorts of what he calls *per se* propositions. See In PA I.10 and I.33.

Given his views about real definition, when Aquinas says that a proposition's predicate belongs to the account of the subject he does not mean that the predicate term is part of the meaning of the subject term, if the meanings of terms are understood as the sorts of things any competent speaker of a language grasps. He distinguishes between knowing the signification of the term (roughly, knowing a description that for the most part succeeds in picking out the objects to which the term refers: e.g., knowing that "thunder" signifies a certain noise in the clouds) and knowing the real definition associated with the term (roughly, knowing the metaphysically precise account – in terms of the genus and differentia – of the things referred to by the term: e.g., knowing that thunder is the noise caused by the quenching of fire in the clouds, or something of the sort). On Aquinas's view, a competent language user will know the signification of the term but not necessarily the real definition of the thing named by the term. Consequently, on his view, a competent language user might know the signification of the subject and predicate terms of an immediate proposition, and so in some sense "understand" the proposition, but nevertheless fail to see that the predicate belongs to the account of the subject because he fails to grasp the real definitions of the subject and predicate. See In PA I.2, I.4, II.8.

33 Aquinas takes the so-called Porphyrian tree to represent the metaphysical relationships holding between natures in the category of substance. Each terminal node on a fully developed tree of this sort represents a lowest species whose immediate essential constituents are the genus represented by the node immediately above the species and the differentia that distinguishes that species from other species of the same genus.

34 He allows that a proposition might be immediate *for some person* without being immediate absolutely speaking; see section VI below.

35 This connection between metaphysics and the logic of demonstration accounts for the connection between the two senses of *scientia* I identified above (n. 13). *Scientia* (the propositional attitude) with respect to P requires demonstration that P. But because demonstration must map reality in the right way, the requirement for demonstration entails a requirement for a kind of true theory into which P fits.

36 We might think of these metaphysically more basic facts as metaphysically prior to – or, as Aquinas prefers, better known *by nature* than – the fact they explain.

37 In PA I.2.9.

38 In PA I.19.2; I.20.6; and I.44.8.

39 ST Ia.79.8; QDV 15.1.

40 "Understanding, considered as the understanding of principles, is always correct. It is not mistaken with respect to them for the same reason that it is not mistaken with respect to what a thing is (*quod quid est*), for principles known *per se* are those that are cognized immediately (*statim*) on the understanding of the terms by virtue of the fact that the predicate is placed in the definition of the subject" (ST Ia.17.3, ad 2).

41 In PA I.19.2; I.36.7; ST Ia.2.1; and In BDH 1.

42 Aquinas suggests that we cannot be in the state of understanding a first principle without being aware of it (In PA II.20.4).

43 Aquinas often says that having a demonstration for some proposition compels or necessitates one's assent to that proposition; see, for example, DV 14.1, ST Ia.82.2.

44 In PA I.42.8; I.44.9; and II.19.5.

45 For example, this is how he introduces the discussion of *scientia* at In PA I.4.4.

46 Aquinas holds that intelligible objects can be distinguished on the basis of their relation to matter: (1) some (corporeal objects) both depend on matter for their being and include matter in their definitions; (2) some (mathematical objects, for instance) depend on matter only for their being and do not also include matter in their definitions; (3) some (God, for instance) neither depend on matter for their being nor include matter in their definitions. He maintains that intelligible objects of the second sort can be objects of strictly *a priori scientia*, and so *scientia* with respect to them will be more certain than *scientia* with respect to objects of the first sort. See In BDT 5; In PA I.25.4; I.41.2–3; and ST. Ia.85.1, ad 2.

47 By contrast, Aquinas asserts that the propositions of first philosophy (or metaphysics), which are the most universal, are better known absolutely speaking; see In PA I.17.5. He suggests that we can attain the paradigm of *scientia* in cases in which the propositions that are better known absolutely speaking are also better known with respect to us, as is the case in purely formal or *a priori* disciplines; see In PA I.4.16. See also n. 46 above.

48 Some of Aquinas's examples appeal to limitations imposed not by our corporeal nature but by our observational location, such as our having to observe a lunar eclipse from the earth rather than from the moon and our being unable to observe the microscopic pores that permit light to pass through glass (In PA I.42).

49 In In PA Aquinas develops the distinction in detail at I.23, but he calls our attention to it at the very beginning of his discussion of *scientia* (I.4.8), as if to warn us that the very strict account of *scientia* he is developing is not the entire story.

50 Aquinas also discusses under the heading of *demonstrationes quia* what he calls subordinate or subalternate *scientia*. One has *scientia* of this sort when one holds a proposition on the basis of a demonstration the ultimate premisses of which one holds because one takes them to be conclusions of strict explanatory demonstrations known to someone but not to oneself. In this case, what functions as ultimate premisses for one (because one has no demonstration for them) are not paradigmatic first principles, since they are demonstrable – Aquinas calls non-paradigmatic first principles of this sort *suppositions* (In PA I.5.7). Demonstrations of this sort are merely factual and not fully explanatory because of our inability to ground them in objective first principles.

51 "Sometimes what is better known to us is not better known absolutely speaking, as happens in the case of natural things in which the essences and powers of things are hidden on account of their being in matter. These are revealed (*innotescunt*) to us, however, by their exterior features

that appear [to us]. Thus, in cases of this sort, demonstrations are frequently (*ut plurimum*) constructed on the basis of effects which are better known with respect to us and not absolutely speaking" (In PA I.4.16).

52 Aquinas maintains that objectively speaking there is paradigmatic *scientia* about God. God himself and the blessed who see God's essence in the beatific vision have the sort of access to objective epistemic foundations that is necessary for *scientia* about these matters.

53 ST Ia.1; SCG I.3–9, 28–29; In BDT 1.2, 2.2–3, 5.4, 6.1. Aquinas also holds that we have cognition of truths about God by means of revelation. Moreover, he holds that the propositions contained in revelation can function *for us* as first principles (see nn. 50 and 51 above), grounding subordinate or subalternate *scientia*. With respect to us those propositions are neither demonstrable nor seen to be immediate, but they are demonstrable absolutely speaking (from God's perspective), and we can take them as starting points on the assumption that they are in fact properly grounded.

54 See also In PA I.42.3: "There can be demonstration of things that are for the most part insofar as there is something of necessity in them."

55 The probability here is understood not in the sense of relative frequencies, but in the sense of natural tendencies. I assume that probabilistic reasoning of the sort Aquinas identifies here differs from what he elsewhere calls dialectical or probable reasoning by virtue of the former's being grounded on truths about the natural tendencies of things.

56 "Necessity is different in natural things, which are true for the most part and fail sometimes (*in minori parte*), and in the disciplines, i.e., in the case of mathematical matters, which are always true. For the necessity in the disciplines is *a priori* whereas in natural things it is *a posteriori*" (In PA I.42.3).

57 See, for example, Plantinga 1983, p. 57.

58 Ibid., pp. 60–62.

59 Notice the exact parallel between the structure of these arguments about epistemic justification and Aquinas's causal proofs for God's existence (ST Ia.3.2).

60 In PA Prologue; In BDT 2.1, ad 5; and SCG I.9.

61 See also ST IIaIIae.2.9, ad 3, and SCG I.6, where Aquinas suggests that we are justified in holding certain propositions by virtue of having good reasons for their truth that are nevertheless not demonstrative.

62 See also In PA I.44; QDV 15.2, ad 3.

63 There were well-developed and widely known theories of dialectical reasoning in the Middle Ages; see Stump 1989.

64 The authority, of course, is God, and Aquinas argues for the divine origin

of revelation by merely probable arguments that appeal to certain historical facts, including the occurrence of miracles. See SCG I.6.

65 We have already seen his answer to the question of what justifies us in
holding immediate principles: we are non-inferentially justified in holding them by virtue of our inability to conceive their contraries, given our
conception of the terms of those propositions.

66 "Someone might hold, however, that sense or memory of particulars is
sufficient by itself to cause intellective cognition of principles . . . and so
for the purpose of ruling out this view the Philosopher adds that one
must presuppose, together with sense, that the soul is of such a nature
that it can undergo this sort of thing – i.e., that it is receptive of cognition of the universal, which of course comes about by virtue of the
possible intellect – and, moreover, that it can be active in this respect
(possit agere hoc) in accordance with the agent intellect, which makes
objects intelligible in actuality by means of an abstraction of universals
from particulars" (In PA II.20.12).

67 For detailed development of the doctrine of abstraction referred to here,
see ST Ia.79 and 84–86. See also Owens's Chapter 2 and Kretzmann's
Chapter 5 above.

68 QDV 10.6; ST Ia.84.4.

69 Aquinas argues against views that hold that human beings can have
access to intelligible objects without any recourse to sense perception by
claiming that cognition of that sort would be unnatural for human beings, given their corporeal nature.

70 Aquinas uses the term "principle" to designate both the propositions
that are premisses of a demonstration and the terms out of which a
demonstration is constructed. See In PA I.2.2–3 (where the conclusion's
subject and the proprium predicated of the subject in the conclusion are
called principles); I.5.9 (where he claims that since the definition cannot
be an immediate proposition – because it is not a proposition of any
kind – it should be taken as an immediate principle); I.18.7; and II.2.9
("Definitions are principles of demonstrations").

71 An example of a non-epistemic, causal process of induction would be
our teaching a child that 1 + 1 = 2 by placing one apple on the table,
then a second, and explaining that we have added one apple to one apple
with the result that we have two apples; then repeating the process with
pennies, wooden blocks, and so on, until the child grasps the principle.
When the child finally grasps (and so can claim to know) that 1 + 1 = 2,
her knowledge will be the causal result of this process of running
through particular instances. It will clearly not be the case that the
child's justification for holding the arithmetical proposition is an inductive inference that appeals to certain particular experiences of apples,

pennies, wooden blocks, and so on. Similarly, we would take facts about how *we* learned that 1 + 1 = 2 (the sorts of facts we could learn from our parents and first teachers) to be utterly irrelevant to our justification for believing that proposition. For a different view about Aquinas's appeal to induction in this passage and others like it, see Stump 1992.

72 "For [intelligible objects to be made actually intelligible] we require, besides the presence of the agent intellect, the presence of phantasms, a good disposition of the sensory powers, and *practice in this sort of activity*" (ST Ia.79.4, ad 3).

73 See Kretzmann 1992.

74 See, e.g., In PA I.4, II.13; ST Ia.29.1; 77.1, ad 7; IIaIIae.8.1; SCG I.3; and QDV 4.1.

75 This strategy is apparent in arguments of the sort found in ST Ia.75.5 and 79.3. In ST Ia.78.4, however, Aquinas suggests that we have *experience* of abstracting universal natures from sense perception of particulars. Perhaps he intends to rest his account in part on a phenomenological appeal of this sort; see section V above.

76 For our purposes we can take externalism in epistemology as the denial of internalism, where internalism claims that for a person to know or be epistemically justified in holding some proposition, that person must in some sense have access to or be aware of the fact that he satisfies the conditions necessary for knowledge or justification with respect to that proposition. For the claim that Aquinas is an externalist, see Jenkins 1989 and Stump 1992.

77 See also the passages cited in n. 20 above.

78 I am assuming that, for Aquinas, to have cognition of something (a thing or a proposition) is to have access to it in the sense of "access" that interests the internalist. (Of course, the internalist requirement of access needn't entail *occurrent* awareness.) Hence, our having cognition of the truth of a given cognition involves our having access to both that cognition and grounds for thinking that it corresponds to reality (in the case of paradigmatic justification, this would involve either direct awareness of the fact itself or direct awareness of facts that necessitate what is cognized – together with awareness of the necessitation).

79 For example, DV 10.4, ad1; ST IIaIIae.1.5.

80 *Contra academicos*, see Augustine 1922, Section I, Part III.

I am grateful to Jan Aertsen, Panayot Butchvarov, Richard Fumerton, Norman Kretzmann, and Eleonore Stump for comments on a draft of this chapter, and I acknowledge support from the Center for Advanced Studies at the University of Iowa.

7   Ethics

I. INTRODUCTION

Whether it be philosophical or theological in character, moral theory for Thomas Aquinas derives from reflection on actions performed by human agents. This truism calls attention to the priority of moral action over moral theory. Since human persons engaged in acting are aware of what they are doing and why, the distinction between theory and action is not one between knowledge and non-knowledge – between knowing and willing, say – but rather a distinction between two kinds of practical knowledge. In what follows I present a summary statement of Aquinas's moral philosophy, stressing the centrality of the analysis of human action to that theory and the way in which his doctrines of virtue and of natural law arise out of his theory of action. I end with a discussion of one topic central to the distinction between, and complementarity of, moral philosophy and moral theology: Have human persons two ultimate ends?

II. HUMAN ACTS

Aquinas maintains that the acts human agents perform are moral acts, which is why the theory of them is moral theory. To be at all plausible, this requires the distinction Aquinas makes between human acts (*actus humani*) and acts of a human being (*actus hominis*). The latter are any and all activities or operations that can truly be attributed to human beings, *but not insofar as they are human*, not *qua* human. Human acts constitute the moral order. "Thus the proper task of moral philosophy, which it is our present intention to

196

treat, is to consider human operations insofar as they are ordered to one another and to the end."¹ This description of moral philosophy grounds its subdivision into ethics, economics, and politics. The subject of moral philosophy is also given as "human operation ordered to an end" and "human beings insofar as they are voluntarily acting for an end."² All human action properly so-called falls to moral philosophy.

But surely Aquinas has thrown too wide a net. If human acts are what humans do, and if humans beings fall when dropped, hunger and thirst, age and wear out, it seems necessary to speak of all these activities or operations as moral acts. But surely to do so would be madly Pickwickian. It makes sense to speak of growing old gracefully, perhaps, but the ineluctable aging of the human organism does not seem blameworthy or praiseworthy in itself, precisely because it is not an object of choice.

It was just such considerations that led Aquinas to make his well-known distinction between human acts and acts of a human being,³ between activities attributed or not attributed to human agents *just insofar as they are human, qua* human. How can we tell whether a given activity falls to the one category or the other?

Human acts are those that are attributed *per se* or as such to human agents, that is, attributed to a kind of thing and of each and every instance of that kind, and of nothing that is not an instance of that kind. Aristotle calls this a commensurately universal property.⁴ Thus, those activities that, while truly attributed to humans, are not attributed to humans alone – that is, are not attributed to them *qua* human, are not commensurately universal properties, are not *per se* attributes – are denied the status of *human* acts. Only those activities that are willingly and knowingly performed or engaged in will count as *human*. Human acts have their source in reason and will, faculties peculiar to humans. "Human beings differ from irrational creatures in this, that they have dominion over their actions. That is why only those actions over which a human being has dominion are called human. But it is thanks to reason and will that human beings have dominion over their acts: free will (*liberum arbitrium*) is said to be the *faculty of reason and will.*"⁵

In this way the initially surprising suggestion that whatever humans do, all their acts, are moral acts is made more precise and more plausible. But difficulties remain.

Would we want to say that all the acts that only humans perform are just as such morally significant? The list we began above contains actions that none but a human could do, yet their proper appraisal does not seem to be a moral one. To be accounted a good golfer or poet or flautist or salesman is not just as such to be accounted morally good. The discussion of this more interesting difficulty is better postponed until we have said something of the role of the good, particularly as end.

III. ACTION IS FOR THE SAKE OF AN END

Human action is ordered to an end; we act for the sake of an end insofar as we have a reason for action. As characteristically human, action proceeds from intellect and will; that is, the agent consciously directs himself to a certain goal and does so freely. Moral responsibility is established by the relevance of the question "Why?" addressed to such actions. "Why are you doing that?" "Why did I do that?" Unlike "acts of a human being," human acts are those over which we have dominion, and dominion is had thanks to reason and will. If I ask someone why she is gaining weight, the answer may very well be an account of the effect of foods of a certain sort on the human body. If I ask, "But why do you eat so much?" Or "Why do you eat foods of that kind?" the answer will be of another sort. A man's beard grows willy nilly, yet some men grow beards and others do not. Not all "acts of a human being" can become elements of a human action in this way, but that some can shows the sweep of the moral. It is insofar as we are taken to bring something about freely or freely to let it occur that we are responsible for it and our doing is accounted a human act. Aquinas takes such a use of our freedom to be unintelligible apart from some end for the sake of which it is exercised.

Aristotle did not want to settle for the claim that all actions aim at some end or other; he holds that there is some end or good for the sake of which all actions are performed.[6] That is, there is an overarching, comprehensive, ultimate end of all that human beings do. Aquinas moves toward the same position by a series of steps.

The first step, of course, is the claim that each and every human act aims at some goood as its end. This is taken to be a property of human action as emanating from reason and will. The action is the action it is because of the objective the agent has in mind in performing it. What

Aquinas sometimes calls the object of an action – cutting cheese, chopping wood, binding wounds, running in place – is the proximate end of the action, what individuates it.[7] We could of course individuate acts by appealing to the individual agents who perform them – Ralph-acts, Thelma-acts, Caesarian acts, Elizabethan acts – but we would use the end the individual has in view to distinguish the different acts performed by the same individual. (When the same end characterizes several acts of the same individual – shaving one's beard – we would of course individuate by time.) This indicates that any individual act is an act of a given type and its type is taken from its end or objective.

The second step is to note that we can speak of a further end for the sake of which an objective is pursued. Granted that you are chopping wood, you can still be asked why you are doing it. The further objective could be winter fuel, needed for a warm hearth, which in turn is conducive to the well-being of the house's inhabitants. Many different kinds of acts can be ordered to the same remote end of physical well-being – sweeping the chimney, wearing a sweater, jogging, eating properly, having the house insulated, and so on. We call a variety of things healthy because of this orientation to the same remote end. This gives rise to the notion of an ultimate end, the goal to which the goals of other actions are subordinated.

Distinguishing between the order of intention and the order of execution, Aquinas argues that in each case there must be something first or ultimate. Intending a given end – getting to the top of Mount Everest – I clarify in my mind the steps that must be taken to get there. The ultimate objective I intend orders my thinking as to what I must do. So too from the point of view of the order of execution, the actual doing of the steps, I do things whose rationale is drawn from the end in view.[8]

Can a person have a plurality of ultimate ends? If health counts as an ultimate end, our answer of course will be in the affirmative. We can have lots of ultimate ends insofar as various acts of ours can be clustered under and subordinated to an objective beyond their particular objectives. Aristotle gave the goals of the building contractor and the general as examples of ultimate end.[9] The contractor orders the ends of the bricklayer, the carpenter, the glazier, the electrician, to the ultimate superordinate but subordinating end of the house; the general directs the ends of the infantry, cavalry, ordnance, quartermaster, and artillery to the end of victory. But talk of ultimate end leads to a far more interesting question: Is there some end to which the ends of all human acts should be subordinate? That there is an ultimate end of human life in this unqualified sense Aristotle took to be clear from two considerations.[10] First, legislators regulate all overt human actions in a community with an eye to the common good of the members of that community. Because that common good is the good of all citizens, it can be the ultimate end of each of them. Second, we have a word for it: happiness. Whatever we do, we do in order to be happy. Happiness is the ultimate end of human life.

It is of course platitudinous, and true, to say that everyone acts for the sake of happiness, but what does it tell us? We must, as Aristotle does, go on to consider the various accounts that have been given of human happiness and ask what the criteria of their truth and falsity, adequacy and inadequacy, might be. Could there perhaps be a plurality of mutually compatible accounts of human happiness? And what then of the claim that there is a single ultimate end for all?

Aquinas has Aristotle very much in mind when he discusses these questions, but his approach differs somewhat. "Whatever a human being seeks, it seeks under the aspect of the good (*sub ratione boni*), and if it does not seek it as its perfect good, which is its ultimate end, it must seek it as tending to that perfect good, since any beginning is ordered to its culmination."[11] Something is seen as good and attracts the will insofar as it is a constituent of the complete and perfect good of the agent. Aquinas relies on two obvious presuppositions. We cannot want what is evil or bad: evil or bad *means* the opposite of desirable. We can only want something insofar as we see it as good for us, see the having or the doing of it as preferable to the not having or not doing of it. Further, there is a distinction between the thing sought and the reason for seeking it, the aspect under which it is sought. The things we seek are innumerable, but each of them is sought because it is good, because it is seen under the aspect of goodness. Our good is what fulfills and completes us. Thus any object of action must be seen as at least a part of our comprehensive good. I do not want food simply as the good of my taste buds, but for my physical well-being, which is a part of my comprehensive good. (It will become clear that my comprehensive good cannot be simply *my* good.)

When Aquinas speaks of every human agent necessarily seeking the same ultimate end, he means that each and every human agent does whatever he does under the assumption that the doing of it is good, that is, fulfilling of the kind of agent he is, viz., a human agent. The notion of the human good is implicit in any human action. It would be absurd to say that all human agents do or ought to do the same kind or even kinds of act, like chopping wood, writing odes, reading Greek, climbing mountains. But it is not absurd to say, indeed it is inescapably true, that insofar as a human agent performs a human act, that action is undertaken on the implicit assumption that to act in that way is perfective of the agent. (Here "perfective" is tied to the act's reaching its term, that is, being a perfected act. Holiness or extraordinary goodness is not meant.) That is Aquinas's basis for saying that all human agents actually pursue the same ultimate end.

But humans live their lives differently; they organize their days and activities in a variety of ways. Indeed, their societies differ in organization: some are members of crude and primitive societies; some live in South Bend, Indiana. And when the mind's eye considers the race's diachronic existence, vertigo threatens. Not only does it then seem inexpressibly banal to say that all humans seek the same end insofar as they all seek what is fulfilling or perfective of them; it seems to be a mistake consequent on what we might dub the fallacy of abstraction. Has Aristotle, and Aquinas with him, gone awry?

People can, of course, be mistaken about what is good for them in individual actions, and they can be mistaken as to the superordinate and subordinating ends they set for themselves. Happiness will consist in the attainment of that which *truly* realizes the *ratio boni*.

The modern reader is likely to wonder whether Aquinas is here talking about what is the case or what ought to be the case. It is important to see that he is talking about both. There is a sense of ultimate end such that no human agent can fail to seek it, since it comes down to the self-evidently true assertion that none of us can act except for the sake of what we take to be good. But just as we can be mistaken about the good in a particular instance of action, so we can be mistaken about what is a worthy superordinate and subordinating objective of our deeds. If we come to see that not-*A* rather than *A* contributes to our happiness, we have the same reason for doing not-*A* that we thought we had for doing *A*. We did *A* in the mistaken belief that it was good for us; when we learn that our judgment was mistaken, we do not need any further *reason* for not seeking *A*. We already and necessarily want what we think is good for us, and we now see that *A* is not. So too, however many quite different things might be taken to be the ultimate objective of life, what is common to them all is the (often unarticulated) supposition that so to organize one's life is good for the kind of agent one is. When we disagree, we do not disagree that humans ought to do what is fulfilling or perfective of them: we disagree about where that fulfillment or perfection is to be found. Disagreements can be profound, even radical, but they can never be total.

IV. VIRTUE

The human agent is precisely one who performs human actions with a view to the good. If we want to know whether something or someone is good, we ask what its function is. This is one of Aristotle's great contributions to moral analysis. I can say that an eye is good if it performs its function of seeing well. The organ is called good from the fact that its operations are good, are performed well. The "well" of an action, its adverbial mode, is the ground of talk of virtue. The "virtue" of any thing is to perform its natural function or proper task well.

Since Aquinas is employing here a variation on the function argument of the *Nicomachean Ethics*,[12] it is not surprising that he encounters many of the same difficulties that have been recognized in Aristotle's argument. Bernard Williams, who acknowledges the force of the function argument as reintroduced by Peter Geach,[13] is typical in objecting that we cannot make the transition from particular functions to *the* human function. Aristotle is right to say that, if man has a function, he will be good insofar as he performs that function well; but there is no such function.

The human act is one that only the human agent performs. But, as we have seen, we can begin a seemingly endless list of such exclusively human actions.

Aquinas's response to this is the same as Aristotle's. What characterizes the human agent is rational activity – having dominion over his acts thanks to reason and will – and the virtue of *that* activity makes the human agent good. But "rational activity" is a phrase common to many acts, and it is common not univocally, but analogously. In a primary sense, rational activity is the activity of the faculty of reason itself. This in turn is subdivided into the theoretical (or speculative) and the practical uses of reason. Second, an activity is called rational not because it is the act of reason as such, but because it comes under the sway of reason even though it is an act of another human faculty. Thus our emotions can become humanized, rationalized, insofar as they are brought under the sway of reason.[14]

If rational activity is an analogous term such that there is an ordered set of kinds of rational activity, and if performing each of these kinds of rational activity well will be a distinct kind of virtue, it follows that the human good consists in the acts of a plurality of virtues. But, just as the activity of which they are the virtues is analogously common, so too is "virtue" an analogous term. Aquinas employs Aristotle's definition to the effect that virtue is that which makes the one having it good and renders his activity good. Good being the object of appetite, it follows, somewhat paradoxically, that the virtues perfective of rational activity in a participated sense of that term (for example, our feelings as they come under the sway of reason) are most properly called virtues, whereas the virtues perfective of speculative intellect, the characteristic human activity par excellence, are virtues only in an extended and diminished sense of the term. Geometry may perfect our thinking about extended quantity, but to call someone a good geometer is not an appraisal of him as a person. If geometry is a virtue; it is not a moral virtue.[15]

A human virtue is any habit perfecting a human being so that it acts well. There are two principles of human action, namely intellect or reason and appetite. . . . Hence any human virtue must be perfective of one or the other of these principles. If it is perfective of speculative or practical intellect so that a person acts well, it is an intellectual virtue; if it is perfective of the appetitive part, it is a moral virtue.[16]

We are now in a position to consider a difficulty we encountered at the outset. Aquinas's identification of human acts with moral acts seems to overlook the fact that we sometimes appraise human acts in ways that are not moral appraisals. An analysis of your golf swing or the way you bid in bridge will doubtless speak of good and bad, well and ill, ought and ought not, right and wrong, but these uses we should perhaps want to call technical rather than moral uses of such terms of appraisal. And Aquinas would agree. The speculative virtues, having geometry and quantum mechanics, say, enable us to perform well certain kinds of mental activity, and to say of someone that she is a good geometer or physicist is not just as such a moral commendation. But if we can appraise some human acts in a nonmoral way, it seems wrong to identify human action and moral action.

Aquinas, however, rightly sticks to this identification. His reason is that any human action that can be appraised technically can also be appraised morally. It makes sense to ask whether it is good for one to do geometry well in such and such circumstances. The fact that one is gaining knowledge of human psychology does not justify every procedure that might be employed. Intellectual virtues, whether those of theoretical intellect or the virtue of practical intellect that Aristotle and Aquinas call art (which has a wide and analogous range, from shoemaking to logic), are said to give us the capacity (*facultas*) to do something, but our employment (*usus*) of that capacity is another thing.[17]

Virtue in the strict and proper sense ensures a steady love of the good and thus involves will essentially, good being the object and love being the act of the will. Virtue in a secondary sense of the term provides only a capacity, but one we may use well or badly depending on the disposition of our will: it is the use, not the capacity, that depends on the will. But Aquinas exempts two intellectual virtues from this limitation, namely, prudence and divine faith.

If I have learned logic, I can reason well, but logic does not dispose me to use the capacity it gives. Intellectual virtues, since they can be used well or badly, are not virtues in the full sense of the term according to which a virtue makes the one having it and his operation good. Only habits that dispose appetite give both capacity and the bent to use the capacity well; indeed, the capacity is the tendency to act well in a certain way.

Practical wisdom or prudence is a virtue of the practical intellect that depends in a special way on the moral virtues, on appetite, and is more properly a virtue than are the other intellectual virtues. "Prudence gives not only the capacity for a good work but also use, for it looks to appetite, indeed presupposes the rectification of appetite."[18]

The good for a human being thus consists of a plurality of moral and intellectual virtues. No single virtue could make the human agent good, because the human function is not something univocally one. In order to be morally good, one needs the moral virtues, and these in turn are dependent on that virtue of the practical intellect Aquinas calls prudence. The moral virtues enable one to order the goods of the sensory appetite to the comprehensive good of the agent: they have, we remember, a greater claim to the designation "virtue" because they have their seat in appetite – they provide not merely a capacity but a disposition or inclination to the good. Justice has will or rational appetite for its subject and enables us so to act that we pursue our private ends with an eye to what is due others, whether because of special business we have undertaken with them or because of the comprehensive good we share as members of the same city, nation and, eventually, species.[19] We are so close to members of our own family that there is not sufficient distance for justice. Justice is concern for the "good of the other," but our parents and children – even our spouse – are insufficiently other for justice strictly speaking to obtain between us and them.[20]

V. ANALYSIS OF ACTION

Aquinas, like Aristotle, seeks to find an interpretation of Plato's thesis "knowledge is virtue" that is true. To do so he makes use of a conception of practical discourse or syllogism, suggesting that a principle or rule of action can be thought of as a first premise. I know what I ought to do. Such knowledge can be expressed in such judgments as "One ought not harm the innocent," "One ought to come to the defense of one's country," and "One ought to protect those put in one's charge." Lord Jim knew the last, but his action negated the knowledge. How could he have done what he knew he ought not to do? The very problem makes the identification of knowledge and virtue seem insane. What if we said that one can know yet not know his particular circumstances in the light of that knowledge? Then one could know and not know at the same time. One just doesn't see the particular circumstances in the light of the common judgment. More interesting for our purposes, one might culpably fail to apply what one knows (generally) ought to be done to these circumstances here and now. This is possible because the circumstances create an oppostion between the principle or rule and what I *really* want, that which is the object of my appetite because of previous behavior. My habits and character are such that my immediate particular good as I see it is opposed to the good expressed in the principle of action to which I give my assent only as long as it is kept general.

This analysis provides a negative approach to the role of moral virtue in the judgment of prudence. Moral virtue disposes to the end and enables prudence to judge efficaciously about means to be chosen. The judgment of prudence is knowledge of a different sort than that expressed in principles. Sometimes Aquinas contrasts general knowledge and the kind of knowledge prudence is by describing the former as rational knowledge (*per modum rationis*) and the latter as connatural knowledge (*per modum inclinationis* or *per modum connaturalitatis*).[21] This connatural knowledge of prudence is tantamount to virtue.[22]

The discourse of practical reason is sometimes described as a movement from a major premise, expressive of the general rule or principle, through the minor premise that is the appraisal of one's particular circumstances in the light of the principle, with the conclusion being the command of prudence as to what one ought to do. But the major premise can only function in such discourse if there is an appetitive disposition to the good action it expresses.[23] When there is a failure of application on the part of someone who knows and accepts the general principle, this can be due to the fact that he is not appetitively disposed to it. Then, Aristotle suggests, there is a suppressed general principle that, if articulated, would perhaps embarrass the agent, a principle such as "No pleasure ought to be foregone." In any case, a practical syllogism that issues in a choice must involve a major premise that is more than just a cognitive stance.

This analysis of human action in terms of end/means is even more prominent in the treatise Aquinas devotes to the constituents of a complete human act.[24] What has sometimes been regarded as a fantastic multiplying of entities has recently been appreciated as a discernment of moments of the complete act revealed when an action is interrupted at various points.[25] The analysis depends on a number of distinctions: first, that between the internal and external act. When I pick up my cudgel, thump my chest, and charge the foe bellowing ferociously, this external act is expressive of an internal command. Second, Aquinas distinguishes between the order of intention and the order of execution. Practical reasoning begins with the end and seeks the means of achieving it, moving from remote means to proximate and arriving ultimately at what I can do here and now. That is what Aquinas means by the order of intention. The order of execution, beginning with the act I can do here and now and proceeding to the achievement of the end, is the reverse of the order of intention.

The analysis of the interior act draws attention to the interplay of acts of intellect and will, first in the order of intention and then in the order of execution. Those in the order of intention bear on the end. A first act of will bears on what the mind sees as good, as an end to be pursued. An object is seen as good when I regard it in such a way that I am moved by it as fulfilling my needs. Continued thinking about it produces enjoyment and pleasure, as I imagine having it. As mind continues to explore the attractions of the good, the will, drawn to what is presented to it as attractive, enjoys the prospect of having it and then may come to intend it, that is, to desire it as something to be reached by as yet unspecified steps. The good willed and taken pleasure in must be attained and thus intended. These three acts of will – volition, enjoyment, intention – pertain of course to the order of intention. The intenal act now moves toward the choice of means, and here too Aquinas distinguishes different acts of will. It may be that there are many ways to achieve the good intended, and we find ourselves approving several among which we are going to have to choose. What Aquinas calls consent (*consensus*) precedes the choice of means when there is a plurality of attractive means. Reason commands the pursuit of the means chosen, and this involves will's use of powers other than will, perhaps most notably those of the body. While this could mean the choice to pursue a certain line of argument, in which case the command bears on the use of our mind, the command is most obviously grasped as bearing on the use of our motor powers, our limbs, various tools and instruments. The three acts of will in the order of execution are thus consent, choice, and use.

We are seldom aware of such complexity in our actions, but then we seldom think of how complicated walking is. The moments of the complete act come to our attention only when the act is aborted. We are constantly aware of goods that stir our will in a preliminary way, but that's the end of it. But we may dwell on and take pleasure in the contemplation of the course of action or state of affairs, yet not make the good an object of intention, an objective to be achieved through intermediate steps. Only if we do intend it will our mind go in search of ways and means of attaining it. If there is only one way across the river and our intention is to cross the river, to consent and to choose would be the same. Since there is usually a plurality of attractive means, consent usually precedes choice. The command then leads will to use another faculty, although sometimes the commanded act can be internal and sometimes it is an external deed. An example is the picking up of the cudgel, and so on, mentioned earlier.

This analysis of the complete human act into its components is another look at practical discourse as issuing in the command of prudence. In both cases, the starting points are said to be ends. Yet, in the case of practical discourse or syllogism, the ends were taken to be embodied in judgments or precepts as to what is the good for us. This is the view of them that leads on to another distinctive feature of Aquinas's moral doctrine, natural law.

VI. NATURAL LAW

It is a feature of the Aristotelian philosophy Aquinas adopted that there are starting points of human thinking that are accessible to all. Conversation presupposes shared assumptions about the way things are and the kind of agents we are, truths so basic that the articulation of them as common or basic seems almost an affectation. Aristotelian principles lie embedded in the practices of our life and thinking and come to mind as implicit in other thoughts and judgments. If your search for your tennis racket in the attic continued to the point where you said, "Well, either the damned thing is here or it isn't," this would seem facetious rather than the enunciation of a principle.

When Aquinas talks about the principles or starting points of thoughts, he means such embedded rockbottom truths, not a set of axioms we would regularly lay out before making another move. They are made explicit under pressure. That it is impossible for something to be and not to be, the most fundamental truth about things, is articulated when it is sophistically called into question. Basic principles of morality, those not tied down to our town or people, come to be expressed when we encounter others who seem to think otherwise and we need to get clear on what it is ourselves think. "Natural law" is the label Aquinas applies to the underlying principles of moral practice and discourse that are teased out of reflection on less general talk.

By the term "law" we mean, if he is right, a rational ordinance for the common good promulgated by one who has governance of the community.[26] Such an account puts us in mind at once of what issues from legislatures, from regulators, from judges and – once upon a time at least – from monarchs more constrained than these in their power: a rule for action proposed, discussed, then voted on, which effectively governs our behavior. The presumed aim of such restraints on our freedom is to preserve the common good of the citizens. Hunting laws; traffic laws; laws governing buying and selling, building and remodeling, the operation of vehicles, the preparation of food – the range of our laws is breathtaking, but theoretically the ultimate end in view is the common good. The use of the term "law" to talk about the rockbottom principles embedded in the moral discourse of human beings involves a meaning of the term that both leans on and is distinct from the term's first and obvious sense. This use does not begin with Aquinas, of course, but he spends some time justifying it.[27]

Civil law provides guides for action like those that function as major premises of practical syllogisms. Of course, not every such precept or guide is a matter of civil law; rather, civil law borrows from such moral judgments for its force. At the least, civil laws ought not be in conflict with fundamental moral truths. Some things are right or wrong because a law has been passed; sometimes a law is passed that expresses what is already recognized as wrong. Driving on the wrong side of the road carries punitive sanctions not because there is something about the right or left side of the road that requires this legal determination, but because traffic has to be regulated in order to avoid chaos. Laws against killing innocents do not establish the wrongness of such action. To engage in such behavior is wrong independent of its sanction in civil law.[28]

It is because civil law is not through and through an arbitrary affair, but sometimes expresses and should always avoid conflicting with moral judgments, that moral judgments came to be spoken of as an unwritten law, a law prior to the written law. To some degree the two have a common source. If a society passed a law making it obligatory to slaughter Irishmen, members of that society could not escape our censure by appealing to the law. Some civil laws, we should say, do not oblige and, while they have the look of law, actually are a perversion of it.

Our actions within society are constrained by laws, but the assumption is that this is a guidance of our freedom to the true shared good of the community of which we are a part. Whence comes the constraining power of the moral law? Why are we obliged by moral judgments? The notion of *ought* depends on the relation of means to an end. If there is but one means to an end, or but one available means, we are obliged to choose that end. "Ought" thus attaches to means rather than ends in the controlling sense of the term. Some means are obligatory, given our ends. This restriction of our freedom is thus hypothetical. He who wills the end must will the means, in the old adage. But what of the ends themselves? What of those ends to which we are disposed by the possession of the moral virtues?

The will as intellective appetite bears on things the mind sees as good, and there are certain things that are seen to be necessary components of the complete human good. Indeed, the mind grasps them as goods to which we are already naturally inclined. Virtue, as second nature, is the perfection of a natural inclination toward the good.[29] Judgments about goods to which we are naturally inclined form the starting points or principles of moral discourse. If particular choices are analyzed in terms of a kind of syllogism that applies a moral rule to particular circumstances, the principles are the non-gainsayable precepts that we articulate when less general guides for action are questioned. The set of the principles of moral discourse is what Aquinas means by natural law.[30] These judgments as to what one ought to do cannot be coherently denied. In this they are likened to the first principles of reasoning in general, and Aquinas has in mind the way in which the principle of non-contradiction is defended. It cannot be proved if it is the first principle, but that does not mean it can be coherently denied. One denying this principle must invoke it, at least on the level of language, as Aristotle argued. In order for "It is possible for something to be and not to be at the same time and in the same respect" to be true, its opposite of course must be false. Even more basically, the terms in which it is expressed cannot simultaneously be taken to mean X and non-X.

The equivalent of the principle of non-contradiction in the moral order is "Good should be pursued and done and evil avoided." It makes no sense to commend evil because one must commend it as a good, as desirable and worthy of pursuit. Is this the only non-gainsayable moral principle? Yes and no. There are others, but they are articulations or specifications of this one. "This is the foundation of all the other precepts of nature's law, such that whatever things practical reason naturally grasps to be human goods pertain to natural law's precepts as to what is to be done or avoided."[31] On what basis will practical reason judge something to be a human good, a constitutent of the comprehensive human good? "Since good has the character of an end and evil the contrary character, all those things to which a man has a natural inclination reason naturally grasps as goods, and consequently as things to be pursued, and it grasps their contraries as evils to be avoided."[32] Human beings have, in common with everything, an inclination to preserve themselves in existence; in common with other animals, they have an inclination to mate, have young, and care for them; and they have a peculiar inclination following on their defining trait, reason – to know and to converse and to live together in society.

Natural inclinations are those we have but do not choose to have: it is not a matter of decision that existence is good or that sexual congress attracts or that we think. We are inclined to do these, so to speak, willy nilly. Of course Aquinas is not offering as the first principles of the moral order precepts that tell us to do what we cannot help doing. If we acted naturally, willy nilly, this would be the negation of, rather than the beginning of, the moral order. It is because we can pursue such goods well or badly as human beings that moral precepts are formed about them. The moral order consists of putting our minds to the pursuit of the objects of natural inclinations, such that we pursue them well. We ought not look after our continued well-being in a way that is detrimental to our comprehensive good. Cowardly action runs afoul of that judgment. We ought to follow the inclination of our nature to mate and procreate in a way appropriate to agents who, like their offspring, have a good that is not exhausted by such activity. If I should take eleven wives and mate morning, noon, and night to see how many children I could produce, my actions would not be justified by the fact that sex and children are undeniable goods. It would be to pursue a good at the expense of the comprehensive good, as would my engaging in sexual activity in such a way that I thwarted the good to which I have a natural inclination.

The way in which natural law precepts are described may lead us to think of moral discourse as an axiomatic system: first set down the most general principles, then articulate less general ones, then proceed systematically toward the concrete and particular. This is not the procedure in the speculative sciences, save for geometry. Principles are starting points in the sense that they express (when formulated) the rockbottom goods embedded and implicit in ongoing human actions. Natural law is a theory about moral reasoning, and we should not assign to what is being discussed what belongs as such to the theoretical account. Natural law is the theory that there are certain non-gainsayable truths about what we ought and ought not do. These truths are described as principles known *per se.* It would be absurd to say that everyone knows what self-evident propositions are or any of the other trappings of the theory. Nor does the theory require that every human agent begin the day, let alone his moral life, by reminding himself that good ought to be done and evil avoided. That truth will be embedded in precepts he may very well formulate: "It's not fair to others to spend so long in the bathroom." "You need a good breakfast." "Wear a hat." The moral life is expressed in such discourse. More general principles, the most general principles, will be uncovered and in that sense discovered under the pressure of temptation or conflict or travel. But they will provide a shock of recognition rather than seem wholly novel. Indeed, when the most general principle is expressed, we are likely to take it as a kind of joke. "Do good and avoid evil" sounds a bit like "The sky is above us." Yet there are times when enunciating it enables us to get our bearings.

VII. MORAL THEOLOGY

Not everyone has a theory of natural law, but every human agent has access to its main tenets. Indeed, at least with respect to the very first principle of moral discourse, "Do good and avoid evil," every human agent already implicitly holds it. Unless one is very corrupt, other precepts of natural law will also be recognized by any human agent. This is not to say that they are a set of formulated rules imprinted on the mind that require only our reflexive attention to make themselves known. Rather, they are judgments we make after only slight consideration.[33] In this way the immorality of lying and stealing and seducing the spouses of others is recognized as inimical to a reasonable, human ordering of our lives. Aquinas maintains that prohibitions of lying and theft and adultery are exceptionless and that anyone is capable of recognizing this. A society that permits such practices will contain the seeds of its own dissolution.

This conviction that there are moral principles in the common domain that are the assumption of intercourse among humans has a long and noble history among pagans as well as among Jews and Christians. Questioning the existence of a natural law also has a long history. From a Christian point of view, the assertion of a natural law has an almost Pelagian insouciance about it, as if humanity had not suffered the aboriginal catastrophe that is original sin. Our wills have been weakened and our minds darkened and, it has seemed to some, only with grace can we know the most elementary moral precepts and abide by them. Thomas Aquinas was a Christian, he held to the doctrine of Original Sin, and he had few illusions about the behavior of most of us, Christian or not. His doctrine of natural law allows for its almost total loss through sin and perversity.[34] But nature is not wholly destroyed by sin; if it were, grace would have nothing to address. "Grace," he observes, "is more efficacious than nature, but nature is more basic to and thus more lasting in man."[35]

This is a large subject, but one facet of it seems necessary to round off this presentation of Aquinas's moral doctrine. It is sometimes suggested, even by students of Aquinas, that there can be no adequate moral philosophy. All moral doctrine, if it is to address human agents as they actually are (that is, fallen, redeemed, and called to a heavenly bliss) must come under the guidance of Christian revelation. Apart from this, it must give false advice as to what we should do and what is good for human persons. A version of this claim is as follows. Such a pagan philosopher as Aristotle, in laying out the ultimate end of human action, laid out an ideal of human conduct that would suffice to fulfill us and make us happy. Christian revelation offers another and conflicting view of the nature of human happiness or fulfillment. They both cannot be right. The Christian will know which is. He must then reject the pagan account.

The fact that Aquinas did not reject Aristotle's account of human happiness, of the ultimate end for human beings, must either convict him of a radical lapse in coherent thought or lead us to another look at the supposed opposition between the Aristotelian and Christian accounts of ultimate end.

We have seen the distinction Aquinas makes between the notion of ultimate end, on the one hand, and that in which that notion is thought to be realized, on the other. This enabled him to maintain that men who set their hearts on quite different objectives and have different ultimate ends nonetheless share the same notion of ultimate end. On the basis of this distinction, we could make short shrift of the difficulty and simply say that Aristotle located the ultimate end differently than Christians do, but that both Aristotle and Christians mean the same by "ultimate end," viz., that which is fulfilling and perfective of human beings.

Aquinas takes a quite different tack. He observes that Aristotle did not think that the notion of ultimate end could be realized by human agents. In laying out the notion, he spoke of a state that would be sufficient, that would be permanent and could not be lost, that would be continuous and not episodic. And then he contrasted the happiness humans can attain in this life with that ideal.

Why then should we not say that he is happy who is active in conformity with complete excellence and is sufficiently equipped with external goods, not for some chance period but through a complete life? Or must we add "and who is destined to live thus and die as befits his life"? Certainly the future is obscure to us, while happiness, we claim, is an end and something in every way final. If so, we shall call blessed those among the living in whom these conditions are, and are to be, fulfilled – but blessed *human beings*.[36]

Human happiness is an imperfect realization of the notion of ultimate end. It is on this basis that Aquinas distinguishes between an imperfect and a perfect realization of ultimate end. The philosophical ideal does not conflict with the Christian as if both were doctrines of what perfectly realizes the ideal of human happiness. The pagan philosopher's realization that our conceptual reach exceeds our practical grasp provides the basis for Aquinas to speak of the complementarity, rather than the opposition, of the philosophical and theological. Moral theology is not a total alternative to what men can naturally know about the human good. Rather, it presupposes that knowledge and would indeed, at least in the form in which we find it in the *Summa theologiae*, be inconceivable without reliance on the achievements of moral philosophy.

NOTES

1 In NE I.1.2.
2 In NE I.1.3.
3 ST IaIIae.1.1.
4 Aristotle's teaching on modes of perseity is found in *Posterior Analytics*, 73a34–73b26, and in *Metaphysics* V 18. See Aquinas's commentaries on these discussions.
5 ST IaIIae.1.1.
6 See MacDonald 1991b.
7 See Finnis 1991.
8 ST IaIIae.1.4.
9 *Nicomachean Ethics*, I 1.
10 *Ibid.*, I 2; I 4.
11 ST IaIIae.1.6.
12 I 7: "Now if the function of man is an activity of soul which follows or implies a rational principle, and if we say 'a so-and-so' and 'a good so-and-so' have a function which is the same in kind, e.g., a lyre player and a good lyre player, and so without qualification in all cases, eminence in respect of goodness being added to the name of the function (for the function of a lyre player is to play the lyre, and that of a good lyre player to do so well); if this is the case [and we state the function of man to be a certain kind of life, and this to be an activity or actions of the soul implying a rational principle, and the function of a good man to be the good and noble performance of these, and if any action is well performed when it is performed in accordance with the appropriate excellence: if this is the case] human good turns out to be activity of soul in accordance with virtue, and if there are more than one virtue, in accordance with the best and most complete."
13 See Williams 1972 and Geach 1956.
14 See the magnificent Chapter 13 of Book One of the *Nicomachean Ethics*, where Aristotle develops the material schematized here.
15 See McInerny 1968, pp. 24–29.
16 ST IaIIae.58.3.
17 ST IaIIae.56.3; 57.4.
18 ST IaIIae.57.4.
19 ST IaIIae.56.6.
20 Given the nature and purpose of the *Summa theologiae*, we expect Aquinas to bring into play so traditional a doctrine as that of the four cardinal virtues. As a theologian, he also must include the theological virtues – faith, hope and charity – and weave into his account as well

the Beatitudes and the Gifts and Fruits of the Holy Spirit. ST IaIIae.60.2 gives a remarkable summary of Aristotle's doctrine of the moral virtues. Aquinas lists ten moral virtues having to do with the passions or emotions. These, plus justice, give a total of eleven moral virtues.

21 ST Ia.1.6, ad 3.

22 ST IaIIae.58.2.

23 See ibid. for the use of *connaturale* in this regard.

24 ST IaIIae.8–17. See Donagan 1982. This is a very perceptive presentation of Aquinas's doctrine. I discuss Donagan's criticisms of the doctrine in McInerny 1992.

25 It is one of the great merits of Donagan's article to have emphasized this.

26 ST IaIIae.90.4.

27 The term 'law' is in short an analogous term, the controlling meaning of which, as far as our use of the term goes, is civil law. As to the real or ontological ranking, eternal law is primary. Aquinas accepts and defends the Aristotelian view that we first know and name the ontologically less perfect things that are accessible to us through our senses and then, on the basis of arguments grounded in our knowledge of such things, come to know and name their transcendent causes. The various meanings of 'law' are discussed in ST IaIIae.91: eternal law, natural law, divine law, the law of the flesh.

28 The way in which human positive law is derived from natural law is discussed in ST IaIIae.95.2

29 See ST IaIIae.65.1 and, for the opposite in vice, 75.2, ad3.

30 ST IaIIae.94.2.

31 Ibid.

32 Ibid.

33 ST IaIIae.100.1. "*cum modica consideratione.*"

34 ST IaIIae.94.6.

35 Ibid., ad 2.

36 *Nicomachean Ethics*, I 10, 1101a14–21.

8　Law and politics

Aquinas's political and legal theory is important for three reasons. First, it reasserts the value of politics by drawing on Aristotle to argue that politics and political life are morally positive activities that are in accordance with the intention of God for man. Second, it combines traditional hierarchical and feudal views of the structure of society and politics with emerging community-oriented and incipiently egalitarian views of the proper ordering of society. Third, it develops an integrated and logically coherent theory of natural law that continues to be an important source of legal, political, and moral norms. These accomplishments have become part of the intellectual patrimony of the West, and have inspired political and legal philosophers and religious and social movements down to the present day.

I. THE LEGITIMACY OF THE POLITICAL ORDER

The challenge to which Aquinas responded was posed to medieval Christianity by the rediscovery of the full corpus of Aristotle's works, which except for some logical treatises had been unavailable to the West before the thirteenth century. Aristotle's *Politics* included descriptions and evaluations of a wide range of political experiences in fourth-century Greece that were different from the experience of the medieval feudal order. His *Metaphysics, Physics* and *Nicomachean Ethics* contained analyses of human conduct and of the external world that contrasted with the approach to legal and scriptural texts that had predominated in the medieval "schools" (which were in the process of becoming the forebears of modern universities). Operating on the basic assumption that reason and

217

revelation are not contradictory, that "grace does not contradict nature, but perfects it," Aquinas combined tradition, Scripture, contemporary practice, and Aristotelian philosophical methods to produce a lasting and influential "Thomistic synthesis" in politics and legal theory. Central to that effort was his reliance on Aristotle's conception of teleology or final causes, which in Aquinas's thought became the working out of God's purposes in the nature of the universe and mankind that he had created.

Aquinas, however, is first a Christian, and his Aristotelianism is a Christian Aristotelianism. In contrast to Christianity, Aristotle had no conception of original sin, and, although he was not optimistic about the possibility of creating the ideal state, he was open to the possibilities of "constitutional engineering" and conscious of the wide variations in the political structures of the 158 Greek constitutions he had studied. For early Christianity and the Fathers of the Church, however, typified in the writings of St. Augustine (381–430), political life was corrupted by man's hereditary inclination to evil, and the state was a coercive institution designed to maintain a minimum of order in a sinful world. The ruler, even if he was a Christian, could only strive to moderate human power drives and impose a minimal justice on the earthly city that would make it possible for the members of the heavenly city to reach their eternal reward.[1] For the Aristotle of Book I of the *Politics*, on the other hand, man is *zoon politikon* – literally, a *polis*-oriented animal – and political life is a necessary part of his full development. "He who is unable to live in society, or has no need because he is sufficient to himself, is either a beast or a god."[2]

In his major political work, *The Governance of Rulers* (*De regimine principum*, 1265–67), Aquinas correctly broadens the translation of *zoon politikon* to argue that "man is by nature a political and social animal" (Chapter 1) who uses his reason and faculty of speech to cooperate in building political communities that respond to the needs of the group and of the individuals who compose it. The political community will be a union of free men under the direction of a ruler who aims at the promotion of the common good. Government then has a positive role and moral justification. Infidel (e.g., Moslem) rulers can rule justly "since dominion and government are based on human law, while the distinction between believers and unbelievers is a matter of divine law, [and] the divine law which is based on grace does not abolish human law which is based on reason."[3]

Having said this, Aquinas then argues that the Church may for religious reasons take away the infidel's power to rule, so that the autonomy of the temporal rule is not absolute. On the question of church-state relations Aquinas is contradictory, since in some passages – notably in *The Governance of Rulers*, Chapter 15 – he appears to argue for papal supremacy over all earthly rulers because "those who are responsible for intermediate ends [that is, the common good of the temporal community] should be subject to the one who is responsible for the ultimate end and be directed by his command", while in other places – STIIaIIae.60.6 and In Sent II.44.2 – he states that the civil ruler is subject to the spiritual only in religious matters (although in In Sent II.44.2 he makes an exception for the pope as possessing both spiritual and secular power). In theory, it would appear that Aquinas should be a dualist or advocate of the "indirect power" of the Church, defending a moral rather than a legal or political supremacy for the Church, but, as far as the texts go, he "waffles."

M. J. Wilks has argued that by admitting the legitimacy of temporal rule in a sacral age, Aquinas was initiating the process of secularization that would ultimately destroy the intellectual and ideological power of the Catholic church.[4] It is certainly true that Aristotle provided a rational justification for government different from that of revelation; but once the claims of reason, as exemplified by Aristotle, were admitted, there was always a possibility of conflict. For Aquinas, however, a belief that faith and reason were both valid and divinely legitimated sources of human knowledge meant that neither should be considered as dominating the other. (In fact, of course, as Aquinas implies in his discussion of divine law,[5] revelation acts as a kind of negative check on reason although, unless the pope is the sole interpreter of the divine law, this does not in itself argue for papal supremacy over the temporal ruler.)

II. AQUINAS AND CONSTITUTIONALISM

In addition to re-legitimizing political life, Aquinas shifted the emphasis in thinking about the best form of government. Until the thirteenth century, it was assumed that monarchy was not only the best form of government but also the only one that was in accordance with divine intention. The Neoplatonic world view of "the great chain of being" coincided with the realities of the feudal structure to support a hierarchical structure in the universe and in society that was profoundly anti-egalitarian in its implications. The hierarchy of the angels under one God was reproduced on earth with various ranks in church, state, and society, each assigned to its position under a single monarch. As Aquinas says in *The Governance of Rulers*, Chapter 1, "In everything that is ordered to a single end, one thing is found that rules the rest," and in Chapter 2, "In nature, government is always by one." Among the bees there is a "king bee," and one God has created and rules the universe. Thus monarchy is the best form of government.

Yet from Aristotle Aquinas had also derived a view of government as rule over free men who are able to direct themselves. Moreover, he admits that a monarch can be easily corrupted and there seems to be no remedy against the tyrant but prayer.[6] The solution, Aquinas suggests, is for the community to take action to get rid of the bad ruler if this is legally possible. (In his *Commentary on the Sentences*, written when he was a young man, Aquinas went further and argued for individual action against tyrants even to the extent of tyrannicide against usurpers, although not against legitimate rulers who abuse their power.) In two other places, Aquinas advocates a mixed constitution that combines monarchy with aristocracy (in its etymological sense of the rule of the virtuous) and democracy, involving an element of popular participation – a system that he describes as both modeled on the government established by Moses and recommended by Aristotle in the *Politics*.[7]

If these passages are combined with Aquinas's belief in the supremacy of law and his recognition of the special claims of the Church as concerned with man's ultimate end, it is easy to understand why Lord Acton described Aquinas as "the First Whig" or believer in the limitation of governmental power. We should add, however, that he was also one of the first to endorse popular participation in government, despite the fact that he was writing before the emergence of national representative institutions.[8] Aquinas may also have been familiar with republican institutions in the Italian city-states, and he cites in his writings the example of the Roman republic. In addition, his *Commentary on the Politics* familiarized students and intellectuals both with Aristotle's discussions of the commonwealth (*res publica*) "in which the multitude rules for the common benefit," and with Aristotle's definition of a citizen as one who rules and is ruled in turn,[9] this tending to undermine the dominant hierarchical and monarchical model.

The admixture of constitutional and republican elements in Aquinas's monarchism meant that centuries later, when neo-Thomists like Jacques Maritain and Yves Simon argued for a Thomistic basis for modern Christian Democratic theory, they did not have to look far to find texts to cite. This is not to say that Aquinas himself was a democrat. There is no mention of the need for explicit consent to law and government, and where he discusses participation, it is participation by corporate groups, not individuals, or by "the people" as a whole rather than through the individual voting and the majority rule of modern democracy.[10] Above all, the modern idea of religious freedom was completely alien to his thought. Heretics "have committed a sin that deserves not only excommunication by the church but their removal from the world by death [since] it is a much more serious matter to corrupt the faith that sustains the life of the soul than to counterfeit money, which sustains temporal life."[11] It is true that Aquinas admits that if there is "an error of reason or conscience arising out of ignorance and without any negligence, that error of reason or conscience excuses the will that abides by that erring reason from being evil";[12] but for him it was unthinkable that a heretic who had known the truth (as distinct from a Jew or "infidel") could be other than culpable for rejecting it.

Aquinas's view of women was also very different from that taken in modern liberal democratic theory. Contemporary feminist critics have focused on a single article in the *Summa theologiae* in which Aquinas argues that God created woman not as a helpmate to man "since he can get more effective help from another man – but to assist in procreation."[13] Even more shocking to modern sensibilities, in the same article Aquinas rejects Aristotle's description of woman as "a misbegotten man," arguing that although, as Aristotle states, women are weaker and passive "because of some material cause or some external change such as a moist south wind, . . . woman is not something misbegotten but is intended by nature to be directed to the work of procreation."[14] He adds that woman is naturally subject to man in a mutually beneficial relationship "because man possesses more discernment of reason."

The most striking difference from modern liberalism is Aquinas's treatment of slavery. Here he is attempting to reconcile two conflicting traditions. On the one hand, Aristotle (in Book I, Chapter 5, of the *Politics*) argued that the enslavement of those who are incapable of living a moral life is justified by nature. On the other hand, the Fathers of the Church wrote that all men are equal by nature and viewed slavery as a consequence of sin. Aquinas's answer is to refer to Aristotle's argument, to describe slavery as an "addition" to the natural law "that has been found to be convenient both for the master and the slave", and to limit the master's rights over his slave in the areas of private and family life as well as the right to subsistence.[15] Yet it is not clear that he rejects Aristotle's view of natural slavery, and as late as the sixteenth century theologians at the court of Spain debated whether or not American Indians were natural slaves.[16]

In modern terms Aquinas's political thought in its original formulation (that is, before the neo-Thomist revisions) is closer to European or Latin American corporatist and integralist conservatism than to modern liberalism. In one area, however, there is less need for a drastic reformulation in order to come up with a theory that is still applicable today – and that is the Thomistic theory of natural law.

III. NATURAL LAW

Next to the Five Ways of proving the existence of God (STIa.2), the Treatise on Law (STIaIIae.90–97) is probably the best-known part of the *Summa theologiae*. Aquinas begins with a definition of law as "an ordination of reason for the common good promulgated by the one who is in charge of the community."[17] Two comments should be made about this definition. First, by defining law as an ordination of *reason* Aquinas is saying more than simply that it is rational in character. As is clear from his explanation, he has in mind a particular type of reason – reasoning that is teleological or goal-oriented: "whenever someone desires an end, reason commands what is to be done to reach it."[18] This rational command is not a mere act of the will. When the Roman law says "the will of the prince has the force of law," it is understood that that will "must be guided by reason . . . Otherwise the will of the prince would be iniquity rather than law."

The second point is that for Aquinas, law is based on the community, since it is ordered to the common good and "making law belongs either to the whole people or to the public personage who has the responsibility for the whole people."[19] Thus even without organized representative institutions, the ruler is obliged to keep the common good in mind when he legislates, and corrupt governments are those that are directed at the private good of the ruler rather than the common good.

Aquinas then outlines his typology of laws. At the top of the hierarchy of laws is *the eternal law*, which he defines as "the rational governance of everything on the part of God as ruler of the universe,"[20] and identifies as divine providence.

Natural law, ranked below the eternal law, is defined by Aquinas as "the participation in the eternal law by rational creatures." That participation is through "a natural inclination to their proper action and ends."[21] What this means, as he explains in Question 94, is that reason has the capacity to perceive what is good for human beings by following the "order of our national inclinations."[22] These Aquinas lists as self-preservation, an end that human beings share with all substances, family life and bringing up offspring, which is shared with all animals, and the goals of knowing God and living in society, which are shared with all rational creatures. These goals in turn are seen as obligatory because practical reason perceives as a basic principle that "good is to be done and evil is to be avoided," which is a self-evident principle like the principle of non-contradiction.

The brief discussion of natural law in Question 94 has been the subject of considerable critical comment and debate. Jacques Maritain used it to argue that Aquinas believed that human beings come to know the natural law intuitively through natural inclination, and that when that knowledge is articulated in rational and universal terms, it becomes something else – *the law of nations* (*ius gentium*).[23] It is clear from the text, however, that Aquinas means that knowledge of the natural law is rational knowledge that is based on our perception of natural goals or inclinations "that are naturally apprehended by reason as good." It is true that in an earlier discussion Aquinas describes *synderesis*, the capacity to understand the basic principles of morality, as beginning with "the understanding of certain things that are naturally known as immutable principles without investigation," but he then goes on to describe the way human beings make judgments on the basis of those principles "concerning what has been discovered by reasoning."[24] Applying this account to the discussion of natural law, it seems that human beings know quasi-intuitively that good is to be done and evil to be avoided, but that they use their reason to make judgments that identify the basic human goods that are the object of our natural inclinations.

Others besides Maritain have attempted to de-emphasize the rational and propositional character of Aquinas's theory. Michael Novak, for example, describes Aquinas's natural law theory as "the traditional pragmatism. . . . not a set of generalizations but a set of individual intelligent actions,"[25] and E.A. Goerner argues that natural law is only an imperfect, second-best standard of morality, while "natural right" (ius naturale) is the "equitable but unformulatable virtue of the prudent and the just."[26] Morton White also misrepresents Aquinas's theory of natural law when he describes it as deductive in character, on the model of a system of logic.[27]

Aquinas states explicitly that adultery, homosexuality, usury, drunkenness, gluttony, suicide, murder, lying, and the breaking of promises are opposed to nature and therefore forbidden by natural law.[28] His argument is not intuitive, pragmatic, or deductive, but teleological in terms of the nature and purposes of human beings in relation to a given type of action. Those purposes can come into conflict, as Aquinas recognizes, but he believes that such conflicts are not irreconcilable, and that apparent contradictions can be resolved by the use of reason, since the world has been created and continues to be guided by a rational and purposive God.

Aquinas built his theory of natural law by taking a number of Aristotelian concepts and combining them in a way that is different from the way they were used by Aristotle. Whether or not he was faithful to the spirit of Aristotle can be argued,[29] but a comparison of Aquinas's discussion of natural law with the relevant passages in Aristotle's writings reveals that Aquinas has combined quite disparate elements in Aristotle – the *phronesis* of the *Nicomachean Ethics*, the description of final causality in the *Physics*, the discussion of the natural basis of government, slavery, property, etc., in Book I of the *Politics*, the ambiguous treatment of natural justice (not natural law) in Book V of the *Ethics*, and the description of law as reason in

Book III of the *Politics* – into a new synthesis that makes the determination of natural ends (based on natural inclinations) a central consideration in the development of a workable theory of natural law.

The originality of Aquinas's theory is evident when it is compared, for example, with discussions of natural law in Gratian's *Decretum* or *Concordance of Discordant Canons*, the major source book for canon law in the thirteenth century. Gratian describes natural law as "what is contained in the Old and New Testaments," following this with quotations from Isidore of Seville's *Etymologies* stating that "Divine laws come from nature" and, in a formulation borrowed from the introductory passages of the *Digest* of Roman law, "Natural law is the law that is common to all nations."[30]

For Aquinas *the law of nations* is related to natural law as "conclusions from principles," conclusions that enable people to relate to one another in all societies.[31] Aquinas therefore classifies the law of nations as a type of *human law*, that is, the particular applications of natural law derived by reason, while he calls the more specific and variable applications of human law "civil law" (from *civitas* = 'city'). Both varieties of human law are derived from natural law, and if human law disagrees with natural law, "it is no longer a law, but a corruption of law."[32]

When Aquinas discusses the application of natural law through human law, he allows for a good deal more flexibility than one might expect, given the absolute character of the prohibitions of natural law. Thus evils like prostitution, usury, and the widespread exercise of the religious rites of heretics or infidels may be tolerated "so as not to prevent other goods from occurring, or to avoid some worse evil."[33] The "secondary" precepts of natural law, which "follow as immediate conclusions from first principles," can be changed "in a few cases because some special reasons make its precepts impossible to observe,"[34] although, except for the mention of polygamy in the Old Testament, there is no further discussion of the difference between the two types of principles.

It is also possible for there to be additions to the natural law of "provisions that are useful to human life." In addition to slavery, already mentioned, property is cited as an addition to resolve the contradiction between the statement of Isidore of Seville, reflecting a common view of the Fathers of the Church, that "possession of all things and universal freedom are part of the natural law" and Aristotle's arguments in favor of the natural character of private property and slavery. For Aquinas, "neither separate possessions nor slavery resulted from nature, but they were produced by human reason for the benefit of human life."[35] Despite what appears to be a parallel treatment of the two cases of property and slavery, however, it is clear from other passages, cited earlier, that Aquinas is much more favorable to Aristotle's view of the natural law basis of private property (within limits such as a starving man's need for the means of subsistence)[36] than he is to his argument for natural slavery.

Two other concepts derived from Aristotle serve to provide flexibility in Aquinas's application of the natural law. The first is prudence, which he describes as a virtue by which human beings choose the right means for the attainment of ends that are identified by practical reason.[37] Some modern interpreters of Aquinas's political thought put great emphasis on prudence, particularly in the area of the conduct of international relations, where, it is claimed, the norms of natural law can be applied only in a modified way. Others are more insistent that even in the case of modern war, natural law prohibitions, against the killing of the innocent, for example, even indirectly, are still binding.[38]

Equity is a second source of flexibility that Aquinas derived from Aristotle's *Nicomachean Ethics* (V 10). Aquinas's word for equity is not its Latin cognate, *aequitas*, but Aristotle's original Greek term, *epieikeia*. This is the power of the ruler to depart from the letter of the law when its literal application would violate its spirit.[39] An example that Aquinas gives is the opening of the gates of a besieged city after the legal hours of closure in order to admit defenders of the city being pursued by the enemy. The exceptions, however, may not violate the divine law or the "general precepts" of natural law.[40]

In the area of sexual morality, which is part of the divine law, there is no departure from the Christian doctrine that sexual expression is permitted only within the bonds of monogamous marriage, although Aquinas admits that polygamy was tolerated in the Old Testament. Fornication and adultery are seriously wrong because they operate against the natural goals of family life, especially the upbringing of children. Because this is "the natural ordering of the sex act that is appropriate to mankind," masturbation, sodomy, and bestiality are also unnatural vices, in increasing order of seriousness.[41]

Did Aquinas believe that these sins should be made the subject of legislation? On the one hand, like Aristotle he believed that the object of government was to promote virtue. On the other hand, as noted above, he was also willing to allow for considerable legislative flexibility "to avoid greater evils," and human law can prohibit only "the more serious vices, especially those that harm others and which must be prohibited for human society to survive."[42]

On the other hand, Aquinas's discussion of sexual pleasure as divinely intended (and as more intense before the Fall) implies a more positive view of sexuality than earlier Christian writers had held.

The teleological approach to natural law also affected Aquinas's discussion of usury, which in the Middle Ages was defined broadly as the charging of interest for lending money. Citing Aristotle's discussion in Book I of the *Politics,* Aquinas asserts that because money is not in itself productive, but only a means of exchange, it is wrong to receive payment for a loan of money. But he admits that "human law allows usury, not because it considers it just, but to avoid interference with the useful activities of many people."[43]

There are two other issues where Aquinas's natural law theory has been relevant for public policy down to the present day, abortion and the just war. Deliberate abortion of the fetus is for Aquinas equivalent to murder, but only after "quickening" or "ensoulment," which Aquinas, following Aristotle, believed occurred forty days after conception in the case of males, and eighty days thereafter for females.[44] However, contrary to what some contemporary polemicists have argued, Aquinas believed that abortion even before ensoulment was a sin, although not the sin of murder. He did not discuss the case where the mother's life is directly threatened, but given his biblically based opposition to doing evil so that good may come of it (Romans 3:8), it is unlikely that he would have approved.

Aquinas was not the originator of the just war theory. Cicero had defended the wars of Rome as just, and Augustine had discussed the problem of the legitimate use of defensive violence by Christian rulers. What Aquinas did was to systematize its conditions, setting out three: declaration by the ruler whose duty it is to defend the commonwealth, a just cause (in particular, self-defense), and a right intention.[45] Possibly equally important was his description of what came to be known in ethics as the principle of "double effect."[46] In discussing whether killing an unjust aggressor in order to defend one's life would be using evil means to achieve a good end, Aquinas argues that one intends only the defense of one's own life but not the killing that may inevitably result, and that only the minimally necessary force may be used. This passage has been cited in connection with the debate on the morality of nuclear warfare, with the defenders of nuclear deterrence arguing that it is not immoral to target military objectives that may incidentally have the unintended (but inevitable) effect of killing innocent people.[47]

IV. AQUINAS'S LEGACY

As we have seen, Aquinas's thought on the topics of this chapter continues to be influential to the present day. Initially, he was only one of many writers of *Summae*, and he was even regarded with some suspicion because of the Church's condemnation of the doctrines of the Latin Averroists.[48] Despite the fact that Aquinas expressly opposed the Averroists in detail, some propositions drawn from his works were condemned by the bishop of Paris in 1277 in a general condemnation of Averroism. In 1323, however, Aquinas was declared a saint; his writings were widely taught, especially by the Dominican order to which he belonged; and when the Council of Trent assembled in the middle of the sixteenth century, his *Summa theologiae* was placed on the altar along with the Bible as a source from which to draw answers to the arguments of the Protestant reformers. In 1879, his teachings were declared to be the official philosophy of the Roman Catholic church by Pope Leo XIII, and, at least until the Second Vatican Council (1962–1965), they were the principal basis of theological and philosophical instruction at Catholic seminaries and in most Catholic universities.

His political ideas were developed by sixteenth-century Jesuit theorists such as Suarez and Bellarmine and through them influenced Grotius and other early writers on international law. His theory of natural law was adapted late in sixteenth-century England by Richard Hooker in his *Laws of Ecclesiastical Polity*, and through Hooker influenced John Locke. Aquinas's views on property, the family, and sexual morality have been widely cited in papal encyclicals; and a modernized version of his politics, which endorses democracy, religious pluralism, and human rights, has become the ideological basis of significant Christian Democratic parties in Germany, the Low Countries, Italy, Chile, Venezuela, and Central America. His statement on the invalidity of unjust laws was cited by Martin Luther King in his *Letter from Birmingham Jail*, and he has inspired many contemporary Catholic social theorists to argue for the establishment of a "communitarian" society that avoids the excessive individualism of capitalism and the collectivism of socialism.

Protestant Christians are critical of the excessive rationalism and optimism of Thomistic ethics, and of his refusal to recognize that there are contradictions between a rationalistic teleological natural law theory and certain aspects of the message of Christ, such as sacrificial love, martyrdom, rejection of wealth and worldly possessions, and "turning the other check." Radicals are suspicious of Aquinas's emphasis on the "natural" character of social systems that they insist are subject to human control and conditioned by economic structures. At least until the twentieth-century Neo-Thomist changes in favor of democracy, freedom, human rights, and religious pluralism, liberals were suspicious of Thomism's clericalism, implicit authoritarianism, sexism, and hierarchical outlook that seemed to prefer order to freedom.

Recognizing that many of Aquinas's views on society and politics that are unacceptable today (such as his monarchism, his qualified acceptance of slavery, his attitudes toward Jews, his defense of the burning of heretics, his belief in the natural inferiority of women) were historically conditioned or the result of an uncritical acceptance of Aristotle, the modern reader, like a number of contemporary moral and social philosophers (such as John Finnis, Alasdair MacIntyre, and Alan Donagan),[49] can still find relevant Aquinas's belief in the human capacity to identify goals, values, and purposes in the structure and functioning of the human person that can be used to evaluate and reform social, political, and legal structures, and to make a sustained argument based on evidence and clear statements of one's assumptions and the conclusions derived from them. This belief, which is really a faith that the meaning of human life is, at least in part, accessible to human reason, is an important element in the continuing attraction of what some of his followers like to call the perennial philosophy (*philosophia perennis*).

NOTES

1 Augustine, *The City of God*, Bk. XIV, ch. 28; Bk. XIX, chs.6,13.
2 Aristotle, *Politics*, I.2.
3 Aquinas, ST, IIaIIae.10.10
4 Wilks 1963.
5 ST IaIIae 91.4.
6 Aquinas, DRP 6.
7 In Sent II.44.2.exp.; ST IaIIae.95.4;105.1.
8 The English Parliament dates its foundation in its present form to 1265, the year Aquinas began to write DRP.
9 Aquinas 1963, pp. 314 and 332.
10 ST IaIIae.105.1.
11 ST IIaIIae.11.3.
12 ST IaIIae.19.6.
13 ST IaIIae.92.1.
14 Aristotle, *On the Generation of Animals*, IV 2.
15 SCG III,81; ST IIaIIae.57.3; Ia IIae. 94.5, ad 3;IIaIIae.104.5.
16 Hanke 1959.
17 ST IaIIae.90.4.
18 ST IaIIae.90.1.
19 ST IaIIae.90.2.
20 ST IaIIae.91.1.
21 ST IaIIae.91.2.
22 ST IaIIae.94.2.
23 Maritain 1951, ch. 4.
24 ST Ia.79.12.
25 Novak 1967, p. 342.
26 Goerner 1983.
27 White 1959, pp. 124 ff.
28 ST IaIIae.94.3; IIaIIae.47.2; 64.5; 78; 88.3; 110.3; 154.2.
29 See, for example, Jaffa 1952.
30 D.1.c.1 and 7, translated in Sigmund 1981.
31 ST IaIIae.95.4.
32 ST IaIIae.94.1. Cf. Kretzmann 1988.
33 ST IIaIIae. 10.11;78.1.
34 ST IaIIae.95.5.
35 Ibid., obj.3.
36 ST IIaIIae.66.7.
37 ST IaIIae.57.5. See also QDVC 13.
38 For the two views see Novak 1983 and Finnis 1987.
39 ST IIaIIae.120.

40 ST IaIIae.96.6;97.4.
41 ST IaIIae.154.11.
42 ST IaIIae.96.1.
43 ST IIaIIae.78.1.
44 In Sent IV.31.2.
45 ST IIaIIae, 40.1.
46 ST IIaIIae.40.7.
47 See Ramsey 1961, pp 39ff.
48 See Aertsen's Chapter 1.
49 Finnis 1980; McIntyre 1988; Donagan 1977.

9 Theology and philosophy

I. AQUINAS THE THEOLOGIAN

Nothing occurs more spontaneously to the modern reader of Aquinas than to ask about the relations between his philosophy and his theology, and no question is more misleading. To ask how his philosophy is related to his theology supposes that he would admit to having two separate doctrines and that he would agree that a doctrine was *his* in any important sense. Aquinas was by vocation, training, and self-understanding an ordained teacher of an inherited theology. He would have been scandalized to hear himself described as an innovator in fundamental matters and more scandalized still to hear himself – or any Christian – called a "philosopher," since this term often had a pejorative sense for thirteenth-century Latin authors.[1] Still, there is certainly something to be queried in Aquinas's ample use of philosophical terms and texts, in his having commented meticulously on a dozen of Aristotle's works, and in his having been regarded by some of his contemporaries as too indebted to pagan thinkers. What, then, is the appropriate formulation of the modern reader's question?

Any appropriate formulation must begin by recognizing that whatever philosophy there is in Aquinas can be approached only through his theology if it is to be approached as he intended it. Indeed, it is very difficult to separate out the philosophical passages in his works. His writings are overwhelmingly on the topics and in the genres of the medieval faculties of theology. He wrote almost always in what is self-evidently the voice of a theologian. Thus the three largest portions of his corpus are, in ascending order, commentaries on Scripture, a required commentary on a theological source-book, and a pedagogically motivated re-thinking of the topics in that source-book.[2]

In some texts Aquinas indeed seems not to write as a theologian, but these texts are at best ambiguous in their classification. The largest block of such texts is the set of commentaries on Aristotle. But these are "literal" commentaries characterized by the intention to explain, with little extrapolation or critical questioning, what Aristotle says. Aquinas did not write the commentaries in order to expound a philosophy of his own, but in order to make sense out of Aristotle's philosophy. Besides the Aristotle commentaries, the other seemingly "philosophical" works are either recapitulations of received doctrine (such as *De fallaciis, De regno*) or polemical pieces (for example, *De unitate intellectus, De aeternitate mundi*) or letters (such as *De principiis naturae*).³ Even the famous *De ente et essentia*, which has often been taken as a programmatic statement of Thomistic metaphysics, is a set of youthful variations on themes by Avicenna. In short, no single work was written by Aquinas for the sake of setting forth a philosophy.

Aquinas chose not to write philosophy. He did so partly because of other choices he had made – for example, to become a Dominican and a Master of Theology. But these earlier choices would not in themselves have settled the issue. After all, Aquinas's teacher Albert wrote at length in philosophical genres, and some of his students or disciples would do so as well. Aquinas's decision to write as a theologian when he wrote in his own voice was chiefly the result of his view that no Christian should be satisfied to speak only as a philosopher.

II. "PHILOSOPHY" AND THEOLOGY

For Aquinas, *philosophia* names, first, a hierarchy of bodies of knowledge.⁴ These can be built up as intellectual virtues in human souls. *Philosophia* is, in the second place, a pattern of teaching such virtues, a pattern enacted in communities of learners and in textual traditions. Aquinas conceived philosophy as embodied in historical communities, in lines of teachers and students who shared ways of life, languages, topics, and procedures. Such philosophical schools were among the glories of pagan antiquity. But membership in them did not, on his view, befit Christians.

One can see this both in his terminology and in the forms of some of his historical arguments. He speaks about philosophy, of course, as a habit of knowing – an acquired grasp of principles and arguments – necessary to an educated Christian believer. Yet when he speaks of a school of philosophy or of philosophers, he speaks of how wisdom was sought by pagans. He never applies the epithet *philosophus* to a Christian.⁵ Again, he never includes Christians in his surveys of philosophical opinions, even when he does include writers beyond those mentioned in the ancient or patristic narratives that are his sources. He is quite ready to posit that the compiler of the *Liber de causis* was one of the Arab "philosophers."⁶ He never speaks of a similar group of Christians. "Philosophers" properly so-called are not always ancient, but they seem always to be unbelievers.

No one can doubt that Aquinas admired pagan philosophers both for their zeal in inquiry and for their way of life. He praises the philosophic pursuit of contemplation, just as he holds up the philosopher's abandonment of earthly goods.⁷ And yet he also diagnoses the origin of philosophic contemplation as self-love, and so distinguishes it sharply from Christian contemplation.⁸ The philosopher's asceticism is also not the Christian's, since the Christian must renounce worldly goods for the sake of Christ.⁹ The philosophers seek authority by dispute, while the Lord teaches believers to come peacefully under a divinely constituted authority.¹⁰ The philosophers can offer a dozen causes for the arrangement of the cosmos, but the believer knows that divine providence has arranged the world so that human beings might have a home.¹¹

If these scattered remarks seem only particular corrections, one can turn to Aquinas's very explicit judgments on the doctrines and the promises of the philosophers. He judges that their doctrines were severely constrained by the weakness of human reason. Before general audiences, Aquinas is reported to have said such things as that all the efforts of the philosophers were inadequate to understand the essence of a fly.¹² In academic writings, whenever Aquinas argues for the appropriateness of God's revealing what might have been demonstrated, he insists on the weakness and fallibility of unaided human reason.¹³ He notes the same failings in distinguishing the philosophical and theological bodies of knowledge about God.¹⁴ He judges philosophy's promises even more harshly. Pagan philosophy presented itself as the love of the best knowledge of the highest things, that is, as a way toward happiness. Yet philosophy was incapable of providing happiness. The ancient philosophers multiplied views on the human good, but they could not achieve it.[15] Philosophers were unable to convince even their fellow citizens, because they could not offer a teaching about life that was firm, comprehensive, and useful.[16] No philosopher had enough wisdom to call men back from error; instead they led many into error.[17] The philosophers could not avoid sin, because they could not undergo the unique purification of the true worship of God, which begins in the philosophically unknowable coming of Christ.[18]

Aquinas gathers these observations into a handful of contrasts. Frequently he draws a line between what the philosophers think or say and what "we" believers say.[19] He makes the contrast clear when he constructs a trichotomy of philosophy, the Law of the Old Testament, and the Gospel of the New. The light of philosophy was false; the light of the Law was symbolic; the light of the Gospel is true.[20] Again, philosophy is "earthly" and "carnal" wisdom, "according to the natures of things and the desires of the flesh"; "we" Christians live rather by grace.[21] It cannot be a surprise, then, that Aquinas glosses the scriptural condemnations of secular pretension as applying specifically to philosophers,[22] or that he groups philosophers with heretics as opponents to the faith.[23]

Nevertheless, Aquinas uses philosophy and explicitly urges its use on writers of theology. How can this be? The use is authorized by what he likens to a miraculous change in the philosophical doctrines: "those who use philosophical texts in sacred teaching, by subjugating them to faith, do not mix water with wine, but turn water into wine."[24] "Subjugating" philosophy to theology seems to mean several things. First, it means that the theologian takes truth from the philosophers as from usurpers.[25] The ground of philosophic truth is thus asserted to be the revealing God who is more fully and accurately described in theology. This suggests, second, that theology serves as a corrective to philosophy. As Aquinas puts it in one of his sermons, "Faith can do more than philosophy in much; so that if philosophy is contrary to faith, it is not to be accepted."[26] Again, in a commentary on Paul, he turns aside to raise a general objection: "Are the reasoning and the traditions of men always to be rejected?" He answers, "No, but rather when matter-bound reasoning proceeds according to them and not according to Christ."[27] To proceed "according to Christ" requires, third, that the impure motives of philosophy – vanity, contentiousness, arrogance – be transformed into the motives of the Christian believer. Philosophical inquiries ought always to serve a theological end. Applied to texts, this rule would seem to require that philosophical argumentation be begun and carried forward only from the believer's motive of the twofold love of God and neighbor.

Even if such procedural rules or admonitions are somehow helpful, they remain abstract. To see how Aquinas enacts them, one has to look carefully at places in which he does change philosophy into theology. I have chosen two such places, both from ST. The passages have been influential historically, but I have not selected them for that reason. While discussions in ST sometimes lack the technical detail of parallel passages elsewhere in Aquinas, they also offer the best chance to see Aquinas using the materials that he considers essential for the construction of a balanced theological pedagogy. ST is Aquinas's last and best experiment in the invention of a literary form that would accommodate his whole view of theology. It is thus the best single work in which to watch him construct theological teaching page by page. I thus turn to ST's definition of the virtues and to its analysis of sacramental efficacy as good examples of Aquinas's conversion of philosophy into theology.

III. DEFINING THE VIRTUES

Readers familiar with Aquinas's teaching on analogy and with his views of philosophical language will not find it surprising that he treats "virtue" explicitly as an analogous term (IaIIae.61.1, ad 1).[28] Still, the analogical range of "virtue" is something more than the richness of any important philosophical term. Aquinas is very clearly aware not only that there are different authorities on the definition of virtue but that the term itself, even on its best definition, must apply to very different types of cases. He must not only collate authoritative texts, he must also show that the various cases covered by them are ordered around one primary case so as to prevent the term from becoming equivocal.

Of course, Aquinas inherited a number of authoritative definitions, including several from Cicero[29] and from Aristotle's physical works.[30] But the main contest is between two definitions of "virtue," one from Aristotle's Ethics and one from Augustine by way of Peter Lombard's Sentences. The Aristotelian definition is the famous conclusion that virtue is a voluntary habit leading to action that lies in the mean with regard to us, defined as reason and a prudent person would define it.[31] Aquinas paraphrases this definition in a number of different ways throughout his discussion of the virtues,[32] although not in IaIIae.55, the Question on the definition of virtue. The reason for the omission will appear in a moment. The competing definition comes from Lombard's *Sentences:* "Virtue is a good quality of mind, by which one lives rightly and which no one uses badly, that God alone works in man."[33] It is, as Aquinas knows, a conflation of Augustinian texts and especially of passages from Book II of his *On Free Choice*, which supplies the middle clause of Lombard's definition.[34] The definition from the *Sentences* is the only one that Aquinas sets out explicitly to defend, even though it is a definition only for divinely infused virtue.[35]

The tension between these two definitions is quite strong. Aristotle's definition has in view chiefly moral virtue (that is, humanly acquired virtue), with the stress on the notion of the mean and on the reference to the prudential judgment of the virtuous in establishing the mean. The definition that Peter Lombard composes out of Augustine is a definition of virtue infused by God, and it is not immediately clear whether it speaks both of the infused theological virtues of faith, hope, and charity and of the infused moral virtues. Aquinas attempts to resolve the tension between these two definitions by constructing a more comprehensive analogy of the term "virtue," one ample enough to contain both Aristotle and Augustine. I think that he succeeds in the attempt but only by subordinating Aristotle to Augustine.

Aquinas introduces virtue, in good dialectical fashion, with a remark on its least specific sense: " 'virtue' names a certain completion of power" (*quandam potentiae perfectionem*) (IaIIae.55.1). This sense is divided between natural powers, which are themselves called *virtues* as determined to a specific end, and "rational" powers, for which *virtus* names the habit or cumulative disposition that determines the power to act. Then the distinction is displaced by a second: virtues can enable being or acting (IaIIae.55.2). In the second part of ST, Aquinas is concerned with peculiarly human virtues of acting and restricts the use of *virtus* accordingly. He can thus add yet another piece for a fuller definition, namely, that virtue is an "operative habit" (IaIIae.55.2). It is very easy to conclude, next, that it must be a good operative habit, since the notion of completeness forms part of the moral notion of virtue. Then something puzzling happens. He turns, in the last Article of the Question, to defend the very different definition of infused virtues taken from Augustine via Peter Lombard.

What is the point of jumping, as it seems, from the general notion of virtue inherited from Aristotle to the much more specific and theological definition provided by Lombard? If a full definition is needed to cap the dialectical development of Question 55, why not supply Aristotle's definition of moral virtue from the *Ethics*? The answer cannot be simply an appeal to Augustine's authority, because Aquinas has a dozen ways of re-reading Augustine or of fashioning revisionary contexts for him when there are things he finds imprudent or misleading in the Augustinian texts. The answer must rather be that the *center* of the analogy of virtue lies not in the civic virtues as Aristotle understood them, but in virtues infused by God. The full definition must be given for the first and clearest member of the analogy, and the clearest case is not acquired, but infused virtue.

Making the principal definition of virtue theological has any number of consequences. One is that Aquinas must rework the notion of habit that he has constructed so carefully in Questions 49–54 using Aristotle and Aristotle's interpreters.[36] Another consequence is that he understands even the pagan virtues as if from above. At the end of his discussion of the cardinal virtues, he introduces a passage from Macrobius that includes a quotation from Plotinus. In it Plotinus multiplies the four cardinal virtues into four steps or stages corresponding to four states of the soul: the political, the purgative, the already purged, and the exemplary (61.5, s.c.). The passage had appeared several times in Albert's *Lectura* on the *Ethics* and was familiar to Aquinas from many other texts as well.[37] He does not correct its teaching, but he follows his predecessors in giving it a thoroughly Christian reading.

It is easy to understand that the political stage of the virtues corresponds to man as naturally political, that is, to man "according to the condition of his nature." The exemplary stage corresponds to the virtues as they are in God – here Aquinas simply follows Macrobius's reading of Plotinus. The two middle stages are thus understood as helping the soul toward its end in God. The purging cardinal virtues are virtues of motion toward God. Thus prudence is reinterpreted as the virtue of despising all worldly things in favor of contemplation. The virtues of the soul already purged are those exercised while possessing the highest end, the virtues of the blessed. Thus prudence becomes, at the third stage, the seeing only of the divine.

This allegorical reading of the four stages of virtue, by which each cardinal virtue is carried upward from the human realm to the divine, extends the analogy of the terms in an unexpected direction. In the first discussions of the cardinal virtues, the whole question of the theological virtues had been held at bay. Now it becomes clear that the political cardinal virtues are the most important virtues for our present condition, but not for our final end, which lies beyond human capacity (61.1, ad 2). But the purging and already purged virtues are clearly related directly to that last end. They are some of the cardinal virtues that last into the state of glory (67.1). Indeed, they must be among the infused moral virtues rooted in charity (63.3).

Here is the difficulty, because the infused moral virtues differ in kind from the acquired moral virtues precisely because they prepare human beings to be citizens of the heavenly city, not of the earthly (63.4). If they are different in kind and take a different definition, it is difficult to see how they can be called by the same name except equivocally. Nor is the difficulty over the unity of the analogy confined just to the infused cardinal virtues. The three theological virtues are ordered to an end different from that of the acquired virtues. They have God as their object, they are infused only by God, they are taught only by divine revelation (62.1). They thus differ in species from the moral and intellectual virtues (62.2). The difference is not merely a formal one; it has consequences for action. The theological virtues are more than supplements in aid of the cardinal virtues. They both enable and require different actions. The theological virtues are not virtues lying in the mean, except accidentally, since their rule and measure is God himself (64.4). So they prescribe different standards even for subject matter considered also by the moral virtues. Thus, for instance, the infused moral virtues will require a degree of bodily asceticism not required by the acquired moral virtues (63.4).

All of this seems to stretch the analogy of virtue almost to breaking. Can it be held together by clarifying the hierarchy of cases within the analogy, that is, by distinguishing proper and improper senses for the term? Aquinas provides a clarification in his discussion of the connection and equality of the virtues. These are, on the surface, topics familiar from ancient philosophy. He knows from a number of sources, such as Simplicius and Augustine, that the Stoics taught the unity of all virtues and the equality of all faults. Aquinas is concerned with these questions. What is more important for him, however, is the connection between the acquired virtues of intellect and will and the infused virtues, whether moral or theological. The ancient philosophical topics become occasions for trying to display the unity-and-difference in the analogy of virtue itself.

Four objections are raised against the connection of acquired moral virtues. Aquinas replies with four authorities in the *sed contra*, three from the Church Fathers and one from Cicero (65.1). His counter-argument depends less on these authorities than on a distinction between complete and incomplete virtue. Incomplete virtue is no more than an inclination to do some good thing, an inclination that can arise as much from natural endowment as from practice. Imperfect virtues are not connected to one another. Someone can have a natural or acquired tendency to do generous deeds without having any tendency to be chaste. By contrast, complete virtue is the habit inclining one to the good performance of a good deed. Complete virtues are connected with one another, whether they are understood as common components of good action or as related to specific cases or matters. First, the connection has to do with the common structure of action. Second, it has to do with the central role of prudence, through which all particular virtues are connected. Without prudence, a habit of repeated self-restraint when faced with one kind of temptation, say, will not become the virtue of self-restraint, because it will lack the relation to prudence by which it could be generalized to similar situations. Indeed, the operations of moral virtue are ordered to one another in such a way that a habit in one operation must require a habit in all (65.1, ad 3).

So far the consideration has proceeded in what seems a philosophical manner. But the next Question asks whether this unified complex of moral virtues can exist without charity (65.2). Aquinas's answer is nuanced. If "virtue" is taken as aiming toward a naturally attainable human end, it can be said to be acquired by human effort. This virtue can exist without charity, as was the case among many pagans. Still, pagan virtues do not "completely and truly satisfy the notion (*ratio*) of virtue." The notion is satisfied only by virtues that conduce to the highest human end, which is supernatural. Strictly speaking, then, there can be no virtue without charity. Moral virtues are infused, together with the prudence on which they depend, after the infusion of charity. "It follows then from what has been said that only the infused virtues are complete, and are called virtues simply, because they order the human being rightly to the last end simply speaking." Aquinas holds that charity cannot be infused without the attendant moral virtues, of which it is the principle (65.3), or without the other two theological virtues, which make possible friendship with God (65.5).

For Aquinas, then, no single inclination toward the good, standing by itself, can be called a virtue without qualification. It is only an incomplete or anticipated virtue that needs to be taken up into the unity of the virtues centered on charity. Pagan virtues are only virtues *secundum quid*, that is, as ordered to some particular good that is not the complete and final good of human life. He thus approves a gloss on Romans that says, "Where acquaintance with the truth is lacking, virtue is false even when connected to good customs" (*in bonis moribus*, 65.2c). Securing the analogy of virtue has led, then, not only to the substitution of a theological for a philosophical definition, but also to judgments on human life very different from Aristotle's. It seems clear that Aquinas has here changed philosophical materials into theology. The further implications of the change will be traced after setting forth the second example.

IV. ANALYZING SACRAMENTAL EFFICACY

Aquinas is often credited with formulating decisively the teaching that sacraments are causes of grace. Part of the credit usually goes to his philosophical account of causality, on the supposition that it was because he understood Aristotle so well that he was able to explain the sacraments. He does show himself an attentive reader of Aristotle on causes, as in his expositions of the *Physics* and the *Metaphysics*. Moreover, he often supplements the Aristotelian classifications of causes – for example, by borrowing from Avicenna and by insisting on the importance of exemplary causality, that is, causality by participative likeness. Aquinas does not hold that there is one and only one proper cause for a natural event. Nor does he teach any strict doctrine of causal determinism in nature. He is careful not to reduce the complex discourse about causes to one or several tightly worded "principles." All of this makes for a complex account of natural causality, and some have concluded that this account should somehow be responsible for the famous conclusion that the sacraments are causes. In fact, the motivation appears to work in the opposite direction. Aquinas's understanding of theologically important cases of causality motivates changes in his teaching about causality in general.

Aquinas was by no means the first Scholastic theologian to call the sacraments causes. The usage goes back at least a century before him. Peter Lombard distinguishes sacraments from other signs by pointing to their causal efficacy: " 'Sacrament' is said properly of what is so much a sign of the grace of God and so much the form of invisible grace, that it produces the image of it and stands forth as a cause" (ipsius imaginem gerat et causa exsistat).[38] Lombard's language is taken up explicitly by such theologians as Guido of Orchelle and William of Auxerre,[39] not to mention such influential Franciscans as Bonaventure.[40] Perhaps more important, assertions of sacramental causal efficacy can be found in many of Aquinas's Dominican predecessors.[41]

If Aquinas is not the first to speak of sacraments as causes, he does give new prominence to sacramental causality by asserting it separately and straightforwardly. In the Sentences, for example, the whole treatment of sacraments is part of the "teaching about signs" (doctrina signorum), and so its discussions of causality seem inevitably surbordinated to discussions of signification.[42] In Bonaventure, a lengthy review of controversies over sacramental causality ends on a note of skeptical reserve: "I do not know which [opinion] is truer, since when we speak of things that are miracles, we ought not to adhere much to reason. We thus concede that the sacraments of the New Law are causes, that they produce effects and that they dispose things, according to the loose sense of 'cause' . . . and it is safe to say this. Whether they have something more, I wish neither to affirm nor to deny."[43] Even Albert is careful to describe their causality as a kind of material disposition, and to deny that saving grace is somehow tied to the sacrament or that the sacraments "contain" grace in any ordinary sense.[44] Against this background, Aquinas's steady assertions of causal efficacy in the sacraments are striking.[45]

The organization of ST, unlike that of the *Sentences*, makes sacra-mental causality more prominent than signification. Aquinas di-vides the common consideration of the sacraments into five topics: what they are, why they are needed, what their effects are, what their causes are, and how many of them there are (ST IIIa.60, prol.). Each topic takes one Question, except for the topic of effects, which is divided into two Questions as between principal effect and secon-dary effect (IIIa.62–63). The topic of sacramental efficacy is thus more highly articulated than the others from the start.

Aquinas begins the whole consideration traditionally enough by defending the claim that sacraments are a kind of sign. He defends it even against the objection that they cannot be signs because they are causes (IIIa.60.1, obj.1 & ad 1). Yet it becomes clear soon enough that he is here speaking most generally of "sacrament" as any sign of something holy that serves to sanctify those appropriately perform-ing or receiving the sign (60.2). In this loose sense, "sacrament" refers not only to the rites of the Old Testament, such as the paschal lamb or priestly blessings (60.2, ad 2; 60.6, ad 3), but also to the worship of God practiced before or beyond the special revelation recorded in Scripture (60.5, ad 3; 61.4, ad 2; 65.1, ad 7). When Aquinas wants to specify the Christian sacraments within the genus of sacrament, he does so by asserting their causal efficacy (62.1; 65.1, ad 6). To state this differently: when Aquinas speaks of sacraments as signs, he has in mind the whole range of human religious ritual. When he wants to restrict himself to the seven sacraments of the Christian church, he speaks of sacraments as causes.

What exactly does Aquinas mean? He does not mean something that can be found immediately in Aristotle. At least, he does not point the reader toward Aristotle for help with the pertinent notion of cause. There are some sixty explicit citations in the two Ques-tions on sacramental effects. Only five are to Aristotle, and he is the only pagan author mentioned.[46] Two of the Aristotelian citations have nothing to do with causality. Two of the remaining three assert only that a power is a cause and that there are powers in the soul.[47] The third asserts that political ministers are instruments – a maxim that Aquinas applies, somewhat disingenuously, in order to bring priesthood under the account of instrumentality.[48] And, just as inter-esting, he seems to avoid citing Aristotle even when he could. He cites Augustine for the common Aristotelian principle that a cause is higher or nobler than its effect (62.1, obj.2). He cites no authority whatever for a Peripatetic maxim on the teleology of nature (62.2, s.c.) or for the logical teaching about the categoreal difference between figure and power (63.2, obj.1).

The importance of the absence of Aristotle is confirmed if one looks to Aquinas's elaboration of an account of sacramental causality. The account begins by distinguishing between a cause and a conventional sign (62.1). The sacraments are asserted to be causes "in many of the authoritative pronouncements of the Saints" (62.1). They are not principal causes as much as instrumental causes. A principal cause works in virtue of its own form, and so its effects are likened to that form. An instrumental cause does its work in virtue of the motion of some principal cause, so that the effects of an instrument are not like its form, but instead like the form of the principal cause moving it. Any instrument thus has two actions, that of its own form and that of its moving cause (62.1, ad 2). These two are connected: the moving cause achieves its effects through the proper action of the instrument.

Aquinas explicitly defends the image of the moving cause working "through" an instrument when he argues that the sacraments can be said to "contain" grace (63.3). His argument is by way of exclusion. Grace is in the sacraments not according to the likeness of species, nor according to some proper and permanent form, but rather "according to an instrumental power (*virtus instrumentalis*), which is flowing and incomplete in the being of nature" (63.3). The puzzling last phrase is not a lapse. Aquinas repeats it when he says that the grace has a "flowing and incomplete being" (*esse fluens et incompletum*) (63.3, ad 3). Indeed, to say that a sacrament is an instrumental cause obliges us to say that there is "some instrumental power" in the sacrament that is "proportioned to the instrument" (63.4). The power has an incomplete being that passes from one thing to another.

It is difficult to imagine this power, but more difficult still when one thinks particularly of the sacraments. In them, physical instruments connect an immaterial being, who is cause, to a partly immaterial being, who receives a spiritual effect. Moreover, the same instrumental power is found in the very different elements of a sacrament – in its verbal formulae, its prescribed actions, its material. Finally, the instrumental efficacy of the sacraments depends on the efficacy of the humanity of Christ, itself an instrument of His divinity (62.5). Whereas the human instrument is conjoined to its principal cause, the sacramental instruments are separated from it. To understand sacramental causality requires of us, then, to conceive of instruments composed of many kinds of material parts that receive and contain their causal power from a remote being of a different order, in order to pass that power along to beings of yet another kind.

Much ingenuity has been spent in trying to explain that Aquinas cannot possibly mean any of this literally, that he must mean something more philosophically familiar. Lonergan, for example, has argued elegantly and emphatically that Aquinas's causality must be spoken of generally either as a "formal content" in the agent or as a relation of dependence in the effect; it cannot be something added to the cause.⁴⁹ Again, Lonergan holds that "a causally efficient influence" passing from agent to patient in cases of efficient causation is "either a mere *modus significandi* or else sheer imagination."⁵⁰ Lonergan's reading of Aquinas on causality has been applied by others to Aquinas on the sacraments. Thus McShane argues that a sign can become an efficient cause of grace without itself changing, without "doing" anything "in any popular sense of the word 'do.' "⁵¹ Again, "action is predicated of the agent only by extrinsic denomination."⁵² Unfortunately, these readings do no justice to Aquinas's language nor to his choice of issues in the Questions on sacramental efficacy. What is required is not to explain away important features of Aquinas's texts, but to see that he uses the sacraments to extend ordinary notions of causality.

A full account of instrumental causality would require the reading of passages in which Aquinas argues at length that creatures are instruments in relation to divine action,⁵³ as well as of other applications of instrumentality, such as to the humanity of Christ. But even without a full development, one can see that Aquinas's notion of instrumental causality far exceeds the Aristotelian account. It exceeds precisely in developing so elaborate an account of instruments, which Aristotle mentions only casually in his main classifications of causes.⁵⁴ Aquinas's notion also exceeds the basic Aristotelian analysis of cause insofar as it stresses the presence in the instrument of a power capable of producing effects quite beyond the instrument's own nature.

The second revision of Aristotelian causality is underscored in ST when Aquinas turns to another kind of effect produced by some sacraments. Here the reader is asked to understand that the unrepeatable sacraments – baptism and priestly ordination – produce not only grace but a permanent "character" in the soul of the recipient (IIIa.63). As Aquinas's scholarly remarks show, theological formulations defining such a "character" were rather new in Latin. His most technical definition of it is an anonymous one to be found no further back than among his immediate predecessors (63.3, s.c.). He uses the notion, however newly formulated, to extend the account of instrumental causality even further.

This sort of bestowed, permanent "character" is a spiritual power (*potestas spiritualis*) that enables its possessor to participate appropriately in the worship of God (63.2; 63.4, ad 2). The power is itself instrumental as far as it creates "ministers" in the divine service. Becoming a minister is not simply acquiring an extrinsic attribution; it requires that something be put into the soul. This something, the "character," establishes a relation that is then signified as the minister's particular office in the service of God (63.2, ad 3). The relation remains in the soul as a permanent intrinsic attribute – more permanent than normal habits or grace, which can be lost. The "character" is permanent because it participates in the permanency of its divine cause (63.5, ad 1), which is, most specifically, the universal priesthood of Christ (compare 63.3).

If one stands back from the particulars, one can see in this teaching a rather remarkable extension of the notion of causality. Aquinas is asserting that there are complex events, involving words, gestures, and physical objects, that can properly be said to be causes of permanent changes in the moral condition of those participating in them. The changes are changes of moral condition because they enable the participants to perform virtuous actions, such as the just worship of God, by which they are brought nearer their end. The recipient who performs these actions is brought closer to the vision of God, which is his highest end and profoundest desire. But Aquinas has explicitly contrasted his account with any appeal to legal ordination or convention (62.1). He wants to assert that there is a causal power in the sacramental instruments and that some of their effects are permanent and morally significant alterations of the powers of the soul.

Now this analysis of sacramental efficacy appears to be another case of turning philosophy into theology. At the very least, Aquinas has added another wing onto the account of causality in developing the instrumentality of events, just as he has required any full survey of causes to include the sacraments among its cases. Indeed, Aquinas has also reversed the analogy of the term "cause" just as he did with "virtue." The richest kind of causality is the causality by which God brings rational creatures into participation of the divine life. That causality is more concretely grasped by us in the sacraments, which thus come to seem not the exceptional cases, but central, from a theological point of view, within the fullest account of causes available to us.

V. PHILOSOPHY WITHIN THEOLOGY

Aquinas likens the theologian's use of philosophy to the miraculous transformation of water into wine. In context, he is answering an Old Testament admonition read allegorically with a New Testament miracle read literally.[55] He thus makes a point about arguing from Scripture, but he also means to suggest that it is by the miracle of grace that the theologian gains the confidence to illuminate what the philosophers labored so hard to see so partially.

Aquinas intends the image of substantial change with some seriousness. Just as the water became wine, so the philosophical materials become something else when taken up by Christian theology. This Johannine image is stronger than the Pauline image with which Aquinas connects it – the image of "subjugating" philosophy to Christ. I suggested above that "subjugation" could be understood as several rights exercised by theologians over philosophy: a right to own philosophical truths, a right to correct philosophical errors, and a right to re-direct philosophical motivation. Yet the image of turning water into wine suggests even more. It suggests that theology strengthens philosophical reflection and improves philosophical discoveries.

We have seen this in the two examples from ST. The theologian's definition of virtue is ampler and more properly ordered than the philosophers' definitions. The theologian's notion of causality both embraces more kinds of causes and deepens the accounts of causes already recognized. What the philosopher thought of as virtues and causes are now seen to be only particular and, indeed, incomplete cases of each. The theologian's acceptance in faith of the data of revelation has allowed a thorough revision of what was thought to be well known by the philosopher.

We are left, then, with two responses from Aquinas to the modern reader's question about the relation of philosophy to theology. The first response is that the question must be reformulated so that it asks about theology's transforming incorporation of philosophy. Theology is related to philosophy as whole to part. The second response is that a Christian theology done well ought to speak more and better things about matters of concern to philosophy than the philosophers themselves can say. If a Christian theology cannot do this, Aquinas would not count it theology done well.

NOTES

1 Chenu 1937.
2 I round off the word counts from the *Index Thomisticus* for the scriptural commentaries (1,170,000 words, 13.5% of the corpus), the *Scriptum* on the *Sentences* of Peter Lombard (1,498,000, 17.2%), and the *Summa theologiae* (1,573,000, 18.1%). It will be seen that these three make up just about half of Aquinas's entire literary corpus. The Aristotle commentaries, including that on the first book of *De anima*, come to 1,165,000 words or just over 13% of the corpus.
3 I leave aside, of course, philosophical treatises falsely or uncertainly attributed to Aquinas, as well as gross re-titlings of his works, such as the early modern custom of calling the *Summa contra gentiles* a "*Summa philosophica.*"
4 I also have discussed some of the relevant texts in the 1990 Gilson Lecture at the Pontifical Institute of Mediaeval Studies (Jordan 1992).
5 The one apparent exception seems to involve a corruption in the text. In most modern versions of In PH, Aquinas refers to a "Joannes Grammaticus" as "philosophus" (1.6, paragraph 4). In Aquinas's In DC 1.8, and throughout Averroes, "Joannes Grammaticus" is John Philoponus, a Christian. But the critical edition now proposes to read "Philonus" for "philosophus," thus removing the puzzling epithet (see *Expos. lib. Peryermenias* 1.6, Leonine 1*/1:34.85–87). In any case, Aquinas would not have known of Philoponus's faith, since he learned of him only at second hand as an Aristotelian commentator.
6 In LDC, prol.: "so that it seems to have been excerpted by one among the Arab philosophers from the already mentioned book by Proclus."
7 On philosophic poverty, see ST IIaIIae.186.3, ad 3; 188.7, ad 5. Compare

Contra impugnantes 2.5 and a passage from the sermon *"Beatus gens, cuius est dominus . . .* /Multis modis sancta mater ecclesia . . ." (Busa 6:40c). In In Po 2.8, Aquinas follows Aristotle in seeing philosophy as a remedy for the loss of material goods.

8 In Sent III.35.1.1.

9 In Matt. 19.2.

10 Sermon *"Beati qui habitant in domo . . .* / Unam esse societatem Dei et . . ." 3 (Busa 6:45a).

11 In Ps 23.1.

12 In Sym Ap, prol.

13 In Sent I, prol.1; In BDT 3.1; QDV 14.10; SCG I.4–5; ST Ia.1.1, where he summarizes his view by saying that philosophic truths about God were discovered "by a few, and over a long time, and with the admixture of many errors."

14 In BDT 2.2; 5.4. See also the contrasts between philosopher's wisdom and the Christian's in ST IIaIIae.19.7.

15 See, for example, In BDT 3.3, 6.4; SCG III.48; CT 1.104; ST IaIIae.3.6.

16 In Matt. 13.3.

17 In John 6.1.

18 In II Cor. 7.1; In Col. 1.6.

19 For example, In Sent II.3.3.2; ST IIaIIae.19.7.

20 In John 1.5. Compare the triplet "light of prophecy," "light of faith," and "light of reason" in In Is 6.1 and the contrast from Avicenna between the way of speaking "among the philosophers" and "in the Law" at In Sent II.14.1.3.

21 In II Cor. 1.4 on II Cor. 1.12, where he is paraphrasing Paul.

22 In Is 19; ST Ia.12.13, s.c.; 32.1, ad 1.

23 Such as In Sent II.14.1.3; ST IIaIIae.2.10, ad 3. For a different view of Aquinas's relation to philosophy, see Aersten's Chapter 1, herein.

24 In BDT 2.4, ad 5. See also Owens's Chapter 2, this volume.

25 In I Cor. 1.3, following Augustine.

26 Sermon *"Attendite a falsis prophetis, qui . . .* / Duo esse in verbis istis . . ." 2 (Busa 6:35b–c).

27 In Col. 2.2.

28 For the system of citation, see Section 4 of Wippel's Chapter 4, herein.

29 Cicero, *De inventione* 2.53.159, quoted by Aquinas in IaIIae.56.5. For some earlier uses, see Augustine, *De diversis quaestionibus 83* q.31 (CCL 41.2–3), and Albert, *Lectura super Eth.* 1.15 (Cologne 14/1:76.67–69).

30 Aristotle, *De caelo* I 11 (281a15), quoted by Aquinas in IaIIae.55.1, obj.1; Aristotle, *Physics* VII 3 (246b23), quoted by Aquinas in IaIIae.55.2, obj.3, and 56.1, s.c. 1.

31 Aristotle, *Nicomachean Ethics* II 6, 1106b36–1107a2.

32 ST IaIIae.58.1, obj.1; 58.2, obj.4; 59.1; 64.1,s.c.; 64.2, s.c.; 64.3, obj.2.

33 Peter Lombard, *Sent.* 2.27.1 no.1 (Quaracchi 1:480).

34 See IaIIae.55.4, s.c., and Augustine *De libero arb.* 2.18.50 (CCL:271).

35 ST IaIIae.55.4c: "Now the efficient cause of infused virtue, for which the definition is given. . ."

36 One sign of this is the explicit invocation of Aristotle in important *sed contra* arguments. Of the nineteen *sed contras* that cite an authority in Questions 49–54, fifteen cite Aristotle and not merely for an intermediate premiss. Another sign is the concerted attention to the exegesis of Aristotle's texts, marked particularly by the reliance on Simplicius Simplicius is cited eight times in these Questions (49.1, ad 3; 49.2c and ad 2; 50.1c and ad 3; 50.4, ad 1; 50.6; 52.1). At least three of these passages contain lines of direct quotation, and one of them (49.2) uses a long quotation from Simplicius as a starting point for Aquinas's reformulation of an important distinction.

37 For Albert's use of it, see *Lectura* 2.3 (Cologne 14/1:100.27–30), 4.12 (272.71–73), 5.3 (320.36–39), and 7.11 (568.1–8).

38 Peter Lombard, *Sent.* 4.1.4 no.2 (Grottaferrata 2:233).

39 See Guido de Orchellis 1953, 3–5, especially 5.10–13; and Guillelmus Altissiodorensis 1980–1988, 4:12.15–16.

40 Bonaventura, *Sent.* 4.1.1.3–4 and *Breviloquium* 6.1.

41 The pertinent texts are collected by H.-D. Simonin and G. Meersseman (1936).

42 Peter Lombard, *Sent.* 4.prol (Grottaferrata 2:231). The large structure of the *Sentences* depends upon Augustine's distinctions between things to be enjoyed and things to be used, and between things and signs.

43 Bonaventura, *Sent.* 4.1.unic.4 at end (*editio minor* 4:18a).

44 Albert, *Sent.* 4.1.B.5 (Borgnet 26.18).

45 Consider the following examples from texts before ST: In Sent IV.1.1.1.3, ad 5, "Now simply speaking a sacrament is what causes holiness"; QDV 27.4, "it is necessary to hold that the sacraments of the New Law are in some way the cause of grace."

46 They are 62.2, obj.3, *Metaphysics* VII 3, 1043b36; 62.3, obj.1, *Physics* IV 14, 212a14; 63.2, obj.4, *Metaphysics* IV 12, 1019a15; 63.2, s.c., *Nicomachean Ethics* II 5, 1105b20; and 63.2, *Politics* I 2, 1253b30.

47 *Metaphysics* IV 12 (paraphrased): "a power takes the account of a cause and principle"; *Nicomachean Ethics* II 5 (quoted): " 'Three things are in the soul: power, habit, and passion.' "

48 *Politics* I 2 (paraphrased): "now a minister possesses the manner of an instrument."

49 Lonergan 1971, p. 69.

50 Lonergan 1946, p. 603.

51 McShane 1963.

52 Ibid., p. 430.

53 E.g., SCG III.70, QDP III.7, ST Ia.105.5.

54 Instruments are mentioned briefly as one kind of means in *Metaphysics* V 2, 1013b3, but not at all in the parallel passage in *Physics* II 3.

55 See In BDT 2.3, obj.5 & ad 5, where the objector cites Isaiah 1.22 and Aquinas replies with an allusion to Jesus' miracle at the wedding feast in Cana (John 2:1–11).

10 Biblical commentary and philosophy

I. THE NATURE AND CHRONOLOGY OF THE COMMENTARIES

Aquinas wrote commentaries on five Old Testament books – Psalms, Job, Isaiah, Jeremiah, Lamentations; on two Gospels – Matthew and John; and on the Pauline epistles – Romans, I and II Corinthians, Galatians, Ephesians, Philippians, Colossians, I and II Thessalonians, I and II Timothy, Titus, Philemon, and Hebrews. The early catalogues of Aquinas's works also list a commentary on the Song of Songs, but no such commentary has been found.[1] In addition, there are two inaugural lectures (*principia*) that are discussions of scriptural texts. The first inaugural lecture is based on a verse from Psalm 103: "Watering the earth from above"; the second focuses on a division of the books of Scripture. Weisheipl argues that both these lectures were given in connection with Aquinas's inception as Master of Theology at Paris in 1256.[2] Finally, Aquinas composed a continuous gloss on all four Gospels, the *Catena aurea* (Golden Chain). It consists in a compilation of relevant passages from the writings of the Greek and Latin Fathers of the Church. This work was commissioned by Pope Urban IV and seems to have been written in the period 1262/3–1267.[3] The *Catena aurea* is useful for understanding the background against which to evaluate Aquinas's own biblical commentaries, but because it is his compilation from commentaries by others, it will not be considered here.[4]

There is considerable disagreement about the date of composition of several of Aquinas's biblical commentaries.[5] I will generally follow Weisheipl's dating, corrected occasionally in accordance with the arguments of Simon Tugwell.[6] Part of the problem in dating

Aquinas's works, and especially the commentaries that originated as lectures, is that they sometimes seem to have been reworked, perhaps even more than once, so that one and the same work may contain material from different periods.[7]

The *Expositio super Isaiam* seems to consist of two main parts. The commentary on Chapters 1–11 contains some theological discussion. For example, Lectura 1 on Chapter 1 consists of an examination of the nature of prophecy; Lectura 1 on Chapter 11 includes considerations of the nature of faith and spiritual gifts. From Chapter 12 to the end, however, the commentary consists in a cursory reading, that is, a brief paraphrase or outlining of the text of Isaiah, accompanied by copious citations of other pertinent biblical texts. Tugwell dates Aquinas's first appointment to Paris to 1251 (a year earlier than the date Weisheipl gives); at this time, before becoming a master, Aquinas would have had to lecture on the Bible. Tugwell argues that, as a lecturer on the Bible (*cursor biblicus*), Aquinas chose to lecture on Isaiah.[8] Weisheipl suggests that the two parts of the Isaiah commentary should perhaps be dated separately.[9]

The *Postilla super Jeremiam* and the commentary on Lamentations (*Postilla super Threnos*) seem to belong to the same period as the Isaiah commentary. Tugwell dates the Jeremiah commentary to the period 1252–1253;[10] Weisheipl dates both commentaries even earlier, to the period when Aquinas was studying with Albert the Great at Cologne. Like the second half of the Isaiah commentary, these commentaries contain little philosophical or theological discussion; after a short summary or division of the text, they consist of the persentation of a collection of related biblical passages.

Aquinas probably produced his *Expositio super Job ad litteram* during his stay at Orvieto in 1261/2–1264, when he seems also to have written the *Catena aurea*,[11] although the commentary on Job as we now have it seems to incorporate later revisions.[12] It is apparently roughly contemporary with Book III of Aquinas's *Summa contra gentiles*.[13] Both SCG III and the commentary on Job have the nature of providence as one of their main concerns. Aquinas's commentary on Job is one of his most fully developed and polished biblical commentaries, and I return to it below.

The *Lectura super Matthaeum* is a *reportatio* (a transcription usually left unrevised by the author) of Aquinas's lectures on Matthew. This commentary has usually been thought to belong to Aquinas's first appointment to Paris, 1256–1259, but Tugwell argues that Aquinas's lectures on Matthew actually belong to his second Parisian period, and that they may even be as late as 1270–1271.[14] In fact, the commentary survives in two versions. The first, a *reportatio* probably made by Peter d'Andria, covers the gospel up to Chapter 12:50. The second, less detailed *reportatio* was made by Leger of Bésançon and goes from 6:9 to the end of the gospel, except for a few missing verses near its beginning.[15]

Whatever the case with the Matthew commentary, it is generally agreed that the *Lectura super Johannem* is a product of Aquinas's second Parisian period, although it seems difficult to determine the exact year in which the lectures were given in the period 1269–1272.[16] The lectures were taken down as a *reportatio* by Reginald of Piperno, Aquinas's secretary and faithful companion for the last fifteen years of his life, but Aquinas himself is said to have corrected the transcription of his lectures on the first five chapters.[17] This commentary also belongs to Aquinas's mature philosophical theology and contains detailed discussions of such subjects as the nature of the Trinity, the beatific vision, and the love of God, as well as sensitive, acute interpretations of the biblical narrative.

The *Postilla super Psalmos*, consisting of a commentary on Psalms 1–54, is also a *reportatio*, probably made by Reginald of Piperno while Aquinas was lecturing in Naples in 1272–1273.[18] Although Aquinas recognizes the importance of the literal sense of the Psalms, he concentrates on their spiritual sense, according to which the events and persons in the Psalms prefigure or typify Christ.[19]

The historical evidence concerning Aquinas's commentaries on the Pauline epistles is complex, and their chronology is particularly controversial. Tugwell maintains that the evidence supports assigning the lectures on the epistles both to Aquinas's second Parisian period and to his stay in Naples. On the other hand, he acknowledges that the evidence is ambiguous; since Aquinas reworked at least some of his commentaries on Paul, it is possible that some of the lectures on Paul might have been given as early as the first Parisian period.[20] The commentaries on Romans, Hebrews 1–11, and I Corinthians 1–7:19 were apparently written and edited by Aquinas himself.[21] The commentaries on Romans and I Corinthians in particular appear to be mature works, and Tugwell assigns them to Aquinas's last years in Naples.[22] The remainder of Aquinas's lectures on Paul are preserved only in Reginald of Piperno's *reportationes*.[23] Although they contain many interesting passages, the commentaries on the smaller epistles (such as Galatians, Ephesians, and Philippians) tend to stay fairly close to the text and to avoid elaborate theological development. The commentary on Hebrews contains detailed discussion of Christ as the incarnate Savior, as the second person of the Trinity, and as the fulfiller of the Old Testament promises; and, besides the well-known discussion of the nature of love, the commentary on I Corinthians includes intriguing discussions of Christian relations within the family, within the church, and with secular authority. The richest and most sophisticated of the commentaries on the Pauline epistles, however, is clearly the commentary on Romans, which includes sophisticated discussions of the nature of a will divided against itself and the way the will is affected by grace.

II. AQUINAS'S APPROACH TO SCRIPTURAL COMMENTARY

By the thirteenth century the Latin translation of the Bible, the Vulgate, existed in several versions, and Aquinas apparently used more than one of them.[24] In some cases it is not clear what particular version of the Vulgate Aquinas was using; in other cases we can determine it with some confidence. For example, in commenting on the Psalms, Aquinas uses the Vulgate's "Gallican Psalter," although he sometimes also uses the "Roman Psalter."[25]

Although Aquinas often mentions an alternate reading, he rarely records any concern over the fact that he has differing manuscripts of a biblical text; and sometimes, rather than choosing one of the alternatives as the more accurate or genuine reading, he simply incorporates an exegesis of each alternative into his commentary. So, for example, in commenting on Hebrews 4:13,[26] he cites a passage from Jeremiah, which does not exactly suit the point he has just made ("the heart of man is wicked," Jer. 17:9), but he goes on to note an alternate reading from the Septuagint ("the heart of man is deep"), which suits his purpose better and which he then weaves into his interpretation. Similarly, in explaining Titus 2:12, which concerns ungodliness or impiety, Aquinas cites Job 28:28 in this way: "where we have 'behold, the fear of the Lord, that is wisdom', another text has 'behold, piety, that is wisdom'."[27] And he goes on to base his interpretation of the passage in Titus on the alternate text, although it is clear that he does not intend to repudiate the reading that identifies wisdom with the fear of the Lord.

Weisheipl maintains that "Aquinas knew almost nothing about biblical and near-eastern languages, archeology, philology, comparative religion, and the historical method, [but] if he had, he would most certainly have used them."[28] It is not clear that the second half of Weisheipl's claim is true. Biblical scholarship and its attendant philological studies, of the sort Weisheipl commends, were not unknown in the Middle Ages. For example, early in the thirteenth century Robert Grosseteste learned Greek, studied the New Testament in Greek, and read Greek commentators; and there were some important Hebrew scholars as well, notably at the school of St. Victor in Paris. And not much after Aquinas's time, there was even some impetus from the Church, which in 1311/12 at the Council of Vienne decreed that chairs for the teaching of Greek, Hebrew, Aramaic, and Arabic should be established at Paris, Bologna, Salamanca, and Oxford.[29] Aquinas himself, however, apparently knew very little Greek and virtually no Hebrew, and he does not seem to have been interested in acquiring these languages. Furthermore, it is interesting to note in this connection that although Aquinas recognized that the biblical manuscripts he was commenting on were differing Latin versions of Greek and Hebrew texts, he shows no sign of a concern to try to recover the text in its original form either through his own work or through the efforts of others. On the other hand, he was quite concerned to understand and have available the works of the Greek fathers; he had various Greek passages specially translated for his *Catena aurea*.[30] And, in general, Aquinas's scholarly concerns seem more focused on appropriating the insights and arguments of earlier philosophers and theologians than on engaging in historical investigation of the biblical texts or acquiring the scholarly tools necessary for doing so. So, for example, Weisheipl claims that in his commentary on John Aquinas cites Augustine 373 times, Chrysostom 217 times, and Origen 95 times,[31] and there are also copious citations of the Fathers and of Aristotle, as well as references to Cicero, Ovid, Seneca, Plato, Democritus, and the Stoics in the other commentaries.[32] In view of these facts, it is not at all clear that Aquinas would have welcomed contemporary historical biblical scholarship if he had known of it.

By the thirteenth century it was taken for granted that Scripture has both a literal (or historical) sense and a spiritual sense. The spiritual sense itself was subdivided into three senses: the allegorical, the moral or tropological, and the anagogical.[33] The allegorical sense is the sense in which some things or events described in Scripture foreshadow some action of Christ's or something in Church history. The moral or tropological sense is the interpretation that shows something about the Christian life. The anagogical sense presents things that have to do with life in heaven. According to Beryl Smalley, the exact sorting out of these senses was the occasion for some confusion.[34] She notes two problems in particular. First, it was not always clear what ought to belong to the literal sense and what to the spiritual sense. If the biblical text employs metaphors, is the metaphorical reading part of the literal sense or part of the spiritual sense? Furthermore, what is the relationship between the literal and the spiritual sense? Medieval commentators sometimes give the impression that they regard the literal sense as too elementary to be interesting, as in the case of Gregory the Great's *Moralia in Job*, which heavily emphasizes the spiritual sense. According to Smalley, the commentaries on the Gospels, Psalms, and Apocalypse of Joachim of Flora "are a *reductio ad absurdum* of the spiritual exposition" and show the need for bringing interpretations based on the spiritual sense under some control.[35]

Aquinas is generally held to have been influential in solving both problems.[36] His definitions of the literal and spiritual sense are clear and have the helpful result that metaphorical interpretations can be assigned to the literal sense. More important, in practice as well as in theory he puts a strong and sensible emphasis on the literal sense.[37]

Aquinas defines the senses of Scripture in this way:

Sacred Scripture manifests the truth which it teaches in two ways: by words and by the figures of things. The manifestation by words produces the historical or literal sense; so everything that can be rightly acquired from the very signification of the words has to do with the literal sense. The spiritual sense, on the other hand, ... consists in the expression of certain things by the figures of other things.... Now the truth which sacred Scripture teaches by means of the figures of things has two purposes: believing rightly and acting rightly. If it has to do with acting rightly, then it is the moral or tropological sense. If it has to do with believing rightly, then we must draw a distinction in accordance with the order of the things to be believed. For . . . the state of the Church is intermediate between the state of the synagogue and the state of the Church Triumphant. Therefore, the Old Testament was a figure of the New Testament, and the Old and New Testaments are figures of heavenly things. And so the spiritual sense that has the purpose of believing rightly can [in the first place] be based on the sort of figures in which the Old Testament is a figure of the New; and this is the allegorical or typical sense, in accordance with which those things mentioned in the Old Testament are interpreted as having to do with Christ and his Church. Alternatively, the spiritual sense can be based on the sort of figures in which both the New and the Old Testament signify the Church Triumphant; and this is the anagogical sense.[38]

And in the *Summa theologiae* he says,

[In Scripture] the primary signification by which utterances signify things, has to do with the primary sense, which is the historical or literal sense. On the other hand, the signification by which the things signified by the utterances in turn signify other things, that signification is called the spiritual sense. It is based on the literal sense and presupposes it.

In sacred Scripture no confusion results [from the multiplicity of senses] because all the senses are based on one sense, namely, the literal sense, and arguments can be drawn only from the literal sense, and not from those senses which are expressed as allegories. . . . There is nothing necessary to faith contained in the spiritual sense which Scripture does not teach plainly elsewhere in the literal sense.[39]

In his own commentaries Aquinas does concentrate on the literal sense, but it would be a mistake to suppose that he avoids altogether the spiritual sense so popular among some of his predecessors. For example, in commenting on Hebrews 7:1, Aquinas refers his readers to the pertinent passage in Genesis 14 in which four kings band together and conquer five kings, in the process taking captive Abraham's nephew Lot. Aquinas begins his discussion of the Genesis passage in this way: "These four kings are the four capital vices, opposed to the four cardinal virtues, and they hold captive [our] affect, which is the nephew of reason." And the commentary continues in this vein, giving a good example of the moral or tropological sense.[40]

Finally, something needs to be said about Aquinas's divisions of the text. In his introduction to the translation of Aquinas's commentary on John, Weisheipl says, somewhat apologetically, "The Scholastics had a penchant for *order;* where none existed, one was imposed. . . . This is why the first thing one notices when reading a medieval commentary is the *division,* or the ordering of the whole into parts."⁴¹ Aquinas generally begins a discussion even of a small passage by dividing it into its parts and the parts into their parts. For example, in commenting on Ephesians 1:8–10, Aquinas says,

Since he has put forward the benefits commonly given to everyone, the Apostle here puts forward the benefits specially given to the apostles. This section is divided into two parts, because he first puts forward the benefits individually given to the apostles, and secondly he shows their cause. [1:11]⁴² With regard to the first [part], he does three things, because he first puts forward the individual benefits of the apostles with respect to the excellence of wisdom, secondly with respect to special revelation of a hidden mystery [1:9a], [and] thirdly he explains what this mystery is [1:9b–10].⁴³

Although this method is hardly unique to Aquinas,⁴⁴ for contemporary readers the chain of textual subdivisions linking the interpretation of one passage with another gives Aquinas's commentaries something of their distinctive character.

III. THE CONTENT OF AQUINAS'S BIBLICAL COMMENTARIES

It is not possible to give a short summary of the philosophical and theological subjects covered in Aquinas's biblical commentaries; they are as varied as the biblical texts themselves. So, for example, in commenting on the prologue to John's Gospel, Aquinas discusses the nature of signs, citing Aristotle's views in *De interpretatione;*⁴⁵ and there is a discussion of Aristotle's account of reproduction in the Commentary on I Corinthians.⁴⁶ As we might expect, the theological and philosophical expositions of the texts in Aquinas's commentaries are generally both able and acute. In dealing with the narrative parts of Scripture, he also shows considerable sensitivity toward the literary side of the text. For example, his thoughtful reflection on the role of Mary in the miracle at the wedding in Cana contrasts favorably with Augustine's apparent lack of appreciation of the human side of the interaction between Mary and Jesus in that story.⁴⁷

Sometimes, of course, one finds medievalisms that will strike many contemporary readers as inappropriate or even absurd. For example, as one of his interpretations of John the Baptist's line about Jesus – "he must increase, and I must decrease" – Aquinas explains that "John dies shortened by decapitation; but Christ died elevated by the lifting up of the cross."[48] Similarly, in explaining why the biblical text refers to the same place sometimes as "Salim" and sometimes as "Salem," Aquinas says, "Among the Jews a reader may use any vowel he chooses in the middle of his words; hence it made no difference to the Jews whether it was pronounced Salim or Salem."[49]

On the whole, the commentaries are clearly the product of the same outstanding mind that composed the *Summa theologiae*. With the possible exception of the cursory commentaries on the prophets and the Psalms, all Aquinas's biblical commentaries repay careful study, but three are worth singling out, the commentaries on Romans, the Gospel of John, and Job. The commentary on Romans is especially rich in interesting philosophical theology; the discussion of grace and free will, particularly in connection with Romans 7, is significant and sophisticated.[50] The commentary on the Gospel of John is a rich and subtle exposition of the narrative together with compendious theological reflections that give important insights into Aquinas's views on such subjects as the Trinity, the Incarnation, grace and free will, and redemption. To give some indication of the usefulness of Aquinas's biblical commentaries for philosophical and theological issues, I will focus on the commentary on Job.

IV. THE COMMENTARY ON JOB

Aquinas's commentary on Job will strike a contemporary reader as interesting or unusual in two ways.

First, it is sometimes difficult for contemporary readers to find any progression in the body of the book of Job, which consists mainly of the speeches of Job and his friends. The friends seem to extend the same false accusation with boring repetitiveness for pages, and Job's responses appear at best a prolonged variation on the theme of his innocence. But Aquinas sees the speeches as constituting a debate, almost a medieval disputation[51] (determined at the end by God himself), in which the thought progresses and the arguments advance, and he is both ingenious and persuasive in his construal of the arguments and their development. He is also sensitive, in a way even contemporary exegetes are often not, to the play of interpersonal relationships in the course of the speeches and to the way those relationships advance or explain the progression of the speeches. So, for example, while Aquinas agrees with a great deal of what Elihu, the fourth "comforter," says, Aquinas holds that it is presumptuous of Elihu, one human being among others, to say such things to Job. Elihu is in effect arrogating to himself the role of determining the disputation about the causes of Job's suffering, but, given the nature of the subject, the only appropriate determiner of the argument is God himself. It therefore comes as no surprise to see that Aquinas affirms much of what Elihu says but also supposes that the first line of God's speech – "Who is this that darkeneth counsel by words without knowledge?" – is addressed to Elihu, rather than to Job, as many contemporary commentators suppose.[52] It needs to be said in this connection, however, that Aquinas's sensitivity is not what one could hope for as regards the most important personal relationship in the book, that between Job and God. An important part of Job's suffering stems from the fact that, in the face of all the evil that has befallen him, he remains convinced not only of the existence of God, but also of his power and sovereignty, and even of his intense interest in Job; but Job has become uncertain or doubleminded about the goodness of God. And so his trust in God, which had formerly been the bedrock foundation of his life, becomes shaken, in ways that leave Job shaken to his roots. Aquinas's presentation of Job is oblivious to this side of his suffering, so that Aquinas's Job lacks something of the bitter anguish many of us think we see in the narrative.

Second, contemporary readers tend to think of the subject of the book of Job as the problem of evil. Since the book itself says that Job was innocent and since the book is equally clear about the fact that Job's suffering is (indirectly) caused by God (although perpetrated by Satan), it is hard for contemporary readers to reconcile this story with the claim that there is an omnipotent, omniscient, perfectly good God. How could an omnipotent, omniscient, perfectly good God allow an innocent person to suffer the loss of his property, the death of his children, a painful and disfiguring disease, and the other sufferings Job endures? And so the story of innocent Job, horribly afflicted with undeserved suffering, seems to many people a nightmarishly difficult case of evil with which any theodicy must come to grips. Much recent work in philosophy of religion on the problem of evil has been marked by a somewhat similar attitude toward most varieties of suffering, so that recent attempts at theodicy have been marked by a quest for a morally sufficient reason for God to permit evil. But Aquinas sees the problem and the book of Job differently. He seems scarcely to recognize that Job's story calls into question God's goodness, or even his existence. As he understands it, the book of Job is an attempt to come to grips with the nature and operations of divine providence. How does God direct his creatures? Does the suffering of the just require us to say that divine providence is not extended to human affairs? Of course, this question is not unconnected to the contemporary question generally stimulated by the book of Job. But the difference between the contemporary approach to Job and the one Aquinas adopts can teach us something about Aquinas's understanding of the relationship between God and evil.

On Aquinas's account, the problem with Job's friends is that they have a wrong view of the way providence operates. They suppose that providence assigns adversities in this life as a punishment for sins and earthly prosperity as a reward for virtue. Job, on the other hand, has a more correct view of providence, because he understands that providence will allow the worst sorts of adversities to befall a virtuous person. And the disputation constituted by the speeches of Job and his friends is a disputation concerning the correct understanding of the operations of providence. What is of more interest to us here than the details of this disputation, as Aquinas understands it, is his analysis of the reasons why the friends take such a wrong view of providence. In connection with one of Eliphaz's speeches, Aquinas says, "if in this life human beings are rewarded by God for good deeds and punished for bad, as Eliphaz was endeavoring to establish, it apparently follows that the ultimate goal for human beings is in this life. But Job intends to rebut this opinion, and he wants to show that the present life of human beings doesn't contain [that] ultimate goal, but is related to it as motion is related to rest and the road to its end."[53]

Aquinas's idea, then, is that the things that happen to a person in this life can be explained only by reference to his/her state in the afterlife. That a medieval Christian thinker's account of the human condition should have an otherworldly emphasis comes, of course, as no surprise, but it is at first glance perplexing to see that Aquinas thinks the emphasis on the other world will allay our concerns about how providence operates. For we might suppose that even if all that happens in a person's life is to be referred to his/her state in the afterlife, nothing in this claim allays the concerns raised by seeing that in this world bad things happen to good people. Because Aquinas has always in mind the thought that the days of our lives here are short while the afterlife is eternal,[54] he naturally values anything having to do with the afterlife more than the things having to do with this life. But nothing in his attitude is incompatible with supposing that things in this life might go well for the just or even pleasantly for everyone.

From Aquinas's point of view, the problem that keeps providence from permitting life on earth to be idyllic is the sinful nature of human beings, who are prone to sin even in their thoughts.[55] But it is not possible for people whose thoughts and acts are evil to live happily with God in the afterlife. And so God, who loves his creatures in spite of their evil, applies suffering medicinally. In discussing Job's lament that God does not heed his prayers, Aquinas says,

Now it sometimes happens that God hearkens not to a person's pleas but rather to his advantage. A doctor does not hearken to the pleas of the sick person who requests that the bitter medicine be taken away (supposing that the doctor doesn't take it away because he knows that it contributes to health); instead he hearkens to [the patient's] advantage, because by doing so he produces health, which the sick person wants most of all. In the same way, God does not remove tribulations from the person stuck in them, even though he prays earnestly for God to do so, because God knows these tribulations help him forward to final salvation. And so although God truly does hearken, the person stuck in afflictions believes that God hasn't hearkened to him.[56]

We might, of course, suppose that this sort of explanation could not possibly apply to Job, even on Aquinas's views, since, as the book of Job explains explicitly, Job is perfectly virtuous, a claim Aquinas is content to accept. Nonetheless, on Aquinas's account, even a perfectly virtuous person is afflicted by a proneness to evil, for which the medicine of suffering is still necessary and important. Furthermore, on Aquinas's view, it is precisely those closer and more pleasing to God who are likely to be afflicted the most. Because God can trust them to handle their suffering without despair or other spiritual collapse, he can give them the sort of suffering that will not only assure their final salvation but will also contribute to their additional and unending glory in heaven. So, for example, Aquinas says,

It is plain that the general of an army does not spare [his] more active soldiers dangers or exertions, but as the plan of battle requires, he sometimes lays them open to greater dangers and greater exertions. But after the attainment of victory, he bestows greater honor on the more active soldiers. So also the head of a household assigns greater exertions to his better servants, but when it is time to reward them, he lavishes greater gifts on them. And so neither is it characteristic of divine providence that it should exempt good people more from the adversities and exertions of the present life, but rather that it reward them more at the end.[57]

Aquinas, then, sees the problems raised by the book of Job differently than the way many contemporary commentators see them, because the worldview with which Aquinas approaches the book assigns a different value to the good things of this world and because what Aquinas holds to be the ultimate standard of value for human affairs is nothing in this world. Whether we approve or disdain his solution will then be a function of the values and worldview we ourselves bring to the text of Job and the problem of evil. I myself think that when the full detail and complexity of Aquinas's approach to the problem of evil is taken into account, as cannot be done in passing here, it must be recognized as a rich, sophisticated account and well worth attending to.[58] It is clear, however, that what makes Aquinas's approach to the problem of evil valuable even to those who find his worldview alien or absurd is that it forces us to be conscious of and reflective about the worldview and the values we ourselves bring to bear in thinking about the problem of evil, since it is clear that the values with which we begin our deliberations will enormously influence their outcome.

The problem of evil does not exhaust what is philosophically interesting about Aquinas's commentary on Job. In this commentary and in his many of his other biblical commentaries, scattered among his exegesis of scriptural texts are many sorts of reflections and discussions important for an understanding of his positions not only in philosophical theology but in other areas of philosophy as well. I have concentrated on this one example of the problem of evil in Job in order to indicate the sort of philosophically interesting material that may be found in the commentaries and to show that Aquinas's biblical commentaries repay careful attention.

NOTES

1 The commentaries on the Song of Songs printed in the Parma and Vives editions are spurious; according to James Weisheipl (1983, p. 369), the first belongs to Hymo of Auxerre, and the second to Giles of Rome.

2 Ibid., pp. 373–74.

3 Ibid., pp. 171–73.

4 The New Testament commentaries, including the *Catena aurea*, are available in the Marietti edition of Aquinas's works; the commentary on John will constitute volume 31 of the Leonine edition. The Old Testament commentaries are available in the Parma and Vives editions; the commentaries on Job and Isaiah are also available in the Leonine edition, in volumes 26 and 28 respectively. For some of the commentaries, there are also English translations. Of the Old Testament commentaries, only that on Job has been translated into English (Aquinas 1989). There is an English translation of the *Catena aurea* entitled *Commentary on the Four Gospels by S. Thomas Aquinas* (1841–45) in 4 volumes. The first part of the commentary on John has been translated as *Commentary on the Gospel of St. John*, Part I (Aquinas 1980). And four of the commentaries on the Pauline epistles are available in English: *Commentary on Saint Paul's Epistle to the Galatians by St. Thomas Aquinas* (Aquinas 1969a); *Commentary on Saint Paul's Epistle to the Ephesians by St. Thomas Aquinas*, (Aquinas 1966b); and *Commentary on Saint Paul's First Letter to the Thessalonians and the Letter to the Philippians by St. Thomas Aquinas*, (Aquinas 1969).

5 For discussion of the controversies and the literature associated with them, see Weisheipl 1983, pp. 368–74, and the discussions earlier in the text cited on those pages.

6 Tugwell 1988.

7 Ibid., p. 245.

8 Ibid., p. 211.

9 Weisheipl 1983, p. 370; see also pp. 479–81.

10 Tugwell 1988, p. 211.

11 Weisheipl 1983, p. 153; Tugwell 1988, p. 223.

12 Weisheipl 1983, p. 368.

13 Tugwell 1988, p. 246.

14 Ibid., pp. 246–47.

15 Ibid. According to Weisheipl, there are two gaps in the commentary in all printed editions. The first goes from Matthew 5:11–6:8, and the other includes 6:14–19. In a sixteenth-century edition, these lacunae were filled with the commentary of Peter de Scala, and the spurious text has continued to be included in subsequent printed editions. See Weisheipl 1983, pp. 371–72.

16 Weisheipl 1983, pp. 246–47; Tugwell 1988, p. 246.

17 Tugwell 1988, loc. cit.

18 Tugwell argues that there is no hard evidence for such a late date (1988, p. 248). In fact, Tugwell suggests that this commentary might well be assigned to the first Parisian regency; ibid., pp. 332–33.

19 Cf. Weisheipl 1983, pp. 302–307.

20 Tugwell 1988, p. 248.

21 Regarding Hebrews, Weisheipl says "up to Chapter 11" (1983, p. 373). He also says (ibid.) that Aquinas's exposition of I Corinthians 1 ends at 7:10.

22 Weisheipl (ibid.), on the contrary, assigns them only to the second Parisian regency.

23 Tugwell 1988, pp. 247–48.

24 Popular in the schools in the early thirteenth century was a version commonly called the Paris text, basically an evolved version of the text of the Vulgate prepared by Alcuin. Its deficiencies seem to have been widely felt. In 1236 the Dominican Chapter General mandated that the order's Bibles be standardized "according to the corrections prepared in the Province of France"; but these attempts at correction appear not to have been successful, because in 1256 the Dominicans, repudiating the earlier efforts, undertook another attempt at standardization, based on corrections made by Hugh of St. Cher, the prior of the Paris house. See Loewe 1988, pp. 146–49.

25 Weisheipl 1983, p. 369. For a discussion of these two versions of the Psalter and their history, see Loewe 1988, p. 111.

26 *Super ad Hebraeos*, Chapter 4, Lectura 2.

27 *Super ad Titum*, Chapter 2, Lectura 3.

28 Aquinas 1980, p. 9.

29 See Smalley 1988, pp. 216–19, and Loewe 1988, p. 152. Loewe says that as far as Oxford was concerned, "this injunction was to remain virtually a dead letter," although "an ex-Jewish convert called John of Bristol was teaching Hebrew and Greek at Oxford in 1320–1."

30 See Aquinas 1980, ibid.

31 Ibid., p. 12.

32 Aquinas 1966b, p. 21. The difference between Aquinas's attitude toward biblical studies and that of our own period is, I think, largely a function

of very different understandings of the authoritativeness of Scripture. For interesting discussions of Aquinas's views of the inspiration of Scripture, see the works of Pierre Benoit, especially his 1988 "Saint Thomas et l'inspiration des écritures," pp. 115–31. An outstanding discussion of Aquinas's attitudes toward the inspiration of Scripture, which tends to be critical of Benoit's views, can be found in Lamb's Introduction to Aquinas 1966b; Lamb also gives copious references to the texts of Aquinas in which the issue is discussed and to the secondary literature occupied with the issue. I explore Aquinas's attitude in a forthcoming article, "Aquinas on the Authority of Scripture."

33 See, for example, Beryl Smalley 1988, pp. 197–219.

34 Smalley 1970, pp. 295ff.

35 Ibid., p. 288.

36 This is a view given currency especially by the work of Beryl Smalley; see also Aquinas 1966b, pp. 11ff. For a dissenting voice, see Lubac 1964, pp. 272–302.

37 For a detailed study of Aquinas's treatment of the literal and spiritual senses, see Arias Reyero 1971 and the literature cited there.

38 QQ VII.6.15.

39 ST Ia.1.10c & ad 1.

40 For several other examples of the same sort, see Aquinas 1966b, pp. 23–24.

41 Aquinas 1980, p. 12.

42 Although the version of the Vulgate Aquinas used very likely had chapter divisions, it lacked divisions into verses, and so Aquinas indicates the verse he has in mind by quoting the first few words of the verse. It is common practice to replace citations by first words with the more customary citation by verse number.

43 *Super ad Ephesios*, Chapter 1, Lectura 3; Aquinas 1966b, pp. 55–56.

44 According to Lamb, it was introduced by Hugh of St. Cher and can be found in Albert and Bonaventure as well; Aquinas 1966b, p. 26.

45 *Lectura super Johannem*, Chapter 1, Lectura 1.

46 *Super I ad Corinthios*, Chapter 6, Lectura 3.

47 Augustine, *Homilies on the Gospel of John*, Chapter 2, Tractates VII and VIII; Aquinas, *Lectura super Johannem*, Chapter 2, Lectura 1.

48 *Lectura super Johannem*, Chapter 3, Lectura 5; Aquinas 1980, p. 214.

49 *Lectura super Johannem*, Chapter 3, Lectura 4; Aquinas 1980, p. 208.

50 For an interesting examination of Aquinas's commentary on Romans 7, see Kretzmann 1988a.

51 See Aertsen's Chapter 1 in this book.

52 *Expositio in Job*, Chapter 38:1; Aquinas 1989, p. 415–16. Cf., for example, Dhorme 1984, pp. 574–75.

53 *Expositio super Job*, Chapter 7:1–4, Aquinas 1989, p. 145.
54 See, for example, *Super ad Romanos*, Chapter 12, Lectura 2.
55 *Super ad Hebraeos*, Chapter 12, Lectura 2.
56 *Expositio super Job*, Chapter 9:11–21; Aquinas 1989, p. 174.
57 *Expositio super Job*, Chapter 7:1–4; Aquinas 1989, p. 146.
58 I examine Aquinas's approach to the problem of evil in more detail in "The Problem of Evil and Aquinas's Commentary on Job," forthcoming.

I am grateful to Norman Kretzmann for helpful comments on an earlier draft of this paper.

BIBLIOGRAPHY

The editors are grateful to Claudia Eisen for her work on the Bibliography.

Aertsen, J.A. 1988. *Nature and Creature. Thomas Aquinas's Way of Thought.* Leiden: E.J. Brill.

1990. "The Eternity of the World: The Believing and the Philosophical Thomas, Some Comments." In J.B.M Wissink, ed., *The Eternity of the World in the Thought of Thomas Aquinas and his Contemporaries.* Leiden: E.J. Brill.

Altman, A. 1969. "Essence and Existence in Maimonides." In A. Altman, *Studies in Religious Philosophy and Mysticism.* London: Routledge and Kegan Paul.

Anscombe, G.E.M., and Geach, P.T. 1961. *Three Philosophers.* Oxford: Basil Blackwell.

Aquinas, Thomas, *see* Thomas Aquinas.

Arias Reyero, M. 1971. *Thomas von Aquin als Exeget.* Einsiedeln: Johannes Verlag.

Aristotle. 1982. *Aristotle: Selected Works.* Trans. Apostle-Gerson. Grinnell, Iowa: Peripatetic Press.

Ashworth, E.J. 1991. "Signification and Modes of Signifying in Thirteenth-Century Logic: A Preface to Aquinas on Analogy." *Medieval Philosophy and Theology* 1.

Augustine. 1922. *Contra Academicos,* P. Knoell, ed. *Corpus scriptorum ecclesiasticorum latinorum.* Vienna: Tempsky.

Averroes. 1562–1574. *Aristotelis opera cum Averrois commentariis.* Venice.

1954. *Averroës' Tahafut al-Tahafut.* Trans. Van den Bergh. Oxford: Oxford University Press.

Avicenna. 1960a. *Al Shifa: Ilâhiyyât (La Métaphysique),* C.G. Anawati and S. Zayed, eds. Vol I. Cairo.

1960b. *Al Shifa: Ilâhiyyât (La Métaphysique),* M.Y. Moussa, S. Dunya, and S. Zayed, eds. Vol. II. Cairo.

1977. *Liber de philosophia prima sive scientia divina*, S. Van Riet, ed. Vol. I. Louvain-Leiden: E.J. Brill.

1978. *Avicenne: La Métaphysique du Shifa*. Trans. G. Anawati Vol. I. Paris: J. Vrin.

1980. *Avicenna Latinus: Liber de Philosophia Prima*. S. Van Riet, ed. Leiden: E.J. Brill.

1985. *Avicenne: La Métaphysique du Shifa*. Trans. G. Anawati, Vol. II. Paris: J. Vrin.

Baumgarth, W., and Regan, R.J. 1988. eds. *St. Thomas Aquinas, On Law, Morality, and Politics*. Indianapolis: Hackett.

Benoit, P. 1974. "Saint Thomas et l'inspiration des écritures." In *Il Pensiero di Tommaso D'Aquino e i problemi fondamentali del nostro tempo* (Congresso internazionale Thommaso d'Aquino nel suo settimo centenario). Rome: Herder.

Bernard of Clairvaux. 1958. *Sermones super Canticum Canticorum*. In J. Leclerq, ed., *S. Bernardi Opera II*. Rome: Editiones Cistercienses.

Bigongiari, D. 1953. ed. *The Political Ideas of St. Thomas Aquinas*. New York: Hafner.

Bonaventure. 1960–1970. *The Works of Bonaventure*. Trans. J. de Vinck. Patterson: St. Anthony Guild Press.

Booth, E.O.P. 1983. *Aristotelian Aporetic Ontology in Islamic and Christian Thinkers*. Cambridge: Cambridge University Press.

Broadie, A. 1987. "Maimonides and Aquinas on the Names of God." *Religious Studies* 23.

Burrell D. 1973. *Analogy and Philosophical Language*. New Haven: Yale University Press.

1979. *Aquinas: God and Action*. Notre Dame: Notre Dame University Press.

1985. "Review of James Ross, *Portraying Analogy*." *New Scholasticism* 59.

1986a. "Review of Booth, *Aristotelian Aporetic Ontology in Islamic and Christian Thinkers*." *MIDEO* (*Mélanges Institut Dominicain d'Études Orientales*) 17.

1986b. "Essence and Existence: Avicenna and Greek Philosophy." *MIDEO* 17.

1986c. *Knowing the Unknowable God: Ibn Sina, Maimonides, Aquinas*. Notre Dame: University of Notre Dame Press.

1991, with N. Daher, trans. *Al Ghazali on the Ninety-Nine Names of God*. Notre Dame: University of Notre Dame Press.

Busa R. 1974–1980. *Index Thomisticus*. Stuttgart–Bad Cannstatt: Fromann-Holzboog.

Chenu, M.D. 1937. "Les 'Philosophes' dans la philosophie chrétienne médiévale." *Revue des sciences philosophiques et théologiques* 26.

1964. *Toward Understanding St. Thomas*. Chicago: Regnery.

Clarke, W.N. 1952a. "The Limitation of Act by Potency: Aristotelianism or Neoplatonism." *The New Scholasticism* 26.

1952b. "The Meaning of Participation in St. Thomas Aquinas." *Proceedings of the American Catholic Philosophical Association* 26.

Cobban, A.B. 1975. *The Medieval Universities: Their Development and Organization*. London: Methuen.

Coleman, J., ed. (forthcoming). *Aquinas: Political Writings*. New York: Cambridge University Press.

Copleston, F.C. 1955. *Aquinas*. Baltimore: Penguin.

Cunningham, F. 1988. *Essence and Existence in Thomism: A Mental vs. the "Real Distinction"?* Washington, D.C.: University Press of America.

Dales, R. 1990. *Medieval Discussions of the Eternity of the World*. Leiden: E.J. Brill.

Denifle, H., and Chatelain, E. 1889. eds. *Chartularium Universitatis Parisiensis*. Paris: De la Lain.

Dhorme, E. 1984. *A Commentary on the Book of Job*. Trans. H. Knight. Nashville: Thomas Nelson.

Doig, J. 1972. *Aquinas on Metaphysics. A Historico-Doctrinal Study of the Commentary on the Metaphysics*. The Hague: Martinus Nijhoff.

Donagan, A. 1977. *The Theory of Morality*. Chicago: University of Chicago Press.

1982. "Thomas Aquinas on Human Action." In N. Kretzmann, A. Kenny, J. Pinborg, eds. *The Cambridge History of Later Medieval Philosophy*. Cambridge: Cambridge University Press.

Drake, S. 1957. *Discoveries and Opinions of Galileo*. New York: Doubleday.

Dumoulin, B. 1986. *Analyse génétique de la Métaphysique d' Aristote*. Montréal–Paris: Bellarmin – Les Belles Lettres.

Dümpelmann, L. 1969. *Kreation als ontisch-ontologisches Verhältnis*. Munich: Verlag Karl Alber.

Dunphy, W. 1983. "Maimonides and Aquinas on Creation: A Critique of their Historians." In L. Gerson, ed., *Graceful Reason*. Toronto: Pontifical Institute of Mediaeval Studies.

1989. "Maimonides' Not-So-Secret Position on Creation." In E. Ormsby, ed., *Moses Maimonides and His Time*. Washington: Catholic University of America Press.

Fabro, C. 1939. "Un Itinéraire de Saint Thomas. L'éstablissement de la distinction réelle entre essence et existence." *Revue de philosophie* 39.

1950, 2nd ed. *La nozione metafisica di partecipazione*. Turin: Società Editrice Internazionale.

1954. "Sviluppo, significato e valore della 'IV Via'." *Doctor communis* 7.

1961. *Participation et causalité selon Saint Thomas d' Aquin*. Louvain and Paris: Publications Universitaires de Louvain/Béatrice-Nauwelaerts.

Feldman, S. 1980. "The Theory of Eternal Creation in Hasdai Crescas and Some of His Predecessors." *Viator* 2.

Finnis, J. 1980. *Natural Law and Natural Rights.* New York: Oxford University Press.

1991. "Object and Intention in Moral Judgments According to Aquinas." *The Thomist* 56.

Finnis, J., with Boyle, J., and Grisez, G. 1984. *Nuclear Deterrence, Morality and Realism.* New York: Oxford University Press.

Foster, K. 1959. *The Life of Saint Thomas Aquinas. Biographical documents.* London: Longmans, Green.

Frank, R. 1956. "The Origin of the Arabic Philosophical Term *anniyya.*" Musée Lavigerie, *Cahiers de Byrsa* 6. Paris: Imprimerie Nationale.

Gadamer, H.G. 1979. *Truth and Method,* 2nd ed. Trans. W. Glen-Doepel. London: Sheed and Ward.

Gardet, L. 1974. "S. Thomas et ses prédécesseurs Arabes." In *St. Thomas Aquinas (1274–1974) Commemorative Studies,* Vol. I. Toronto: Pontifical Institute of Mediaeval Studies.

Geach, P. 1956. "Good and Evil." *Analysis,* 17.

Geiger, L.B. 1953. *La participation dans la philosophie de S. Thomas d' Aquin,* 2nd ed. Paris: J. Vrin.

Gerson, L.P. 1990. *God and Greek Philosophy.* London: Routledge and Kegan Paul.

Gilby, T. 1955. *The Political Thought of Thomas Aquinas.* Chicago: University of Chicago Press.

Gilson, E. 1940. *The Spirit of Mediaeval Philosophy.* Trans. A.C.H. Downes. New York: Charles Scribner's Sons

1952. *Being and Some Philosophers,* 2nd ed. Toronto: Pontifical Institute of Mediaeval Studies.

1960a. *Introduction à la philosophie chrétienne.* Paris: J. Vrin.

1960b. *Le Philosophe et la théologie.* Paris: Librairie Arthème Fayard.

1962. *The Philosopher and Theology.* Trans. C. Gilson. New York: Random House.

1986. *Pourquoi Saint Thomas a critiqué Saint Augustin.* Paris: J. Vrin.

Gimaret, D. 1988. *Les Noms Divins en Islam.* Paris: Cerf.

1990. *La Doctrine d' al-Ash' ari.* Paris: Cerf.

Goerner, E.A. 1983. "Thomistic Natural Right." *Political Theory* 2.

Gredt, J. 1937. *Elementa Philosophiae aristotelico-thomisticae,* 7th ed. Freiburg: Herder and Co.

Guido de Orchellis. 1953. *Tractatus de sacramentis ex eius summa de sacramentis et officiis ecclesiae,* D. and O. Van den Eynde, eds. Franciscan Institute Publications, Text Series 4. St. Bonaventure NY: Franciscan Institute.

Guillemus Altissiodorensis. 1980–1988. *Summa Aurea*, J. Ribaillier, ed. Paris: CNRS/Grottaferata: Collegio S. Bonaventurae.

Hanke, L. 1959. *Aristotle and the American Indians*. Chicago: Regnery.

Hanley, T. 1982. "St. Thomas' Use of Al-Ghazali's Maquasid-al-falasifa." *Mediaeval Studies* 44.

Hassing, R. 1991. "Thomas Aquinas on *Phys* VII.I and the Aristotelian Science of the Physical Continuum." In D. Dahlstrom, ed., *Nature and Scientific Methods*. Washington: The Catholic University of America Press.

Henle, R.J. 1956. *Saint Thomas and Platonism*. The Hague: Martinus Nijhoff.

Hissette, R. 1977. *Enquête sur les 219 articles condamnés à Paris le 7 mars 1277*. Louvain: Publications Universitaires/Paris: Vander-Oyez, S.A.

Hodgson, M. 1974. *The Venture of Islam*. Vol. I: *The Classical Age of Islam*. Chicago: University of Chicago Press.

Hoenen, M.J.F.M. 1990. "The Literary Reception of Thomas Aquinas's View on the Provability of the Eternity of the World." In J.B.M. Wissink, ed., *The Eternity of the World in the Thought of Thomas Aquinas and His Contemporaries*. Leiden: E.J. Brill.

Hooker, R. (1977–). *Of the Law of Ecclesiastical Polity*. In W. Speed Hill, ed., *The Folger Library Edition of the Works of Richard Hooker* (5 vols.), Cambridge: The Belknap Press of Harvard University Press.

Irwin, T.H. 1991. "Aristotle's Philosophy of Mind." In S. Everson, ed., *Companions to Ancient Thought*. Vol. II: *Psychology*. Cambridge: Cambridge University Press.

Jaffa, H.V. 1952. *Thomism and Aristotelianism*. Chicago: University of Chicago Press.

Jenkins, J. 1989. "Knowledge, Faith and Philosophy in Thomas Aquinas." D. Phil. dissertation, Oxford University.

——— 1991. "Aquinas on the Veracity of the Intellect." *The Journal of Philosophy* 88.

Jordan, M.D. 1983. "Names of God and the Being of Names." In A. Freddoso, ed., *Existence and Nature of God*. Notre Dame: University of Notre Dame Press.

——— 1986. *Ordering Wisdom. The Hierarchy of Philosophical Discourses in Aquinas*. Notre Dame: University of Notre Dame Press.

——— 1992. "The Alleged Aristotelianism of Thomas Aquinas." 1990 Gilson Lecture. Toronto: Pontifical Institute of Mediaeval Studies.

Kahn, C.H. 1982. "Why Existence Does Not Emerge as a Distinct Concept in Greek Philosophy." In P. Morewedge, ed., *Philosophies of Existence Ancient and Medieval*. New York: Fordham University Press.

Kenny, A. 1969. "Intellect and Imagination in Aquinas." In A. Kenny, ed.,

Aquinas: A Collection of Critical Essays. Garden City, NY: Doubleday–Anchor Books.

1980a. *Aquinas.* New York: Hill and Wang.

1980b. *The Five Ways. St Thomas Aquinas' Proofs of God's Existence.* Notre Dame: University of Notre Dame Press.

1982. With Pinborg, J. "Medieval Philosophical Literature." In N. Kretzmann, A. Kenny, J. Pinborg, eds., *The Cambridge History of Later Medieval Philosophy.* Cambridge: Cambridge University Press.

Klubertanz, G. 1959. "St Thomas' Treatment of the Axiom *Omne Agens Agit Propter Finem.*" In C.J. O'Neil, ed., *An Etienne Gilson Tribute.* Milwaukee: Marquette University Press.

1960. *St. Thomas Aquinas on Analogy.* Chicago: Loyola University Press.

1963. *Introduction to the Philosophy of Being,* 2nd ed. New York: Appleton-Century-Crofts.

Knasas, J. 1980. "Making Sense of the *Tertia Via.*" *The New Scholasticism* 54.

Knowles, D. 1962. *The Evolution of Medieval Thought.* London: Longmans, Green.

Kraemer, J. 1986. *Humanism in the Renaissance of Islam.* Leiden: E.J. Brill.

Krapiec, A.M. 1956. "Analysis formationis conceptus entis existentialiter considerati." *Divus Thomas* 59.

Kremer, K. 1971. *Die neuplatonische Seinsphilosophie und ihre Wirkung auf Thomas von Aquin.* Leiden: E.J. Brill.

Kretzmann, N. 1988a. "Warring Against the Law of My Mind: Aquinas on Romans 7." In T. Morris, ed., *Philosophy and the Christian Faith.* Notre Dame: University of Notre Dame Press.

1988b. "Lex Iniusta Non Est Lex." *The American Journal of Jurisprudence* 33.

1992. "Infallibility, Error, and Ignorance." *Canadian Journal of Philosophy,* Supp. vol. 17.

Leaman, O. 1988. *Averroës and His Philosophy.* Oxford: Clarendon Press.

Leo XIII. 1879. Encyclical 'Aeterni Patris,' in *Acta sanctae sedis* 12.

Leroy, M.-V. 1948. "*Abstractio et separatio* d'après un texte controversé de saint Thomas." *Revue Thomiste* 48.

1984. "Review of Wippel, *Metaphysical Themes.*" *Revue Thomiste* N.S. 4.

Loewe, R. 1988. "The Medieval History of the Latin Vulgate." In G.W.H. Lampe, ed., *The Cambridge History of the Bible.* Cambridge: Cambridge University Press.

Lonergan, B. 1946. "Review of Iglesias's *De Deo in operatione naturae vel voluntatis operante.*" *Theological Studies* 7.

1971. *Grace and Freedom: Operative Grace in the Thought of St. Thomas Aquinas*, J. Patout Burns, ed. New York: Herder and Herder.

Lubac, H. de. 1964. *Éxegèse médiévale, les quatre sens de l'Écriture*, 2e partie, t.II. Paris: Aubier.

Lyttkens, Hampus. 1952. *The Analogy between God and the World. An Investigation of Its Background and Interpretation of its Use by Thomas of Aquino*. Uppsala: Almqvist and Wiksells Boktryckeri AB.

MacDonald, S. 1984. "The *Esse/Essentia* Argument in Aquinas's *De ente et essentia*." *Journal of the History of Philosophy* 22.

1991a. "Aquinas's Parasitic Cosmological Proof." *Medieval Philosophy and Theology* 1.

1991b. "Ultimate Ends in Practical Reasoning. Aquinas's Aristotelian Moral Psychology and Anscombe's Fallacy." *The Philosophical Review* 100.

MacIntyre, A. 1988. *Whose Justice? Which Rationality?* Notre Dame: Notre Dame University Press.

Macken R. 1979. "Le statut de la matière première dans la philosophie d'Henri de Gand." *Recherche de Théologie ancienne et médiévale* 46.

Madison, G.B. 1988. "Hermeneutics and (the) Tradition." *Proceedings of the American Catholic Philosophical Association* 62.

Maimonides. 1956. *Guide of the Perplexed (Dalâlat al-hâ'irîn)*, Trans. Friedländer. New York: Dover Publications.

1963. *Guide of the Perplexed (Dalâlat al-hâ'irîn)*. Trans. S. Pines. Chicago: University of Chicago Press.

1974. *Guide of the Perplexed (Dalâlat al-hâ'irîn)*, ed. Hüseyin Atay. Ankara: Ankara Universitesi Basimevi.

Mansion, A. 1956a. "Philosophie première, philosophie seconde et métaphysique chez Aristote." *Revue philosophique de Louvain* 56.

1956b. "L'objet de la science philosophique suprême d'après Aristote, Métaphysique, E.I." In *Mélanges de Philosophie Grecque offerts à Mgr. Diès*. Paris: J. Vrin.

Maritain, J. 1938. *True Humanism*. New York: Scribner's.

1951. *Man and the State*. Chicago: University of Chicago Press.

McCabe, H. 1969. "The Immortality of the Soul: The Traditional Argument." In A. Kenny, ed., *Aquinas: A Collection of Critical Essays*. Garden City, NY: Doubleday–Anchor Books.

McInerny, R. 1961. *The Logic of Analogy. An Interpretation of St. Thomas*. The Hague: Martinus Nijhoff.

1968. *Studies in Analogy*. The Hague: Martinus Nijhoff.

1982. *Ethica Thomistica: The Moral Philosophy of Thomas Aquinas*. Washington: Catholic University of America Press.

1990. *Boethius and Aquinas*. Washington: Catholic University of America Press.

1992. *Aquinas on Human Action*. Washington: Catholic University of America Press.

McShane, P. 1963. "On the Causality of the Sacraments." *Theological Studies* 24.

Miller, C.L. 1977. "Maimonides and Aquinas on Naming God." *Journal of Jewish Studies* 28.

Montagnes, B. 1963. *La doctrine de l'analogie de l'être d'après Saint Thomas d'Aquin*. Louvain–Paris: Publications Universitaires de Louvain/Béatrice Nauwelaerts.

Novak, M. 1967. *A Time to Build*. New York: Macmillan.

1983. *Moral Clarity in the Nuclear Age*. Nashville: Thomas Nelson.

Owens, J. 1965. "Quiddity and Real Distinction in St. Thomas Aquinas." *Mediaeval Studies* 27.

1978. *The Doctrine of Being in the Aristotelian Metaphysics*, 3rd ed. Toronto: Pontifical Institute of Mediaeval Studies.

1980a. "Aquinas on Knowing Existence." In J.R. Catan, ed., *St. Thomas Aquinas on the Existence of God: Collected Papers of Joseph Owens*. Albany: State University of New York Press.

1980b. "*Quandoque and Aliquando* in Aquinas's *Tertia Via*." *The New Scholasticism* 54.

1980c. *St. Thomas Aquinas on the Existence of God: Collected papers of Joseph Owens*, J. Catan, ed. Albany: State University of New York Press.

1981. "Stages and Distinction in *De ente*: A Rejoinder." *The Thomist* 45.

1982. "The Doctrine of Being in the Aristotelian *Metaphysics* – Revisited." In P. Morewedge, ed., *Philosophies of Existence*. New York: Fordham University Press.

1986. "Aquinas's Distinction at *De ente et essentia* 4.119–123." *Mediaeval Studies* 48.

Patt, W. 1988. "Aquinas's Real Distinction and Some Interpretations." *The New Scholasticism* 62.

Pegis, A.C. 1946. "A Note on St. Thomas, Summa Theologiae I, 44, 1–2." *Medieval Studies* 8.

1948. ed., *Introduction to St Thomas Aquinas*. New York: Modern Library.

1983. *St Thomas and the Problem of the Soul in the Thirteenth Century*. Toronto: Pontifical Institute of Mediaeval Studies.

Peirce, C.S. 1960. *Collected Papers*. Cambridge: Belknap Press of Harvard University Press.

Plantinga, A. 1983. "Reason and Belief in God." In A. Plantinga and

N. Wolterstorff, eds., *Faith and Rationality*. Notre Dame: University of Notre Dame Press.

Prado, N. Del. 1911. *De veritate fundamentali philosophiae christianae*. Fribourg: Consociatio Sancti Pauli.

Quinn, J.F. 1973. *The Historical Constitution of St. Bonaventure's Philosophy*. Toronto: Pontifical Institute of Mediaeval Studies.

Rahman, F. 1958. "Essence and Existence in Avicenna." In R. Hunt et al., eds., *Mediaeval and Renaissance Studies* 4. London: Warburg Institute.

Ramsey, P. 1961. *War and the Christian Conscience*. Durham: Duke University Press.

Regis, L.M. 1959. *Epistemology*. New York: Macmillan.

Renard, H. 1956. "What is St. Thomas' Approach to Metaphysics?" *The New Scholasticism* 30.

Rickaby, J.J., 1896. ed. and trans. *Aquinas Ethicus*. London: Burnes Oates.

Roland-Gosselin. 1926. *Le "De Ente et Essentia" de S. Thomas d'Aquin*. Kain: Le Saulchoir.

Ross, J.F. 1981. *Portraying Analogy*. Cambridge: Cambridge University Press.

  1984. "Aquinas on Belief and Knowledge." In G. Etzkorn, ed. *Essays Honoring Allan B. Wolter*. St. Bonaventure, N.Y.: Franciscan Institute.

Samuelson, N.M. 1977. ed. and trans. *Gersonides on God's Knowledge*. Toronto: Pontifical Institute of Mediaeval Studies.

Schmidt, R.W. 1960. "L'emploi de la séparation en métaphysique." *Revue philosophique de Louvain* 58.

Shehadi, F. 1982. *Metaphysics in Islamic Philosophy*. Delmar: Caravan.

Sherry, P. 1976a. "Analogy Reviewed." *Philosophy* 51.

  1976b. "Analogy Today." *Philosophy* 51.

Siger de Brabant. 1981. *Siger de Brabant. Quaestiones in Metaphysicam*, W. Dunphy, ed. Louvain-la-Neuve: Editions de l'Institut Superieur de Philosophie.

  1983. *Siger de Brabant. Quaestiones in Metaphysicam*, A. Maurer, ed. Louvain-la-Neuve: Editions de l'Institut Superieur de Philosophie.

Sigmund, P.E. 1981. *Natural Law in Political Thought*. Washington: University Press of America.

  1988. ed. and trans. *St. Thomas Aquinas on Politics and Ethics*. New York: W.W. Norton.

Simonin, H.D., and Meersseman, G. 1936. eds. *De Sacramentorum efficientia apud theologos Ord. Praed.*, Fasc. 1: 1229–1276. Rome: Pontifical Institute Angelicum.

Smalley, B. 1970. *The Study of the Bible in the Middle Ages*. Notre Dame: University of Notre Dame Press.

1988. "The Bible in the Medieval Schools." In *The Cambridge History of the Bible*, vol.2, G.W.H. Lampe, ed., Cambridge: Cambridge University Press.

Stump, E. 1989. *Dialectic and Its Place in the Development of Medieval Logic*. Ithaca: Cornell University Press.

1990. "Intellect, Will, and the Principle of Alternate Possibilities." In *Christian Theism and the Problems of Philosophy*, M. Beaty, ed. Notre Dame: University of Notre Dame Press.

1992. "Aquinas on the Foundations of Knowledge." *Canadian Journal of Philosophy*, Supp. vol. 7.

(forthcoming). "Aquinas on the Authority of Scripture." In E. Stump, ed., *Reasoned Faith*. Ithaca: Cornell University Press.

Sweeney, L. 1963. "Existence/Essence in Thomas Aquinas's Early Writings." *Proceedings of the American Catholic Philosophical Association* 37.

Tavuzzi, M. 1991. "Aquinas on Resolution in Metaphysics." *The Thomist* 55.

Thomas Aquinas. 1841–45. *Commentary on the Four Gospels by S. Thomas Aquinas*. Trans. M. Pattison, J.D. Dalgrins, and T.D. Ryder. Oxford: John Henry Parker.

1949. *On Kingship to the King of Cyprus*. Trans. G.B. Phelan and T. Eschmann. Toronto: Pontifical Institute of Mediaeval Studies.

1954. *Sancti Thomae de Aquino super librum de causis expositio*, H.-D. Saffrey, ed. Fribourg: Société Philosophique.

1963. "Commentary on the Politics." In R. Lerner and Muhsin Mahdi, eds., *Medieval Political Philosophy*. Ithaca: Cornell University Press.

1966a. *Commentary on Saint Paul's Epistle to the Galatians by St. Thomas Aquinas*. Trans. F. Larcher. Aquinas Scripture Series, vol. 1. Albany: Magi Books.

1966b. *Commentary on Saint Paul's Epistle to the Ephesians by St. Thomas Aquinas*. Trans. M. Lamb. Aquinas Scripture Series, vol. 2. Albany: Magi Books.

1969. *Commentary on Saint Paul's First Letter to the Thessalonians and the Letter to the Philippians by Saint Thomas Aquinas*. Trans. F. Larcher and M. Duff. Aquinas Scripture Series, vol. 3. Albany: Magi Books.

1980. *Commentary on the Gospel of St. John*, part I. Trans. J. Weisheipl and F. Larcher. Albany: Magi Books.

1981. *Aquinas, Selected Political Writings*, A.P. D'Entreves, ed. Totowa, N.J.: Barnes and Noble.

1983. *On Being and Essence*, 2nd ed. Trans. A. Maurer. Toronto: Pontifical Institute of Mediaeval Studies.

1986. *Expositio super librum Boethii De trinitate*, 4th ed. qq. 5 and 6.

Trans. A. Maurer. In *The Division and Method of the Sciences.* Toronto: Pontifical Institute of Mediaeval Studies.

1987. *Expositio super librum Boethii De trinitate* qq. 1–4. Trans. A. Maurer. In *Faith, Reason and Theology.* Toronto: Pontifical Institute of Mediaeval Studies.

1989. *Thomas Aquinas. The Literal Exposition on Job. A Scriptural Commentary Concerning Providence.* Trans. A. Damico and M. Yaffe. The American Academy of Religion. Classics in Religious Studies. Atlanta: Scholars Press.

Tugwell, S. 1988. *Albert and Thomas. Selected Writings.* The Classics of Western Spirituality. Mahwah, N.J.: Paulist Press.

Van Steenberghen, F. 1980a. *Le problème de l'existence de Dieu dans les écrits de S. Thomas d'Aquin.* Louvain-la-Neuve: Editions de l'Institut Superieur de Philosophie.

1980b. *Thomas Aquinas and Radical Aristotelianism.* Washington: Catholic University of America Press.

Verbeke, G. 1980. "Une Nouvelle Theologie Philosophique." Introduction to S. van Riet, ed., *Avicenna Latinus: Liber de Philosophia Prima.* Leiden: E.J. Brill.

Vollert, C., et al. 1984. eds. *On the Eternity of the World.* Milwaukee: Marquette University Press.

Weisheipl, J. 1965. "The Principle *Omne quod movetur ab alio movetur* in Medieval Physics." *Isis* 56.

1983. *Friar Thomas D'Aquino. His Life, Thought, and Works.* Washington: Catholic University of America Press.

1985. *Nature and Motion in the Middle Ages.* Washington: Catholic University of America Press.

White, M. 1959. *Religion, Politics, and the Higher Learning.* Cambridge: Harvard University Press.

Wilks, M.J. 1963. *The Problem of Sovereignty in the Later Middle Ages.* Cambridge: Cambridge University Press.

Williams, B. 1972. *Morality: An Introduction to Ethics.* New York: Harper and Row.

Wippel, J.F. 1977. "The condemnations of 1270 and 1277 at Paris." *The Journal of Medieval and Renaissance Studies* 7.

1979. "Aquinas's Route to the Real Distinction: A Note on *De ente et essentia,* c.4." *The Thomist* 43. Reprinted in Wippel 1984b.

1984a. "A Reply to Fr. Owens." In Wippel 1984b.

1984b. *Metaphysical Themes in Thomas Aquinas.* Washington: Catholic University of America Press.

1984c. "Metaphysics and *Separatio* in Thomas Aquinas." In Wippel 1984b.

1985. "Thomas Aquinas on the Distinction and Derivation of the Many from the One: A Dialectic between Being and Nonbeing." *The Review of Metaphysics* 38.

1987a. "Thomas Aquinas and Participation." In J.F. Wippel, ed., *Studies in Medieval Philosophy*. Washington: Catholic University of America Press.

1987b. "Thomas Aquinas on Substance as a Cause of Proper Accidents." In J.P. Beckmann, L. Honnefelder, G. Schrimpf, and G. Wieland, eds., *Philosophie im Mittelalter: Entwicklungslinien und Paradigmen*. Hamburg: Felix Meiner Verlag.

1987c. "Thomas Aquinas's Derivation of the Aristotelian Categories (Predicaments)." *Journal of the History of Philosophy* 25.

1989. "Truth in Thomas Aquinas (part I)." *Review of Metaphysics* 43.

1990. "Truth in Thomas Aquinas (part II)." *Review of Metaphysics* 43.

Wolfson, H.A. 1973. "Amphibolous Terms in Aristotle, Arabic Philosophy and Maimonides." In *Studies in History and Philosophy of Religion*. Vol. I. Cambridge: Harvard University Press.

Wolter, A.B. 1965. "The Ochamist Critique." In E. McMullin, ed., *The Concept of Matter in Greek and Medieval Philosophy*. Notre Dame: Notre Dame University Press.

Zimmermann, A. 1965. *Ontologie oder Metaphysik? Die Diskussion über den Gegenstand der Metaphysik im 13 und 14 Jahrhundert*. Leiden–Cologne: E.J. Brill.

(Page numbers appear after the colon in each entry. Note numbers appear in parentheses after the page numbers.)

Attendite a falsis prophetis . . .
2: 249(26)

Beati qui habitant . . .
249(10)

Beatus gens . . .
249(7)

Catena aurea (1262–1267)
252

Contra impugnantes (1256)
2.5: 249(7)

CT *Compendium theologiae*
(1269–1273)
18: 124(85), 125(101)
80: 152(20)
87: 152(20)
104: 249(15)

DAM *De aeternitate mundi* (1270)
26
1: 72
6: 72
7: 72
10: 72
11: 72

DEE *De ente et essentia* (1252–1256)
82(5)
2: 152(19)
2–5: 120(30)
3.68–70: 59(26)
4: 23, 100–3, 113, 116, 117(4), 122(61),
  125(103), 126(111), 151(14)

4.6: 62
4.7: 62
4.8: 63, 69
4.94–146: 59(22)

DPN *De principiis naturae* (1252–1256)
90, 119(19–22)

DRP *De regimine principum*
  (1265–1267)
58(7)
1: 218, 220
2: 220
6: 230(6)
15: 219

DSS *De substantiis separatis*
  (1271–1273)
8: 120(30), 123(76)

DUI *De unitate intellectus contra*
  Averroistas (1270)
152(17)
2: 25
3: 152(20)

Expositio super Job (1261–1264)
253, 260–5
7.1–4: 268(53) (57)
9.11–21: 268(56)
38.1: 268(52)

In BDH *Expositio in librum Boethii De*
  hebdomadibus (1256–1259)
1: 191(41)
2: 120(32)

INDEX

(This index refers to the notes only when they introduce material that is not also in the text to which they are attached.)